Not in My Neighborhood

Not in
My Neighborhood

HOW BIGOTRY SHAPED A GREAT AMERICAN CITY

ᒥᒲᒥᒲᒥᒲᒥᒲᒥᒲᒥᒲᒥ

Antero Pietila

Ivan R. Dee

CHICAGO 2010

www.ivanrdee.com

Maps by Lucidity Information Design

Library of Congress Cataloging-in-Publication Data:
Pietila, Antero, 1943–
  Not in my neighborhood : how bigotry shaped a great American city / Antero
Pietila.
    p. cm.
  Includes bibliographical references and index.
  ISBN 978-1-56663-843-2 (cloth : alk. paper)
  1. Baltimore (Md.)—Race relations—History—20th century. 2. Racism—
Maryland—Baltimore—History—20th century. 3. Antisemitism—Maryland—
Baltimore—History—20th century. 4. African Americans—Segregation—
Maryland—Baltimore—History—20th century. 5. Jews—Segregation—
Maryland—Baltimore—History—20th century. 6. Discrimination in
housing—Maryland—Baltimore—History—20th century. I. Title.
  F189.B19A285 2010
  305.8009752'6—dc22   2009038807

To Barbara,
who told me to write a book

Contents

Preface: Harlem on My Mind

THIS BOOK examines how real estate discrimination toward African Americans and Jews shaped the cities of the United States in which we live. It covers a period from early suburbanization in the 1880s to the consequences of post–World War II white flight, ending in the first decade of the twenty-first century. The narrative centers on residential real estate practices in Baltimore, Maryland's largest city; but, like the city it depicts, the story is all-American. The tools of discrimination were the same everywhere: restrictive covenants, redlining, blockbusting, predatory lending.

A summer-long visit to New York in 1964 sparked my interest in these matters. It was my first encounter with the United States. I was a twenty-year-old aspiring journalist from Finland, a country so homogeneous that eye and hair color marked the chief differences among its four and a half million people. No blacks lived in Finland in those days, and only fifteen hundred Jews. New York's polyglot metropolis stunned me. While reporting one day in Harlem, I found myself naked and sweating in an old Finnish steam bath operated by an immigrant from Jamaica. It had been a popular gathering spot among residents of the Finnish community, which thrived in Harlem from the 1910s until the 1950s. Few traces of that population of several thousand survived. Rival socialist halls, including one with an indoor swimming pool and a bowling alley, were long gone, as were Finnish churches.

One vestige still remaining was a hat shop on 125th Street belonging to an elderly Finnish woman, who had stayed after other whites ran. Another relic was the steam bath, with its black owner, a professional masseur, at Madison Avenue and 122nd Street.

Harlem exemplifies succession, which is the sociologists' term for ethnic, racial, and economic change. In the space of four decades between the 1870s and 1910s, that section of New York City went from a white upper-class community of American-born residents to one populated by recent Irish, Jewish, German, Italian, and Scandinavian immigrants. Soon thereafter, as a result of white abandonment, Harlem became African American and Puerto Rican, as Gilbert Osofsky chronicled in his 1971 classic *Harlem: The Making of a Ghetto*. Racial succession is not over, either. Beginning in the late 1990s, Manhattan's overheated real estate market made Harlem's values so irresistible that whites began returning to live on some streets north of Central Park.

Each transition is different, but one common dynamic is noteworthy: the make-or-break role of real estate agents. In her long-out-of-print 1969 work, *Racial Policies and Practices of Real Estate Brokers*, Rose Helper examined the prejudices of the National Association of Real Estate Boards (NAREB) and the discriminatory policies of the Federal Housing Administration (FHA). This book goes further. It also details the stratagems of blockbusters, freebooters who prospered outside the controls of local real estate boards. They sought out declining white neighborhoods near African-American districts. They bought from panicked whites at rock-bottom prices and then resold to blacks at huge profits. Aging populations, the absence of normal ownership rotation due to the unavailability of financing, and a deteriorating housing stock hastened change.

Unlike New York, Chicago, Detroit, Boston, Philadelphia, and Los Angeles, Baltimore is not usually a prominent part of the American urban narrative. It should be. In 1910 the city enacted the first law in American history that prohibited blacks from moving to white residential blocks, and vice versa. When the U.S. Supreme Court seven years later struck down such laws, Baltimore again became a model that other cities copied because private agreements had barred blacks and Jews from certain neighborhoods for years. Until the Supreme Court in 1948 declared them unenforceable, such restrictive covenants were the backbone of residential segregation throughout the nation. Baltimore was also a forerunner in blockbusting. Large-scale, panic-induced racial turnover began during World War II, earlier by about a decade than in many other cities.

From the 1910s onward, neighborhood succession usually happened in the following order: non-Jewish to Jewish to African American. The pattern was due to Baltimoreans' embedded aversion to Jews. Whenever Jews started to move in, neighborhoods emptied of non-Jews. If Jewish housing demand then also weakened, such areas became transitional zones where sellers ultimately tapped the black market. The prejudice against Jews was so strong that while separate housing markets developed in many other American cities for whites and blacks, in Baltimore an additional market tier emerged to cater to Jews, who were prohibited by private agreements or custom from living in certain neighborhoods. The three-tiered market was so pronounced that even in the early 1970s a separate multiple-listing service sold suburban homes in areas open to Jews.

Finally, in Baltimore the experiences of an increasingly black city may be contrasted with overwhelmingly white Baltimore County, where the percentage of African Americans *declined* between 1950 and 1970, even though the county's overall population more than doubled, from 270,273 to 621,077. This book documents how the county contained blacks through zoning and other government actions. During our period of examination, first Spiro T. Agnew and then Dale Anderson led the suburban county. Agnew, who later became Richard M. Nixon's disgraced vice president, continued longstanding policies that eradicated old black settlements. Anderson, for his part, in 1972 ordered that real estate agents must report to police any home sales they made to blacks.

The narrative covers some 130 years of neighborhood transition, with an evolving story line that establishes causal links. One such link connects to eugenics, a controversial international scientific, political, and moral ideology in vogue from the 1910s to the 1930s. This book shows how eugenics influenced the federal government's policies and actions. For example, the government redlined 239 cities according to white-supremacist eugenic assumptions that ranked nationalities according to race, religion, and pseudoscientific stereotypes. The eugenic mind-set also guided the Federal Housing Administration's far-reaching policies until the 1960s.

Several chapters deal with blockbusting, a hot-button issue after World War II when millions of whites fled America's city neighborhoods because they feared blacks. Victims of their own hysteria, they sold their homes below the market value to panic-peddling blockbusters, who then flipped them to blacks at extraordinary markups. The book reveals a previously overlooked initial motivation of blockbusting—transferring the astronomical modernization liabilities of substandard housing to unsuspecting black buyers.

Previous authors have described blockbusting mostly from the viewpoint of fleeing whites, without any consideration of the black experience. With the addition of that prism, two diametrically opposite responses to blockbusting emerge: whites saw blockbusters as enemies who enabled a black invasion; blacks acknowleged blockbusters as profiteers but also welcomed them as agents of liberating desegregation. This fundamental disagreement split Baltimore fair-housing advocates. They were further weakened by mutual mistrust: black leaders were suspicious of Jews, Jewish leaders did not trust blacks.

Over the years the term "blockbuster" has been used indiscriminately to tar everyone who participated in racial change, regardless of the circumstances or motives. Many true blockbusters were indeed villains—greedy and unscrupulous opportunists. But however reprehensible their tactics, they acted generally within the law after the Supreme Court moved toward legalizing residential desegregation in 1948. Blockbusters also were not a monolith. A central figure in this narrative is an African-American blockbuster who saw the breaking of white neighborhoods as his civil rights mission, similar to the restaurant sit-ins in which he was repeatedly arrested.

The chapter about anti-Semitism describes a leading Christian real estate broker who excluded Jews from apartments he rented, neighborhoods he developed, swimming pools and a golf course he owned. He had many counterparts in all corners of the country. But the same chapter also profiles one of the most powerful men in Baltimore's Jewish community, a celebrated builder, generous philanthropist, and untiring fund-raiser for Israel, who nevertheless refused to sell or rent to fellow Jews. He was not the only one. Snapshots like these create nuanced pictures of complicated and often conflicted motives behind individual real estate practices. The totality produces an approximation of the hurdles that blacks and Jews had to overcome in their struggle for equal housing opportunities not only in Baltimore but in cities throughout the nation.

Baltimore became my urban observatory in 1969 when I joined *The Sun* to write about neighborhoods, politics, and local government. The city was a sad and dispirited place, still reeling from the 1968 riots following the assassination of Dr. Martin Luther King, Jr. I witnessed its turnaround, for which it received All-America City awards. Baltimore remained my beat for thirty-five years, interrupted by eight years spent as a foreign correspondent in South Africa and the Soviet Union. "The Queen City of the Patapsco Drainage Basin," as *The Evening Sun* columnist John Goodspeed called Baltimore, fascinated me more than the Kremlin. First as a reporter and later as a member of *The Sun*'s editorial board, I tried to share that fascination with readers.

The setting for most of the narrative is west and northwest Baltimore. That's where the trendsetting early cycles of ethnic and racial succession occurred and future real estate patterns were established. Baltimore County is the focus of the post–World War II white flight for the same reason: it was the earliest, most common destination of whites abandoning the changing city.

The active research and writing phase of this book took seven years. When I started, Mark Reutter, a native Baltimorean, made a prediction: "You will soon find out that Baltimore is a small town of closely kept secrets." This is a book about those secrets.

Not in My Neighborhood

Part One: 1910–1944

A WHITE MAN'S CITY

"This government was made by white men and
shall be ruled by white men as long
as the republic lasts."
—Maryland's Democratic boss
Arthur P. Gorman, 1889

1

⊓⊔⊓⊔⊓⊔⊓⊔

1910

THE FATE of a local sea captain, Peter Eriksson, his twenty-one-year-old daughter, and an eleven-man crew agonized Baltimore on June 9, 1910. Their three-mast bark, *Good News*, had sunk in a storm off the North Carolina coast three days earlier. Had they survived? All that was known was that the aging wooden ship occasionally carried dynamite to South America.

Seafaring had been Baltimore's lifeline ever since 1729 when a small settlement of mariners, farmers, and iron smelters on the western rim of the Chesapeake Bay was named in honor of Cecilius Calvert, Lord Baltimore and proprietor of the Maryland colony. The town exploited its pivotal position at the border between North and South. In 1910, Washington, D.C., just forty miles south, slumbered as the seat of the still-puny federal government, but Baltimore thrived as a hive of trading and manufacturing. Its busy port was an entry point for foreign immigrants second only to New York's Ellis Island; its garment district and sweatshops knew few rivals. Railroading and steelmaking were big business.

As that rainy Thursday wore on, Baltimoreans were relieved to learn that the missing sailors, their two dogs, and a cat had been rescued, drenched and shivering, after spending three days in lifeboats. *The Sun*'s interview with the captain's daughter, Elizabeth, made their ordeal sound almost lyrical. "Of course, the waves were high and battered us around, but as long as the men said there was no danger I didn't mind," she was quoted as saying. "The nights were beautiful and we had a grand view of Halley's comet. We looked at it and talked about it. Riding over the waves at night has a certain pleasant sensation . . ."

A routine real estate deal that same day went unreported in the press and unnoticed by the public. Barely two miles uphill from the port, on the fringes of one of the city's best neighborhoods, Margaret G. Franklin Brewer sold 1834 McCulloh Street to W. Ashbie Hawkins. Constructed of red brick, the structure was like most residences in Baltimore then and now, a rowhouse. While other cities built apartment houses, most Baltimoreans lived in rowhouses, always written as one word. Some attached rowhouses were grand, but most were not. The humblest were one-story structures only nine feet wide; the house that Hawkins bought boasted three stories but was only thirteen feet wide.

Three weeks later *The Sun* printed the sensational news that Hawkins was an African American. The city was under a "negro invasion," the newspaper's headline warned. By then, all of Baltimore was on edge. So was the nation. Just two days earlier, on the Fourth of July, the flamboyant black boxer Jack Johnson had knocked out his white challenger, James J. Jeffries, in the fifteenth round of a world heavyweight championship fight in Reno, Nevada. Outraged whites rioted in several cities, and eleven people were killed nationwide. Baltimore escaped without fatalities, but seventy blacks, half of them women, were locked up in City Jail. "One negro was badly cut by another and two other negroes were assaulted and severely injured by whites in arguments over the big fight," a newspaper reported. Hoping to curtail violence, Mayor J. Barry Mahool ordered theaters not to show a newsreel of Johnson's victory. *The Sun*, the city's newspaper of record, supported the ban. The fight film was "contrary to public morals and a peril to the public peace," said an editorial in the morning paper.

Race had become an intensively contentious issue in the United States in the half-century following the Civil War. First, the North imposed its will on the vanquished rebel states, requiring them to extend civil rights to African Americans freed from slavery. But in 1877 a political deal led to the withdrawal of federal troops, including large numbers of African-American soldiers, from South Carolina, Florida, and Louisiana. With the occupiers gone, the revengeful old Confederacy ended Reconstruction. Democrats in state after state barred African Americans from voting and took other measures to deny their newly won rights. Racial segregation spread to a dozen Northern states, where "WHITES ONLY" and "NO BLACKS" (or, in some cases, "NO NIGGERS ALLOWED") signs appeared to enforce separation at shops, toilets, drinking fountains, restaurants, hospitals, and amusement parks.

Popular culture promoted separateness. Among the Tin Pan Alley ditties that America sang at the time were "All Coons Look Alike to Me" and "Coon, Coon, Coon, I Wish My Color Would Fade." A revolutionary new medium, film, spread racial stereotypes. In 1896, the same year the Supreme Court's *Plessy v. Ferguson* ruling established "separate but equal" as the law of the land, inventor Thomas Alva Edison released a novelty film, *The Watermelon Eating Contest*. It showed two blacks devouring watermelons and spitting seeds. Such other pictures as *Sambo* and *Aunt Jemima* and *Nigger* emphasized the inferiority of blacks. Thus many whites were scandalized in 1901 when President Theodore Roosevelt treated the educator Booker T. Washington as his social equal by inviting him to dine with his family at the White House, the first African American to be so honored. Among the more extreme reactions was that of South Carolina's populist senator Benjamin R. Tillman—"Pitchfork Ben" to his friends. "The action of President Roosevelt in entertaining that nigger will necessitate our killing of a thousand niggers in the South before they will learn their place again," Tillman warned.

Such a threat was real. Each year people were lynched for lesser offenses. Lynching gauged the change in race relations. Between 1882 and 1885, 481 whites and 227 blacks were lynched in various parts of the United States. Then a startling reversal occurred, and lynching became a weapon used chiefly against African Americans: from 1886 to 1935, 3,282 blacks were lynched, against 903 whites. Overall the position of blacks eroded so seriously that the historian Rayford W. Logan described the period after Reconstruction as "the nadir of the Negro's status in American society." The actual low point began around 1890, when Northern Republicans ceased supporting Southern black rights, and extended through 1940. McCulloh Street in Baltimore became an emblem of worsening race relations.

After purchasing the house from Margaret Brewer, W. Ashbie Hawkins rented 1834 McCulloh Street to his law partner, George W. F. McMechen, a Yale University law school alumnus and the first graduate of Baltimore's Morgan College. "We did not move up there because we wished to force our way among the whites," McMechen told the *New York Times*. "Association with them in a social way would be just as distasteful to us as it would be to them. We merely desired to live in more commodious and comfortable quarters." Meanwhile whites formed the McCulloh Street–Madison Avenue Protective Association. "The colored people should not be allowed to encroach on some of the best residential streets in the city and force white people to vacate their homes," the association resolved. Whites threw stones through the McMechens' door and windows, dumped tar on the front steps, and smashed bricks through skylights. Although there was no shortage of vandals, only two were caught. Arthur B. Rice and Irwin Scholl, both nine years old, lived next door in the 1700 block. A juvenile court judge fined the boys one dollar each.

In its early history Baltimore had expanded without much racial fuss. Main streets and alleys were racially, ethnically, and economically mixed. By 1835, however, whites had taken over the main streets. Blacks remained scattered throughout the city's twenty wards, but most of them lived in alley dwellings behind the whites' houses. After the Civil War, surging European immigration produced ethnic enclaves, many anchored by Roman Catholic parishes created for specific nationalities. Even so, borders between Germans, historically the largest immigrant group in Baltimore, and Bohemians generally shifted without discord, as did dividing lines among the Irish, Hungarians, Poles, and Lithuanians. Jews too participated in this ethnic recycling, replacing other whites—and sometimes blacks—in east Baltimore's slums, only to be succeeded by a more recent immigrant group, Italians.

The cause of this ethnic churn was suburbanization. Amid record immigration, suburbanization had gathered momentum throughout America, thanks to transportation provided by horse-drawn trolleys and, after 1890, electric streetcars. The revolutionary automobile shortened distances, freed motorists from preplanned itineraries, and made previously faraway parcels attractive for year-round residence. Baltimore was particularly ripe for suburbanization. Plenty of land was available for development because large estates hugged the city. That additional space was desperately needed too. In just three decades between 1880 and 1910, Baltimore's population nearly doubled to 558,485 residents, of whom 88,065 were black.

The population explosion exposed a scandalous civic dereliction: the nation's seventh-largest city was the biggest without a sewer system. The low-lying areas of the city reeked. Outbreaks of typhus and yellow fever were common. Even cholera. Experts had despaired over waste-management and public health issues since the 1850s, but the ruling Democratic machine took no action. There was a reason: key leaders shared ownership in lucrative companies that monopolized the twin businesses of cleaning cesspools and processing wastes. They made money, and their money did not stink.

A catastrophe jerked Baltimore into the twentieth century. On February 7, 1904, a freezing Sunday morning, a burning cigar ignited a 30-hour firestorm that incinerated 140 acres of downtown, destroying 1,526 buildings. Despite record low temperatures, it took a week for the ruins to cool after the fire was put out. No time was wasted in beginning reconstruction, including the planning and building, over 15 years, of a sewer system. Other long-overdue concerns also were addressed, including the deepening of the port's vital navigation channel.

The Great Fire opened the floodgates of suburbanization. Fearing that living close to downtown was dangerous, better-off families fled, moving to suburbs that were being created on land that the city had annexed from the county. Aside from everything else, moving made economic sense. As a result of a political deal, the property tax rate in the annex was barely one-fourth of what homeowners paid in the old city.

No area was more affected by this redistribution of population than the Mount Royal district, which included McCulloh Street. Although desirable because of high ground, old plantation lands had been too far away to attract developers until the early 1850s, when Henry Tiffany, a relative of the stained-glass wizard, began building Eutaw Place. Baltimore had never seen anything like it. Evoking Europe, the neighborhood had a boulevard lined with shade trees and decorated with a flowering median, with pathways curving amid cast-iron fountains and marble monuments. Graceful homes lined the boulevard. After a mile, Eutaw Place dead-ended at Druid Hill Park, nearly as big as New York's Central Park. Reachable by streetcars, the park boasted a narrow-gauge railroad that transported visitors around, stopping at a Victorian boat lake and whimsical structures built in Moorish and Chinese styles. Period postcards showed another cherished tradition of Druid Hill Park, a flock of some three hundred lambs under a shepherd. It kept the lawns from overgrowing.

Eutaw Place connoted social status. Captains of commerce and industry built mansions there. After Johns Hopkins University was established nearby in 1876, president Daniel Coit Gilman moved to 1300 Eutaw Place. Dr. William Stewart Halsted, the father of American surgery, took residence at 1201. A Ph.D. candidate of some promise, Woodrow Wilson, the future president, soon joined them, moving across the street. Lesser lights occupied McCulloh and other side streets.

Beginning in the 1880s, moguls of the German Jewish merchant and manufacturing classes began replacing those early notables. Mostly from Bavaria, they took on the trappings of aristocracy, much like the great Jewish families of nineteenth-century New York. They

Eutaw Place during construction in the 1880s. Its mansions became a magnet to the city's most influential but also an early example of ethnic succession. *(Maryland Historical Society)*

built grand landmark temples along Eutaw Place, some with organs and mixed choirs of male and female singers. Christmas trees adorned magnificent homes. Exclusive private clubs sponsored sumptuous dinner galas and fancy debutante balls for "Hebrew Maidens," as one headline put it. That's why the self-selecting elite exhibited discomfort when, soon after 1900, the scene changed once more. The most successful recent Jewish immigrants from Eastern Europe broke out of east Baltimore's slums and took over side streets near Druid Park Lake in an area that later became known as Reservoir Hill. Mostly Orthodox and soon outnumbering Eutaw Place's German Jews, they spread to neighborhoods around the park and also along North Avenue, a gateway to the city's northwest suburbs.

The remaining predominantly non-Jewish area consisted of the southeast corner of Eutaw Place, below North Avenue, and later became known as Bolton Hill. A varied Christian population lived there in stately rows, near handsome churches. Some residents were well-heeled old Baltimoreans. Others included a good-sized contingent of impoverished erstwhile slaveowners, rebel soldiers, and other unrepentant refugees from the South. They treasured their customs, erecting a memorial for fallen Confederate soldiers on Mount Royal Avenue, which constituted Bolton Hill's eastern border. It depicted an avenging angel, wings spread wide, triumphantly holding up a laurel wreath while supporting a wounded soldier, really just a boy. *Deo Vindice* read the Latin inscription, "God vindicates." Bolton Hill was a "haven from the rigors of the Reconstruction Era," one resident wrote.

African Americans too were on the move. In the 1880s, expanding railroads got them evicted from slums around the downtown harbor. The process displaced hundreds of families at a time when migration from rural Maryland made Baltimore's black population the second largest of any city in the nation. Housing-starved African Americans gravitated toward St. Mary's Seminary, on Paca Street, where a community of educated, French-speaking Haitian refugees of both races had existed since 1793. Then, replacing a German population, blacks marched northwest along Pennsylvania Avenue. That onetime turnpike evolved into a busy shopping and entertainment strip, the heart of west Baltimore's expanding black district.

Considerable racial elasticity existed in some neighborhoods radiating from Pennsylvania Avenue. Ephraim Macht's weekly ads in the *Afro-American Ledger* in 1909 attested to that. "Buy now!" the white real estate man exhorted, listing addresses on several predominantly white streets intersecting Pennsylvania Avenue. "Stop paying rent. We have placed hundreds of people in homes and can do the same for you."

That elasticity had increased after Johns Hopkins University announced in 1901 that it would leave its original campus at Howard and Centre streets, just a few blocks from Pennsylvania Avenue's growing black district. Hopkins's move to the old Homewood plantation, several miles north, had been underfoot a long time. It created a real estate vacuum, as there would no longer be a need for staff or student housing. Whites were not interested, but members of

The Eutaw Place Corridor

✝ Churches
★ Synagogues
■ Points of Interest

0   ¼ Mile

Druid Lake

PARK TERR
RETREAT ST

PARK TERR

WHITLOCK ST
RESERVOIR ST
LENNOX ST
NORTH AVE

GOLD ST
BLOOM ST
PRESTMAN ST

ROBERT ST
LAURENS ST
DIVISION ST

RIGGS AVE
MOSHER ST
LAFAYETTE AVE
W LANVALE ST
HARLEM AVE
EDMONSON AVE
FRANKLIN ST

DRUID HILL AVE
MADISON AVE
EUTAW AVE
LINDEN AVE
BOLTON AVE
CALLOW AVE
PARK AVE
MT ROYAL TERR
MT ROYAL AVE
FALLS TURNPIKE

Jones Falls

21ST ST
20TH ST

N CHARLES ST

E LAFAYETTE AVE
E LANVALE ST
E FEDERAL ST
E OLIVER ST
MT ROYAL AVE
E PRESTON ST
E BIDDLE ST
E CHASE ST
E EAGER ST
E READ ST
E MADISON ST
E MONUMENT ST
CENTRE ST

BARCLAY AVE

Confederate Monument

1834 McCulloh St.

Marbury House

BOLTON ST
WILSON ST
MCMECHEN ST
MOSHER ST
JOHN ST
MT ROYAL AVE
DOLPHIN ST
FOSTER AVE
PARK AVE

EUTAW PL
MCCULLOH ST
DRUID HILL AVE
MADISON AVE
LINDEN AVE

W LANVALE ST
HOFFMAN ST
PRESTON ST
ROSE ST
BIDDLE ST
RICHMOND ST

CHARLES ST
MARYLAND AVE
ST PAUL ST
CATHEDRAL ST

Jones Falls

Johns Hopkins University

Preston Gardens

City Hall

MYRTLE AVE
ARGYLE AVE
PENNSYLVANIA AVE
FREEMONT AVE

ST MARY'S ST
ROSS ST

GEORGE ST

FRANKLIN ST
MULBERRY ST
W SARATOGA ST
W LEXINGTON ST
W FAYETTE ST
W BALTIMORE ST
HOLINS ST
W LOMBARD ST
PRATT ST

CAREY ST
CARROLLTON AVE
ARLINGTON AVE
SCHROEDER ST
POPPLETON ST
PARKIN ST
PINE ST
ARCH ST
N PACA ST
N GREEN ST
N EUTAW ST
N HOWARD ST
FAYETTE ST
LIBERTY ST
S SHARP ST

E SARATOGA ST
E LEXINGTON ST
E BALTIMORE ST
E LOMBARD ST
PRATT ST

CALVERT ST
GUILFORD AVE
HOLLIDAY ST
CHARLES ST
LIGHT ST
N GAY ST

Mount Clare

MCHENRY ST
DOVER ST
COLUMBIA AVE
RAMSAY ST

CAMDEN ST
PERRY ST
CONWAY ST

Harbor

Map of Eutaw Place, circa 1915, shows the concentration of houses of
worship. Note the original site of Johns Hopkins University, also Preston
Gardens, which replaced a mixed-race neighborhood near City Hall and the
courthouse.

the African-American elite eagerly acquired elegant Victorian homes along Druid Hill Avenue, which started at the old Hopkins campus. Prestigious black churches relocated there, some buying existing sanctuaries from white congregations and others constructing new buildings. The *Afro-American Ledger* newspaper bought a headquarters building across from the departing university. Booker T. Washington was impressed. He was America's most influential black leader of the day, well traveled and knowledgeable. "So far as I know there is no city in the United States where the coloured population own so many comfortable and attractive homes in proportion to the population, as in the city of Baltimore," he marveled in 1909 about a fifteen-block stretch of Druid Hill Avenue.

The progress that Washington perceived was in fact illusory. Ample evidence pointed to the African Americans' worsening position. In 1905 the *Afro-American Ledger* had reported that whites and blacks could be seen eating together in public places; two years later the paper noted that most public eateries were segregated. Between 1907 and 1910 blacks were made to feel uncomfortable in parks, theater segregation was stepped up, and more and more hotels excluded blacks. In 1910 racial tolerance ended in department stores. A leading store decreed that black customers could try on hats and other merchandise only in the basement. Evidently it "does not desire colored trade," said the *Afro-American Ledger*. Soon all the major department stores prohibited blacks from trying on garments altogether, and nothing that blacks might purchase could be returned, though exceptions were made for servants running errands for their employers. Baltimore became segregated from cradle to grave. Hospitals were segregated, so were cemeteries. Eventually even music. In 1922 the city created a separate Colored Band. Six years later a white donor gave the city seed money so that a municipal symphony orchestra could be established for "coloreds." Two conditions were attached to the gift—"one that my identity remain concealed and the other that I will not have to attend any concerts." The city barred blacks from attending regular symphony concerts as well as from performances at the Peabody Conservatory of Music.

McCulloh Street was at the racial divide. Although Eutaw Place glistened two blocks to the east, only a narrow alley separated whites from the backyards of Druid Hill Avenue blacks. That was not the only thing that unnerved many would-be renters and buyers. In 1895 the city's leading Conservative Jewish congregation, Chizuk Amuno, had built an imposing stone sanctuary at 1501–1505 McCulloh. Eight years later the Orthodox Shearith Israel Congregation erected a large stone synagogue at 2105–2107. They mirrored the extent of Jewish presence. All the officers listed on the letterhead of the Madison Avenue Protective and Improvement Association had Jewish names; the Jewish Social Directory included seventy-seven families with McCulloh Street addresses, and there must have been many more who did not meet its criteria. The more the street became viewed as Jewish, the fewer non-Jewish homebuyers and renters chose to live there. By 1910, with blacks advancing, even McCulloh Street's Jewish real estate market had collapsed.

It is impossible to estimate how much of this collapse was due to suburbanization and how much to aversion to Jews and fear of blacks. This much is known: the white abandonment was so severe that of a citywide total of 5,655 vacant houses, 1,407 were located in a west Baltimore district that included McCulloh Street, the highest number in any of the eight sections recorded. A peculiar Baltimore real estate tradition was born. A dual real estate market was a fact of life in many other American cities—one for whites and a separate one for blacks. In Baltimore a third separate market emerged. It served Jews who were prohibited by custom from residing in neighborhoods northeast of the Jones Falls, a stream that divided the city, and from many west side areas as well.

McCulloh Street introduced a succession pattern that would shape Baltimore: neighborhoods first transitioned from non-Jewish to Jewish and then to African American. When Jewish neighborhoods adjoining black districts experienced extended slumps in demand, some strapped property owner—who may not have been Jewish—eventually tapped an eager clientele: blacks. Once a neighborhood was "broken," others felt free to sell or rent to blacks.

In 1910 most everyone in Baltimore either used public transportation or walked. Among McCulloh Street's attractions was an excellent streetcar service. In the absence of white demand "this property is doomed sooner or later to pass into the hands of the negroes," predicted the real estate lawyer William J. Ogden. "In a large number of cases," he said, "it is not kept in repair and when it begins to go down the white people refuse to live in it, with the result that negroes are placed in the houses by the owners." Another lawyer, David Stewart, concurred: "The negroes seldom drive the white people away. They come after the white people have moved from a neighborhood. This leaves a number of houses vacant, and when the owner cannot get a white tenant he finally leases or sells his property to a negro." That is exactly what happened at 1834 McCulloh Street. W. Ashbie Hawkins was able to buy the property because the real estate market had deteriorated to the point where an offer from a black was better than no offer at all.

Hawkins was no ordinary man. At forty-eight he was a prominent lawyer who had been a leader in the Niagara Movement that the sociologist W. E. B. DuBois had founded in 1905 to oppose Booker T. Washington's policies of racial subordination. When a successor organization, the National Association for the Advancement of Colored People, emerged four years later, Hawkins eagerly participated. He was a featured speaker at NAACP conventions and wrote occasionally for *The Crisis*, the magazine edited by his friend DuBois, and for other journals. But it was in civil rights litigation where he made his mark. His work eventually led to the formation of the NAACP's legal department, whose stars included Charles Houston and Thurgood Marshall. When Hawkins argued, he argued forcefully. Once he delivered such a fiery speech against Marcus Garvey, the foremost proponent of the Back to Africa movement, that local Garvey zealots roughed him up.

Nothing was known about the seller, Margaret Brewer, except that she was white. *The Sun*, referring to her as "a Mrs. Nieda Brewer," said that she was a former schoolteacher. Other newspapers neither mentioned her nor named her.

W. Ashbie Hawkins's purchase of a house at 1834 McCulloh Street triggered Baltimore's residential segregation laws. He successfully challenged them in the courts.

Because Hawkins changed the trajectory of segregation, it would be tempting to interpret his acquisition of 1834 McCulloh Street as a heroic act to force the race issue. Nothing was farther from the truth. Hawkins was motivated by profit. In a city where only 933 blacks—or 0.1 percent of the African-American population—owned real estate, he was a rarity: a black speculator chasing properties in areas being vacated by whites.

A demarcation line soon formed along McCulloh Street. All black families settled on the west side; the east side of the street remained white, as did blocks leading to Eutaw Place. Newcomers on the west side included William B. Hamer, who had worked nearly twenty years as a clerk at the post office, a solid citizen. He said that he simply wanted to rent a better house. His brother-in-law, William H.

Valentine, moved in next door. As the headwaiter at a popular local inn, he had been tipped well and could afford the rent, which
was higher than what whites had paid. Another house's renters were
women teachers.

Real estate agents as a rule refused to sell to blacks, saying that
they had reputations to protect. That forced whites to deal directly
with black buyers, as Brewer apparently did in selling 1834 McCulloh
to Hawkins. This was also the case when Robert Taylor joined the
nucleus of blacks on McCulloh Street in the autumn of 1910. Taylor
bought his house from a white owner who had displayed "FOR RENT"
and "FOR SALE" signs for eighteen months. Since there were no white
takers, the owner finally decided to sell to a black.

The Sun repeatedly printed nonattributed claims that blacks destroyed property values. It backed up the claims by reporting that
Hawkins had paid only $800 for the house, whose previously ac-
cepted value was said to be $2,400. There can be no doubt that the
absence of demand had suppressed McCulloh Street prices. Nevertheless The Sun's report was demonstrably false. According to court
records, Hawkins obtained a $1,900 mortgage for the house. Since a
substantial down payment was required in those days, he must have
paid about what The Sun said the real value should be, perhaps even
more. Issuing the mortgage was Ridgely Building Association, an established white institution. The Afro-American Ledger denied that
blacks were the cause of falling values. Eutaw Place's price slide had
begun years earlier during a real estate slump caused by "the rush of
Gentiles to escape the incoming families of prosperous Hebrews," the
paper wrote.

Emotions were raw. After a white resident, M. Z. Hammen, one
day crossed the street on foot to taunt Hamer, the postal clerk told
him, "I am as good as you are. You move on or I brain you with this
chair." Hammen sought a warrant for Hamer's arrest. The magistrate
regretted that he could do nothing. "As a matter of fact," he said,
"the negro has not committed a crime. He only threatened you with
bodily harm. Had he struck you, the case would have been different. The fact that he is an undesirable neighbor does not constitute a
crime. According to the laws of the State and the nation he has all the

rights and immunities of a white man. In truth you were the aggressor and no controversy would have happened had you not instigated the conversation."

The magistrate's words angered Hammen. He launched a campaign for a City Council ordinance that would make it a crime for a black to move to a white block, and vice versa. Logic was on his side, he argued. Hadn't the Supreme Court's 1896 *Plessy v. Ferguson* ruling established the principle of separate but equal, in effect codifying racial segregation? Didn't laws already differentiate between black and white? "Some may say that such a law would interfere with personal freedom," Hammen acknowledged, but he asked: "Are whites and blacks allowed to intermarry? Could not this also be interpreted as interfering with personal liberty? If in our public schools colored and white children are legally kept apart for five hours a day, why should it not be legal for us to have a law to keep the two races from living in the same block, where they will be forced to intermingle for 24 hours a day?"

With elections approaching in 1911, two Democratic City Council members, Milton Dashiell and Samuel L. West, recognized residential segregation as a potent political issue. William L. Marbury eagerly volunteered his services as their legal adviser. A resident of Bolton Hill, Marbury was a leading lawyer and a Confederate nostalgic. To him, Hawkins's purchase of 1834 McCulloh was a personal affront. In 1884, when the neighborhood was in its ascendancy, Marbury had acquired the land beneath that very house as an investment. Even though records are somewhat unclear, Marbury probably still owned the ground and received regular ground-rent payments from Hawkins under an antiquated system that dated back to colonial times. But he had no veto over the sale of "improvements," such as the separately owned rowhouse built on the land. Hawkins described Marbury as "a rampant Negro hater, like so many others of his kind he has often allowed his prejudice against us to blind him."

The first bill introduced in the City Council proposed to freeze existing racial housing patterns in a quadrangle bounded by Charles and Baltimore streets, the defining north-south and east-west downtown crossroads. North Avenue, some twenty blocks away, would form the northern boundary and Fulton Avenue the western. But that approach was rejected, and Councilman West amended the bill to cover the whole city. Each block was to be designated as either white or black. The final form of the bill decreed that "no negro can move into a block in which more than half of the residents are white," and "no white person can move into a block in which more than half of the residents are colored." Existing residents of either race were grandfathered in; black live-in servants were exempted. Violators could be fined up to $100 or sentenced to a maximum of one year in prison.

The Sun supported residential segregation. It quoted Ogden, the real estate authority, as predicting that a residential segregation law would benefit taxpayers. "It would do more than anything else to reduce your tax rate. It would keep the people from going to the suburbs. It would keep our people together, our population solid and would let us live where we want to live," he said. The newspaper's editorial conduct was intriguing. Among Baltimore's numerous daily newspapers, it seemed to be the only one preoccupied by race. Even its new sister newspaper, *The Evening Sun,* downplayed tensions. Stranger yet was the pattern of apparent provocations. One ad in *The Sun* suggested that blacks would soon spill over to other blocks: "FOR SALE—Cheap to Colored People a modern three-story HOUSE in the 1900 BLOCK MCCULLOH STREET." Next *The Sun* printed a long letter, purportedly from a black resident. The letter claimed that it was "the expressed intention of the colored people to invade every block on each of the following streets: North Charles, St. Paul, Calvert, North Avenue, Mount Royal Avenue, Mount Vernon Place, Madison Avenue, Park Avenue, Bolton Street, McCulloh Street and Eutaw Place—all the best streets in Baltimore." The letter further predicted that a war would soon break out between Japan and the United States. "You will find that not only will the entire 10,000,000 colored people in America be on the side of Japan and actively assisting that country, but also the 200,000 Indians, the 125,000 Chinese and the 100,000 Japanese."

Incensed readers demanded that *The Sun* identify the writer. The newspaper's editors contended that the author could not be located. They described the writer likely as "a wily white man posing as a 'colored gentleman' in the 'woodpile.'" Without expressing any regrets for the bogus letter, *The Sun* then offered its opinion: "An effort is now [being made] in the City Council to pass an ordinance to segregate the white and black races in this city. Those who are promoting the movement are going about it in a spirit free from prejudice and passion. Precisely that spirit is needed to solve so great and complex a problem. There is reason to hope that the better element among the Negroes will co-operate in an effort to remove the most fruitful single source of race friction and feeling."

The Sun's agitation had begun the preceding year with a headline warning "NEGROES ENCROACHING." The accompanying article detailed gradual racial change that was taking place along white side streets of Pennsylvania Avenue and ran nearly a column. What was unusual was the prominence the article was given. At a time when the use of photos in *The Sun* was rare and typography conservative, the paper placed six columns of pictures at the top of the page. "WHERE THE BLIGHT OF THE NEGRO IS MOST SERIOUSLY FELT IN THE CITY," read the headline. The entire article was based solely on a single interview with a man who was identified only as "a well-known taxpayer in the Seventeenth ward." Was it Marbury? Perhaps. At the time Marbury was campaigning for a constitutional amendment to take away black voting rights, and the article trumpeted disfranchisement as the solution that would also stop black residential expansion. The article concluded with the following quotation: "It is up to the white people, without regard to political affiliation, to come to the aid of the city and State by wiping out the negro in the Fourth District of this city, and if for no other reason, it seems to me that every white man should come to the relief of the residents and property owners in the Seventeenth ward by passing the amendment and passing out the negro as a political factor in this city."

The Sun went so far as to write approvingly about the docklands community of Locust Point, near Fort McHenry, where no blacks were tolerated after dark. According to the news story, the peninsula's Irish longshoremen told blacks "that if they moved into that section they would also die." *The Sun* saw merit in such bluntness. "It may not be an ethical position to take," the writer suggested, "but it is successful."

Such was Baltimore in 1910.

2

꒤꒦꒤꒦꒤꒦꒤꒦

Good Government

THE RESIDENTIAL segregation bill won the City Council's approval on December 9, 1910. The very title of the bill suggested that African Americans undermined neighborhood stability: *Ordinance for preserving order, securing property values and promoting the great interests and insuring the good government of Baltimore City*. The bill's adoption was "a great public moment," exulted City Solicitor Edgar Allan Poe, a grandnephew of the famous poet, because "wherever negroes exist in large numbers in a white community, [it] invariably leads to irritation, friction, disorder and strife."

The United States Civil Rights Act of 1866 had decreed that blacks enjoyed the same property rights as white Americans. That Reconstruction-era law, enacted by a congressional override of President Andrew Johnson's veto, still stood. But it had been weakened in 1896 after the Supreme Court's *Plessy v. Ferguson* ruling gave the force of law to segregation. Race separation was nothing new. It was a principle that even Abraham Lincoln embraced in campaigning for a seat in the United States Senate from Illinois. In his fourth debate with Stephen A. Douglas, the Democratic incumbent, Lincoln declared on September 18, 1858: "I will say, then, that I am not nor have ever been in favor of bringing about in any way the social and political equality of the black and white races—that I am not, nor ever have been, in favor of making voters or jurors of negroes, nor of qualifying them to hold office, nor to intermarry with White people; and I will say in addition to this that there is a physical difference between the white and black races which will ever forbid the two races living together on terms of social and political equality. And inasmuch as they cannot so live, while they do remain together, there must be the position of superior and inferior, and I, as much as any other man, am in favor of having the superior position assigned to the White race."

Segregated housing existed in many Northern cities, including Boston and New York. More extreme measures were taken in the countryside. The historian James W. Loewen has documented how, from the Civil War onward, thousands of counties and small towns across the United States, mostly outside the old Confederacy, expelled black residents altogether, sometimes at gunpoint. The precipitating event was usually an alleged outrage by an African American, who often was lynched. Those who refused to obey the mob were beaten or pistol-whipped, sometimes fatally, and their properties ransacked and often burned. A phenomenon of all-white "sundown" towns emerged. Such towns had road signs declaring, "WHITES ONLY WITHIN CITY LIMITS AFTER DARK." Some sounded sirens or whistles at nightfall, alerting blacks to leave.

Baltimore's innovation was the use of government legislation to achieve systematic, citywide race separation. "Nothing like it can be found in any statute book or ordinance record of this country," the *New York Times* wrote. "It is unique in legislation, Federal, State, or municipal—an ordinance so far-reaching in the logical sequence that must result from its enforcement that it may be said to mark a new era in social legislation." Baltimore thus became a national leader in residential segregation. Richmond, Norfolk, Roanoke, and Portsmouth in Virginia passed similar laws; so did Winston-Salem in North Carolina, Greenville in South Carolina, Birmingham in Alabama, Atlanta in Georgia, Louisville in Kentucky, St. Louis in Missouri, Oklahoma City in Oklahoma, New Orleans in Louisiana, Indianapolis in Indiana, and Dallas in Texas. Like Baltimore, all those cities were trying to cope with a black influx. One letter of inquiry came all the way from the Philippines: the U.S. occupation authorities wanted to know how Baltimore had done it.

Soon after the law took effect, about twenty persons were charged with violating residential segregation, their cases investigated by police and sent to the grand jury for action. Most prosecutions involved rentals on blocks where neither race was indisputably in the majority. Several other offenders were not prosecuted; they were simply prevented from moving to houses they had bought on blocks where a different race formed the majority of residents. One white complained to newspapers about losing his down payment because the property he wanted to buy was on a block that the law classified as black. Blacks too expressed unhappiness. A pastor wrote to Mayor Mahool, who had signed the bill: "When colored Methodist preachers living in parsonages owned by their churches, but located in blocks where the majority of residents are white, are ordered by their bishops to move, and a new colored preacher is sent to take the charge, will the law prohibit the new colored preacher from moving into that house owned by his church and located in a white block?"

The mayor referred the letter to Councilman Dashiell. His reply was curt and condescending. "I am only able to say that the colored person, considered to represent the most enlightened of the negro race, should have established his home in the midst of his race, and that he should have encouraged others of his race to do likewise. . . . The inquiry seems to me like a hypothetical one, and can be answered by the person, unaided, save by the ordinance itself."

In fact the law was hopelessly unclear and unspecific. Baltimore had no shortage of racially mixed blocks. In most cases a simple head count determined how a block was to be segregated. But was a block white or black when one side of it was all white, the other all black, and each side had an equal number of homeowners? The law failed to resolve such conundrums. This gave lawyers ammunition for challenges. At a trial involving segregation violations, the prosecutor sprang a surprise: he conceded that the law had fatal defects, including inexactness of language and a failure to define what constituted a city block. When a judge struck down the law, the City Council, undeterred, swiftly passed another segregation ordinance.

Drafting those ordinances was William L. Marbury; leading the court challenges was W. Ashbie Hawkins. The latter's demeanor had changed. When he bought 1834 McCulloh Street, it was just another speculative purchase. After racial controversy erupted, he did not talk to newspapers or otherwise involve himself in the matter. But once the City Council passed the residential segregation law, he pledged to contest it. "The courts are open and to them we should go," Hawkins declared. "The citadel of our rights is in the courts, but courts are not self-acting institutions. They are formed and maintained for our protection, but their protection in private matters is not wholly vouchsafed us unless we appeal to them." That he did. Hawkins managed to invalidate the second version of the segregation ordinance and the next one as well. Finally the City Council's fourth version, passed in 1913, met the legal requirements.

The City Council's residential segregation push was a continuation of a campaign against African Americans that Democrats had been conducting for fifteen years. Maryland, as a border state, frequently exhibited racial attitudes that separated it from both the North and the South. In 1860, just before the Civil War, 90 percent of the city's 27,000 blacks were free, giving Baltimore the largest free black population of any U.S. city. Free blacks were nearly equal, and many slaves exercised considerable freedom. Like the future abolitionist Frederick Douglass, they "hired out" in the labor market with the permission of their owners. Slave or free, they were paid equal wages, and skilled black workers sometimes made more money than whites doing the same job. Blacks dominated many occupations until waves of European immigrants muscled them out. The Irish, in particular, were eager to undercut prevailing wages. Once hired, they refused to work with blacks. Through strikes they ousted blacks from shipyard jobs, including caulking, which was Douglass's trade. In 1860, Colonel Curtis W. Jacobs, a white Eastern Shore planter-delegate to the Maryland General Assembly, proposed the reenslavement of all free blacks. "Free-Negroism is an excrescence, a blight, a mildew, a fungus—hanging on to and corrupting the social and moral elements of our people in Maryland," he wrote. "I would have all negroes to be slaves in order that all whites be free." At a referendum, voters rejected his proposal. Yet such was the state's political climate on the eve of the Civil War that Abraham Lincoln polled just 2,294 votes, or 2.5 percent, in the 1860 presidential election, which was fought in Maryland between two pro-slavery candidates from the South, John Breckinridge and John Bell.

Maryland never seceded from the Union. Many Marylanders wanted to join the Confederacy, but the governor refused to convene the General Assembly. No one was fooled. Union occupation troops in Baltimore trained their cannons on City Hall; soldiers rounded up high officials and civic leaders and jailed them in the dungeons of Fort McHenry. Habeas corpus was suspended, several newspapers were suppressed and their editors arrested. Nominally with the Union, occupied Baltimore was a deeply divided town.

The Northern victory in the Civil War ended slavery in Maryland but not Southern attitudes and sympathies. The prospects for blacks improved in 1895 when a Republican landslide ousted Democrats from power for the first time since the Civil War. With black votes providing the decisive edge, Republicans took over the offices of governor, attorney general, and comptroller. The party also captured an overwhelming majority in the lower house of the General Assembly. Nineteen of the state's twenty-three counties fell into Republican hands. And in a feat not duplicated since, a Republican alliance, bolstered by the bipartisan Reform League, which had become an influential progressive agent for change, won the mayor's office in Baltimore and took control of the two-chamber City Council.

Democrats did their best to prevent the Republican victory. In keeping with a political tradition that had earned Baltimore the nickname "Mobtown," they imported "hundreds of rough-looking strangers" to conduct election fraud. The brunt of serious violence was aimed at scaring blacks away from the polls. One black was reported shot and killed and two others wounded as gangs of armed whites pulled voters out of the ballot lines or fired gunshots into alleys. White liberals also were targeted. One tough assaulted Johns Hopkins University physics professor W. J. A. Bliss, a poll watcher for the Reform League, breaking his jaw; other notable reformers also were attacked and bruised.

The Democrats' humiliation continued the following year when Maryland again voted Republican and supported William McKinley for president. There were obvious explanations for their machine's drubbing. The country was still suffering from the deep depression that followed the Panic of 1893, and voters were up in arms over tax issues and—if they lived in Baltimore—over the acute sanitation crisis. The Democrats had not delivered. Voters simply wanted to throw the rascals out. Instead of confronting these factors, Democrats blamed blacks. Maryland, with its past Confederate sympathies, proved receptive.

Democrats got their revenge in 1899 when they embarked on a comeback campaign with a slogan, "This Is a White Man's City." Street agitators were more graphic. They urged all white men, regardless of party, to "keep down the 'niggers,'" the *New York Times* reported. The call resonated, accentuated by scandals involving two leading African Americans. One was Dr. George Wellington Bryant, an army veteran and nationally known orator who entertained white audiences with stories about how his mother supposedly was a descendant of a pirate king from Borneo. Dr. Bryant, a practicing physician, had been hired to supervise the city's first contingent of black municipal workers—garbage men, janitors, and messengers—whom the Republican administration hired in 1896. When Bryant was sentenced to six months in prison for stealing from the city and demanding kickbacks from his hires, Democrats could point to him as a cautionary example of how permissive race policies spawned lawlessness. That scandal was hardly over when Everett J. Waring skipped town. He was a celebrated lawyer, prominent civic leader, and president of the Lexington Savings Bank, the proudest symbol of African-American economic achievement. As receivers went through records inside the bank, some five hundred anxious depositors milled outside, demanding to know what had happened to their money. It took locksmiths a full day to crack the combination to the bank vault. That night, when the vault's door finally swung open, bank receivers counted $28.70 in the cash box. That was all the bank had.

After regaining power in 1899, Democrats moved to undermine African-American rights. The party scuttled the election reforms that

Republicans had enacted and excluded as many blacks as possible from the voting rolls. This rollback was touted as a progressive reform: Democrats argued that Maryland's 26,616 illiterate black voters in 1900—47 percent of all blacks registered in the state—were an easy and gullible prey to demagogues and charlatans, as could be seen from the mere fact that most voted Republican. "This election is a contest for the supremacy of the white race in Maryland," declared Edwin Warfield, the Democratic gubernatorial candidate who was elected in 1903. "I am not willing that an ignorant, prejudiced, irresponsible, non-taxpaying negro's vote shall outweigh a vote cast by an intelligent, educated white man. The founders of this nation, when laying the cornerstone of our country, never intended any such monstrous perversion of the principle of manhood suffrage and of that principle that declared the right of the majority to rule."

The 1903 election platform declared the Maryland Democratic party's commitment to white supremacy. It stated: "We believe that the political destinies of Maryland should be shaped and controlled by the white people of the State, and while we disclaim any purpose to do any injustice whatever to our colored population, we declare without reserve our resolute purpose to preserve in any conservative and constitutional way the political ascendancy of our race." Disfranchising black voters became an obsession. Borrowing from the so-called Mississippi Plan that defeated Confederate states had so successfully used to emasculate Reconstruction reforms, Maryland Democrats tried three times through referendums to take away blacks' voting rights. After voters rejected the first attempt in 1905, another referendum was held in 1909. Under its remarkable language, voting rights could be extended to

> a person who, in the presence of the officers of registration, shall in his own handwriting, with pen and ink, without any aid, suggestion and memorandum whatsoever and without any question or direction addressed to him by any of the officers of registration, make application to register correctly, stating in such application his name, age,

date and place of birth, residence and occupation, at the time and for
the two years next preceding, the name and names of his employer or
employers, and whether he has previously voted and if so, the State,
county or city and district or precinct in which he voted last, and also
the name in full of the President of the United States, of one of the
Justices of the Supreme Court of the United States, of the Governor of
Maryland, of one of the Judges of the Court of Appeals of Maryland
and of the Mayor of Baltimore City, or of one of the County Commissioners of the county in which the applicant resides.

Voters saw those traps for what they were, rejecting the 1909
referendum and yet another one in 1911. But it was a sign of the
times that even the Republicans, who led the fight against these constitutional amendments, were not concerned so much about blacks as
about the possibility that such arbitrary stratagems might deny the
vote to new white immigrants, who were arriving in the United States
in record numbers.

*

The Reverend Palestine S. Henry was a man of the cloth whose day
job was as a trusty messenger for the United States Fidelity and Guar-
anty Company in Baltimore. On a Wednesday evening in June 1913,
he stood up at a black Methodist Episcopal preachers' meeting and
recited a poem. It was about a matter much on every mind and was
widely circulated as a printed leaflet:

Come, O come thou great anointed,
Thou for us who was appointed;
Save us in our tribulation
From this hateful Segregation.

We never engaged in insurrection
But have been loyal to perfection.
We shed our blood to save the nation,
And now being paid for Segregation.

In 1913 some 560,00 people lived in Baltimore. A sixth were African Americans, whose numbers were steadily climbing due to migration from rural Maryland. As white abandonment of west Baltimore neighborhoods continued, segregation laws could not prevent blacks from spilling over. Spreading from Pennsylvania Avenue in the opposite direction from McCulloh Street, African Americans approached the prestigious Lafayette Square. Whites hurled stones and bricks at newcomers' houses. Blacks gave back as good as they got.

Families belonging mostly to the German merchant class lived in Lafayette Square's stately Victorian homes. Intricate cast-iron balconies decorated some houses; constantly polished long brass handrails graced the entrances of others. The fanciful, turreted edifice of the State Normal School, a teachers' college, occupied one corner of the fountain-decorated square like a fairy-tale castle. Five prominent Protestant churches surrounded the square, interspersed with huge rowhouses. The pastors of those churches were among the most outspoken supporters of segregation; they had their buildings and mortgages to worry about. But nothing stemmed the tide. In a frantic letter, one desperate Lafayette Square resident urged Mayor James H. Preston to put "an end to this hideous negro invasion" in "some way short of wholesale murder." Preston expressed sympathy to another white resident and said he was "heartily in favor of the Segregation Ordinance for the protection of our people and property." But he added that "it would be foolish" to continue introducing such laws if they were to be struck down on the basis of challenges by W. Ashbie Hawkins, the very lawyer whose purchase of 1834 McCulloh Street had led to residential segregation legislation in the first place.

Hawkins exemplified the agility that was required of a black wanting to succeed in segregated Maryland. Born in 1861 in Lynchburg, Virginia, the son of a Methodist Episcopal minister, after graduating from Morgan College he taught in "colored schools," serving three years in Cambridge, on Maryland's Eastern Shore. During a subsequent four years in Towson, just eight miles north of Baltimore, he enrolled in the University of Maryland School of Law. In 1889, the year he entered, the law school graduated its first two African-American students, with honors. This greatly upset white students.

The next year nearly all of the ninety-nine white students in the law, medical, and dental schools signed an ultimatum, threatening to withdraw unless Hawkins and another black student were expelled. On the advice of John Prentiss Poe, dean of the law school—city solicitor Edgar Allan Poe's father and the chief architect of the Democratic party's later legislative attempts to disfranchise black voters—the regents submitted to the white students' demand. They decided that the two blacks had to go "for the protection and preservation of the school." For a while Hawkins was at his wit's end. He was married, with a family, but had no money. Ultimately he was able to obtain his law degree from Howard University in Washington, D.C.

One of Hawkins's challenges against Baltimore's residential segregation law, which he filed on behalf of the local NAACP chapter, reached the Maryland Court of Appeals in 1915. The court delayed a decision, pending a U.S. Supreme Court ruling on the constitutionality of a Louisville law that had been patterned on Baltimore's own residential segregation ordinances. It was an important case. The Baltimore city solicitor filed a Supreme Court brief defending Louisville's right to prevent a black from buying on a "white" block. Hawkins filed a brief opposing the Kentucky city's segregation law.

The Supreme Court's unanimous 1917 decision in *Buchanan v. Warley* nullified the Louisville residential segregation law and Baltimore's as well. It supported an owner's right to sell real estate to whomever he or she wished, even if that person was black and a local law prohibited such a transaction. That put an end to further efforts to impose residential segregation through legislation, opening the way for other segregation tools.

3

꓃꓃꓃꓃꓃꓃

Race Science

JUST FOUR MILES from McCulloh Street's turmoil, Roland Park was
an island of calm. Located just outside Baltimore's city limits at the
time, it was a garden suburb where fine families moved if they had
the money. "This is an ideal community," raved the Civic League
president at the annual banquet in 1910. "We have here the spirit
of neighborly forbearance and neighborly love." As a reaffirmation,
dinner guests sang:

> Take of the past its sunniest days,
> And of memory, its rarest rays.
> A song for the future, this refrain,
> God be with us till we meet again.

Such compatibility was the goal of "romantically planned suburbs," as they are called in urban affairs literature. The earliest included Llewellyn Park, the nation's first gated community, which
began rising in West Orange, New Jersey, in 1853, and Chicago's Riv-
erside, launched in 1868. Each was a trendsetter. Roland Park was
not only a trendsetter but also a barometer. Because its development
uniquely spanned the whole Progressive Era, from the 1890s to the
1920s, and also coincided with the peak of the national interest in
eugenics, Roland Park gauged changes in the American upper crust's

attitudes and behavior, including growing class-consciousness and shrinking social tolerance toward other races and religious groups. Roland Park demonstrated how a belief was taking hold in real estate that Jews, in addition to blacks, were bad for property values.

Progressivism, a movement led by intellectuals, was a big tent where many ideas germinated to cure the social ills that rapid industrialization and record immigration had bequeathed to the nation. Republican leaders included President Theodore Roosevelt and Robert M. La Follette, the firebrand known as "Fighting Bob," who started his own Progressive party after serving as a GOP congressman, governor, and senator from Wisconsin. Democratic progressive champions ranged from President Woodrow Wilson to Oliver Wendell Holmes, the great jurist. Progressives of various stripes spurned calls to join forces with socialists and anarchists. Instead they campaigned on their own for workers' rights and environmental safeguards. They demanded direct election of public officials instead of boss rule.

Although Progressives all agreed that child labor was evil, they were divided on many other issues of the day. They argued about the desirability of women's suffrage. White, male, often upper class and Protestant, leading Progressives showed scant interest in blacks, most of whom were still confined to the rural South and who had their own advocates in Booker T. Washington, W. E. B. DuBois, and Marcus Garvey. In 1910 Baltimore, blacks were the only population group that the city's progressive movement did not embrace.

This was the hothouse of ideas in which Roland Park was born in 1891 on eight hundred acres of woods, steep ravines, and rolling fields just north of Baltimore's city limits. The lands had been part of large estates since colonial times but were ultimately acquired by land speculators from Kansas City, Missouri, who were bankrolled by British investors. Kansas City, a primitive outpost of America's westward expansion just a few decades earlier, had become a national promoter of parklike residential communities to counter the ill effects of urban living. "Life in cities is unnatural life," the Kansas City Board of Park and Boulevard Commissioners declared in an 1893 resolution. "It has a tendency to stunt physical and moral growth. The monotony of brick and stone, of dust and dirt, the absence of the colors with which nature paints, the lack of a breath of fresh air, write despair on many a face and engrave it upon many a heart."

Progressives deemed Baltimore's prevalent form of rowhouse living to be a strange hybrid, less than desirable. Their ideal was home-ownership. That would be good for America, wrote Lawrence Veiller of the influential Russell Sage Foundation in 1910: "Where a man has a home of his own he has every incentive to be economical and thrifty, to take his part in the duties of citizenship, to be a real sharer in government. Democracy was not predicated upon a country made up of tenement dwellers, nor can it so survive." Although it would take decades—and such radio and television hit series as *Ozzie and Harriet* and *Leave It to Beaver*—to popularize homogenized suburbs as an American dream, the vision of white picket fences was grounded in Progressive Era planning.

Edward Bouton fully subscribed to such sentiments. He was Roland Park's developer and a Kansas City native. To perfect the new garden district, he hired Frederick Law Olmsted, Jr., the genius's son and an important landscape architect in his own right. Olmsted, working with his brother, John, retained the old growth and planted chestnut, oak, hickory, and poplar trees in barren fields. Homes ranged from imposing mansions to relatively modest clapboard designs that buyers chose from architectural catalogs. This assortment produced such a pleasing ambience that many of the prominent families listed in the *Blue Book*, Baltimore's social register, moved to Roland Park from places like Eutaw Place during early suburbanization. James F. Waesche's community history likened Roland Park to a siphon "plunged into the city's social heart."

At the center of communal activity there stood the Baltimore Country Club, created by the Roland Park Company to foster congeniality and homogeneity. Three churches on company land welcomed residents—Episcopal, Presbyterian, and Methodist Episcopal. No provision was made for Catholics, even though Baltimore was a heavily Catholic city with its own upper class. Thus Roland Park developers made it plain from the outset that financial ability was merely one test that a prospective home buyer had to pass; ethnicity, class, and religion were others.

Roland Park followed the best practices and most forward-looking planning principles of the Progressive Era. The community exercised self-government through its Civic League, which had an elected board. A separate corporation taxed homeowners and took care of maintenance and infrastructure, including roads. Twenty-five years before New York introduced municipal zoning, Roland Park guaranteed orderly development through legal deeds containing binding covenants that restricted homeowners' land use and regulated their behavior. The Roland Park Company set the lot sizes and approved house plans. It established a minimum construction value for any new home. Outhouses, cesspools, private stables, chickens, livestock, and other nuisances were forbidden. The number of pets was strictly limited. The restrictions were a condition of sale and transferred from one owner to the next. All this was in keeping with the philosophy of the Kansas City park commissioners: "The man desiring to build a handsome residence will expect to be able to select a street which is sure to be used for residence purposes only, and for residences of the same class as that which he intends to build. It is such uniformity of use in a restricted territory that gives special value to lands."

When construction began in 1892, the Roland Park Company evicted scattered blacks from its property. Many moved to the nearby black village of Cross Keys on Falls Road and later returned as servants. As early as 1893, Bouton sought to prohibit "negroes or persons of African descent" from residency, but his lawyers counseled that such a ban would be illegal. He was not happy with that advice. Race was a problem that needed to be contained; one had to be forever watchful. In 1910, only months before W. Ashbie Hawkins's acquisition of 1834 McCulloh Street, Bouton explicitly prohibited nonservant blacks from residency in Roland Park. He did so for competitive reasons: with rival suburbs rising in numbers, he wanted Roland Park and his company's new Guilford community (formally opened nearby in 1913) to be known as the most exclusive in the city.

They became some of the earliest communities in the nation to bar African Americans through property deeds. *The Sun* supported the approach. When the first residential segregation bill was introduced in the City Council, the newspaper said that Baltimore would be on a firmer legal footing if it ostracized blacks through binding private agreements instead of government legislation.

Jews were excluded next. In 1911 one Charles T. Levine could be found among Roland Park homeowners and even as an elected director of the Civic League. His was not the only Jewish family. The celebrated portrait photographer David Bachrach also was a resident. During the Civil War he had followed the Union Army with his cumbersome apparatus. Later he took the only known photograph of President Lincoln delivering the Gettysburg Address. Another resident was Julius Levy, an immigrant from Britain. He lived in a stone mansion with his German-born wife. Levy was the world's leading manufacturer of straw hats, which in those days before air-conditioning were de rigueur in summer wardrobes throughout America and nicely accented the pin-striped blue-and-white seersucker attire that Baltimoreans favored.

Bouton's position on Jews, however, was clear: he believed they hurt property values. Like blacks, they had to be kept out. True, he had been forced to sell a handful of lots to Jews during the 1893 depression, when Roland Park teetered on the verge of bankruptcy. But once the nation and the company recovered, Bouton toughened screening methods. A community must decide whether it "is to be Jewish or Gentile. It cannot be both and be satisfactory," he wrote. In 1913 Bouton ended sales to Jews. Unlike the prohibition against blacks, the ban on Jews remained an unwritten company rule and was never recorded in deeds. Nevertheless it was diligently enforced by the Roland Park Company, which had the right to approve all sales, including resales. For the ensuing fifty years, not a single house was sold to a Jew in Roland Park, or in Guilford, Homeland, and Northwood, which the Roland Park Company developed in north Baltimore. Many rival communities followed Bouton's exclusion policy with real estate brokers' participation and homeowners' approval.

Little in Bouton's early life suggested that he would be a success as a real estate developer. His career included a grocery business, law studies at night, and a stint in Colorado, where he raised sheep and cattle. In Roland Park he found his calling, his fame rising as a leading national authority on creating exclusive garden suburbs. Beginning in 1909 he participated in the development of the Sage Foundation's Forest Hills Gardens in Queens, New York, doubling as the model suburb's general manager. He also advised J. C. Nichols, the Kansas City developer of country club estates. In each case Bouton advocated the exclusion of blacks and "a Jew of any character whatever." His closest friends regarded such discrimination as only natural. Three of them were among Baltimore's most prominent Progressives.

By lineage, the lawyer William Cabell Bruce was the most illustrious of the three. Two of his distant forebears had reigned as ancient kings of Ireland and Scotland, respectively; another far-flung relative would become prime minister of Australia. The wide-ranging American branches of his family tree included John Cabell Breckinridge, James Buchanan's vice president and Confederate secretary of war. Born in Virginia in 1860, Bruce grew up in a turreted Gothic Revival castle on a hill that reigned over his family's five thousand acres of tobacco fields in Charlotte County. As early as 1891, after he moved to Maryland, the former slaveowner's son predicted that the North would adopt the South's attitudes on race. His pamphlet *The Negro Question* called the Maryland Republican party's black supporters an "alien, unassimilable, ignorant, immoral, thriftless, corrupt mass of voters, darkening the face of the South like the overhanging skirts of a nimbus cloud." Bruce's racial views were so unexceptional that triumphant Republicans, after their stunning 1895 landslide in Maryland, elected him to preside over the state Senate, even though he was a Democrat.

Bruce was an effective writer. He won a 1917 Pulitzer Prize for his two-volume biography of Benjamin Franklin. In 1923, at the age of sixty-three, he became a U.S. senator from Maryland. "Progressivism for him meant clean, honest government by the better sort of people in place of squalid machine politics that catered to the lower classes," wrote the biographer of his son, the diplomat David K. E. Bruce.

An even better friend of Bouton's was Charles H. Grasty, a crusading newspaper editor who was to end his career as a roving correspondent in Europe for the *New York Times*. Born in Virginia in 1863, the son of a Presbyterian minister, and raised in Missouri, he entered college at the age of thirteen and became managing editor of the *Kansas City Times* at twenty. The newspaper company aggressively engaged in land speculation, and in 1890 Grasty was sent to Baltimore to attract the needed British capital for Roland Park. After accomplishing his mission, Grasty stayed in Baltimore. In 1892 he acquired the *Baltimore News* and turned the struggling evening paper into a fiery campaigner for progressive reform. Although a Democrat, he was a strong voice against machine rule in the seminal 1895 election that produced the Republican landslide. That made him a power broker. His clout grew in 1910 when he put together a group of investors who bought *The Sun*, just months before the McCulloh Street confrontation. Grasty was both editor and publisher. Under him *The Sun* became a vocal supporter of residential segregation. "The white race is the dominant and superior race, and it will, of course, maintain its supremacy," *The Sun* editorialized while Grasty headed the newspaper. "The attitude of the Southern man and the attitude of an average Baltimorean toward colored people is one of helpfulness. He sees in them not simply wards of the nation but descendants of those whom he and his ancestors trusted and respected for their loyalty and affection."

In later years *The Sun* would gain a certain reputation for institutional anti-Semitism. Such were the newspaper company's personnel policies that no Jewish journalist was hired for three decades after Philip S. Perlman, the city editor of *The Evening Sun*, left for a law career in 1917.

William L. Marbury was Grasty's lawyer and confidant and had saved the newspaperman from ruin. Two years before the 1895 election, Grasty's *News* had published exposés of an illegal lottery racket operated by the Democratic party in Maryland. The operation was so big, the newspaper reported, that it employed two thousand runners and netted $5,000 a day, or well over $150,000 in 2009 dollars. With affidavits from a police marshal and seven captains, the *News* printed names and addresses of the kingpins. They sued for libel. "The experience of the City of Baltimore in the alliance of officers with the gamblers was not different from that of Chicago, New York, New Orleans and the other great cities of the Republic," the jurist John D. Lawson wrote in *American State Trials*, a 1916 book that described the case and Marbury's role in it.

The Democratic party's numbers racket was supremely profitable. Of the turnover, 25 percent was used for expenses and 10 percent for payouts, leaving a staggering 65 percent as profits for the backers. During the three-day trial, key witnesses invoked the Fifth Amendment or pleaded amnesia. Grasty seemed headed for a conviction, but Marbury rescued him. Assuming that the jury knew enough about Baltimore to recognize that the newspaper's articles were true, Marbury put up a show that was skimpy on evidence but big on legal theatrics. The jury found for his friend Grasty.

Grasty lived in Roland Park along a street named after him; Marbury lived in a big rowhouse in Bolton Hill, just seven blocks east of McCulloh Street. His household at 159 West Lanvale Street included six black servants, one of whom had his master's sorrel mare saddled at 6:30 every morning in good weather so that Marbury, attired in a tweed riding ensemble, complete with a bowler hat, bow tie, smart white pocket handkerchief, and shiny dress boots, could join other gentlemen of his class and circumstances for a leisurely ride along Druid Hill Park's bridle paths. He was a wealthy man due to his successful representation of railroad companies in important cases, but he constantly worried about money.

Marbury had been born in 1858 on a tobacco plantation in southern Maryland, on the outskirts of today's sprawling District of Columbia. He was a descendant of Francis Marbury, who had emigrated from England around 1680, and of Josiah Fendall, one of Maryland's early colonial governors. His father was a planter-lawyer and a member of the Maryland General Assembly. His mother was a niece of John Marshall, the first chief justice of the U.S. Supreme Court.

The Marbury plantation, named Wyoming, was a magical place. The family's big white frame house overlooked a scenic valley of ancient Piscataway hunting grounds where trees burst into a riot of color each autumn. Next to the house, ringed by some of the earliest boxwoods planted in North America, mossy headstones marked the graves of ancestors who had mercifully been spared from the humiliation that followed the War of Northern Aggression. At the outbreak of hostilities, the Marburys owned sixty-two slaves who provided the economic foundation for tobacco cultivation; after the Northern victory, the family was forced to free its remaining twenty-five slaves. The devastating property loss was nothing compared to the emotional toll. Young William took it hard. He had knelt down each night to pray for his heroes—Robert E. Lee, Stonewall Jackson, and Jefferson Davis. He was not alone in feeling crushed. A neighbor, Mary Surratt, aided John Wilkes Booth in the assassination of President Lincoln. She was the tavern keeper and postmistress of Surrattsville, where the Marburys lived. She was tried and hanged; the town's name was changed and erased from maps.

Marbury studied at Johns Hopkins University, graduated from the University of Maryland law school (where his co-valedictorian was Bruce), and joined the law firm of his uncle, Colonel Charles Marshall, who had been General Lee's military secretary and an eyewitness to the surrender at Appomattox. His professional breakthrough came when he was appointed U.S. Attorney for Maryland. All the while his keen legal mind was fixated on one goal: keeping blacks in their place. "It is an anomalous condition that an inferior race should share the government with the superior one," he believed. He advised the City Council on residential segregation laws and the legislature on disfranchisement, and served as board chairman of the State Hospital for Colored Insane. After Maryland voters failed to disfranchise blacks for the third time in the 1911 referendum, he took the matter to the U.S. Supreme Court. He contended that since Maryland had

William L. Marbury, a Confederate nostalgic, devoted his life to legal challenges of the rights of African Americans. *(Special Collections, University of Maryland Libraries)*

never ratified the Fifteenth Amendment, the U.S. Constitution's voting rights provisions could not apply to the state's blacks. He lost that argument and many similar ones. Never mind. Such legal cases were his belated contribution to the Lost Cause. To "serve in the cause of political righteousness under those who had fought for the Confederacy was his idea of pure happiness," his son wrote.

Many influential whites shared Marbury's bigotry, and his peers in the legal profession admired it. In the summer of 1910, as racial tensions mounted in Baltimore, Marbury was elected president of the Maryland State Bar Association, and there was talk about a mayoral run in the following year. Instead, in 1913 he declared for the U.S. Senate with the encouragement of President Wilson, a Southern Progressive whose election campaign Marbury had managed in Maryland. He ultimately dropped out of the race, but not before a face-to-face meeting with his friend in the White House. Newspapers reported that President Wilson considered nominating Marbury to the U.S. Supreme Court.

Marbury was a disciple of Arthur de Gobineau, a French count whose theory of the Aryan master race gained popularity among pro-slavery thinkers on the eve of the Civil War. When the eugenics movement emerged, Marbury adopted the belief of millions of other Progressives that science supported white supremacy. The pioneering eugenicist, in the 1880s, was Sir Francis Galton, a half-cousin of Charles Darwin. Eugenicists initially involved themselves in the study of inheritance traits in plants and animals, but their attention soon shifted to improving human stock. Eugenicists advocated selective breeding. Birth control, castration, forced sterilization, and, in extreme cases, euthanasia, were among methods discussed and practiced for weeding out the "unfit." Gradually eugenics grew into an influential worldwide movement. It molded Germany's National Socialist ideology and South Africa's white-supremacist apartheid doctrine.

Eugenicists prepared elaborate rankings of the different races and nationalities. Together with anthropologists, they studied skin color, hair texture, skull shape, brain size, and the characteristics of buttocks in their efforts to determine the developmental level of various races and ethnic groups. They correlated these characteristics with judgments involving the different groups' reputed intelligence and their tendency to commit crimes. Many deemed Anglo-Saxons, particularly the peerage, to be the peak of human existence, followed by Northern Europeans. Not surprisingly, the Church of England and the Episcopalian branch of the Anglican Communion were regarded as the highest expressions of Christianity.

The fresh immigrants streaming to the United States were not Aryans, however, but consisted largely of Irish and Italian Catholics or Jews from Eastern Europe. That uneducated flood worried eugenicists, though many predicted that assimilation—Americanization—would alleviate many concerns. Some nationalities were more desirable than others. The movement's driving force, the zoologist Charles Benedict

Davenport, presented thumbnail sketches of several large immigrant groups in his 1911 work *Heredity in Relation to Eugenics.*

"Germans are, as a rule, thrifty, intelligent and honest," he wrote. "They have a love of art and music, including that of song birds, and they have formed one of the most desirable classes of immigrants."

Davenport's assessment of the Irish was mixed. "Many of Irish, most strikingly those from the north part of that island, were among the nation's most intrepid frontiersmen and their descendants have served the nation in many important posts." But "the traits that the great immigration from the south of Ireland brought were, on the one hand, alcoholism, considerable mental defectiveness and a tendency to tuberculosis; on the other, sympathy, charity and leadership of men. The Irish tend to aggregate in cities and soon control their governments, frequently exercising favoritism and often graft."

Davenport next assessed the Italians. "Aside from his tendency to crimes of personal violence, the average Italian has many excellent characteristics, not one of the least of which is his interest in his work, even as a day laborer," Davenport wrote. "He assimilates fairly rapidly, especially in rural districts; not a few Irish girls marry Italians when both are Catholics; and this assimilation will add many desirable elements to the American complex." This was true, however, only about northern Italians, who thrived in New York as truck farmers. The southern Italians, darker because "doubtless they have derived part of their blood from Greece and Northern Africa," have "not the self-reliance, initiative resourcefulness that necessarily marks the pioneer farmer."

Davenport was conflicted about Jews. The urban "mass of Hebrew immigrants occupy a position intermediate between the slovenly Servians [Serbians] and Greek and the tidy Swedes, Germans and Bohemians," Davenport wrote. "In earning capacity both male and female Hebrew immigrants rank high and the literacy is above the mean of all immigrants. Statistics indicate that the crimes of Hebrews are chiefly 'gainful offenses,' especially thieving and receiving stolen goods, while they rarely commit offenses of personal violence. On the other hand they show the greater proportion of offenses against chastity and, in connection with prostitution, the lowest crimes. There is no question that, taken as a whole, the hordes of Jews who are now coming to us from Russia and the extreme southeast Europe with their intense individualism, and their ideas of gain at the cost of any interest, represent the opposite extreme from the early English and the more recent Scandinavian immigration."

The United States soon became the world leader in the eugenics movement. In 1903 the American Breeders' Association (later renamed the American Genetic Association) was established to improve humans through selective mating. The movement's patrons included the industrialist Andrew Carnegie; Mary Harriman, the wife of the Wall Street railroad magnate; the corn flakes inventor John Kellogg; and the oil baron John D. Rockefeller. Their largesse enabled the movement to open a headquarters, the Eugenics Record Office, at Cold Spring Harbor, New York, in 1910, just as the Baltimore City Council was debating its pioneering residential segregation law.

Baltimore eagerly embraced eugenics. Dr. William H. Welch, the famous first dean of the Johns Hopkins School of Medicine, and Dr. Lewellys F. Barker, the chief physician at the Johns Hopkins Hospital, directed eugenics research at the Cold Spring laboratory, serving as vice chairmen under Alexander Graham Bell, inventor of the telephone. Several other Hopkins luminaries made a name for themselves in eugenics. They included William Howell, the university's first professor of physiology, who succeeded the irrepressible William Osler as dean of the medical faculty and later played a defining role at the new School of Hygiene and Public Health. Other Hopkins notables shaping the eugenics movement included James McKeen Cattell, who smoked hashish during his explorations; Thomas Hunt Morgan, who made important discoveries about the role played by the chromosome in heredity; and Raymond Pearl, one of several scientists who studied the brain of African Americans. (Pearl later became a critic of eugenics.)

Countless scientific and popular books propagated eugenic ideas. So did *The Birth of a Nation*, D. W. Griffith's provocative 1915 film that took the country by storm. Based on the novel *The Clansman* by Thomas Dixon, the film depicted white Southerners' humiliation during Reconstruction and characterized the Ku Klux Klan as heroic in its efforts to restore "order." In a splendid publicity stunt, Dixon persuaded Woodrow Wilson, who had sat next to him at Johns Hopkins seminars, to show *The Birth of a Nation* to a White House audience that included members of the cabinet and the Supreme Court. Afterward Wilson was greatly exercised about the film's vivid imagery. Leaping to his feet, he exclaimed: "It is like writing history with lightning. And my only regret is that it is all so terribly true."

The years from 1880 to 1914 marked the apex of foreign immigration to the United States. With few Anglo-Saxons and Northern European Protestants arriving, President Theodore Roosevelt in 1903 warned that Anglo-Saxons risked committing "race suicide" by not replenishing their stock in adequate numbers. He pointed to "the Jew, the Russian, the Hungarian [and] the Italian . . . darkly outshading the Americanized descendants of the English . . . the German and the Swede." Later, in the heyday of anti-foreign sentiment during World War I, President Wilson was equally harsh. "Any man who carries a hyphen about with him carries a dagger that he is ready to plunge into the vitals of this Republic whenever he gets ready."

The onset of the war in 1914 halted immigration to the United States. Two years later the race theorist Madison Grant published *The Passing of the Great Race*, a best-seller that advocated strict curbs on immigration. An open-door immigration policy, he argued, had resulted in America's becoming overrun by uncouth Eastern and Southern European immigrants. Not only did these groups exhibit dubious racial characteristics and pose a threat of mongrelization, he wrote, they also tended to espouse alien political philosophies, including anarchism and bolshevism. All that was needed was for such troublemakers to infect the blacks with such dangerous ideas.

Grant's fears came true in 1919. Radical agitation—often by immigrant firebrands—over inflation, joblessness, and racism sparked race riots in twenty cities during the "Red Summer," with the most lethal confrontations occurring in Washington, D.C., Chicago, and

Elaine, Arkansas. The political reaction was swift. With the involvement of such leading eugenicists as Davenport, the United States
enacted immigration curbs in 1920 and 1924. Stringent admission
quotas were imposed, based on the number of foreign-born already in
America in 1890, a cutoff date that favored Protestant Anglo-Saxons
and Northern Europeans at the expense of immigrants from Russia,
Poland, Austria, the Balkans, and Italy who had begun arriving in
great numbers after 1890. The law excluded Japanese immigrants altogether, and no immigration quota existed for Africa.

The eugenics influence continued to grow. In another decade it
would guide the Federal Housing Administration and its policies. So
important is the role of eugenics that much of what follows in this
book has some obvious or indirect connection to the movement's
legacy.

4

꒐꒐꒐꒐꒐꒐

Segregation by Collusion

THE HALT of European immigration in the 1920s brought unforeseen consequences to both the South and the North. In their scramble to replace immigrant workers, big-city industries began recruiting African Americans. For the first time blacks had a way out of the South. By the thousands every month they rode the trains to the industrial Promised Land of the North. It was Hallelujah time. The weevil, a voracious insect, had decimated cotton crops throughout the South in the early 1910s, and severe flooding in 1927 destroyed homes and fields along the Mississippi River. With the entire South in an economic crisis, the North's factories offered hope and redemption. The nation's black urban population doubled, from 2.6 million in 1910 to 5.2 million in 1930.

Few blacks from the Deep South gravitated to Baltimore, but a steady trickle came first from Virginia and then also from the Carolinas. Perceiving overflowing black districts as a threat that needed to be contained, uneasy whites sought protection in restrictive covenants. The covenant that Carl and Matilda Schoenrodt recorded in the Baltimore courthouse in September 1925 was typical. It covered a block of modest rowhouses on North Appleton Street, just a few blocks from Fulton Avenue. Fulton had been the racial demarcation line since the city's 1910 segregation law, and it marked the western boundary of the black district, which extended all the way to McCulloh Street in the east. While there were still plenty of all-white pockets within that district, they resembled islands disappearing amid a rising tide.

The Schoenrodts and twenty-six homeowners on their Appleton Street block built a floodwall. They agreed that "none of said respective properties nor any part of them shall at any time be occupied or used by or conveyed, mortgaged, leased, rented or given to any Negro or to any person or persons in whole or in part of Negro or African descent. Persons of negro or African descent may be employed as servants by any of the owners or occupant of said respective properties and whilst so employed may reside in said premises as servants as long as the premises are occupied by their respective employers. . . ."

No population group remained immune to prejudice. In some white neighborhoods, covenants excluded blacks and Jews; some Jewish neighborhoods barred blacks and, verbally, Eastern European Jews. And in 1917, when a rare African-American residential development was launched on the outskirts of the city near the new campus of Morgan College, George R. Morris, the white real estate man advising the college, recommended a covenant. Morgan Park residents followed the advice, prohibiting whites.

Some of the earliest covenants in the United States had targeted Chinese in California before 1892, when the federal judiciary struck them down as a violation of the most-favored-nation clause of an 1868 U.S. treaty with China. While that ruling halted restrictive covenants at the time, whites in California resorted to alternative means, expelling Chinese with beatings, killings, and burnings. In big cities like San Francisco, they were herded to Chinatown, the officially designated ghetto.

Covenants became the new instrument of race separation after the U.S. Supreme Court abolished residential segregation laws in 1917. If municipalities or states could not constitutionally inhibit the purchase and occupancy of property solely because of the color of the proposed resident, what would prevent private parties from doing so voluntarily? Absolutely nothing. Communities in various parts of the country enacted restrictive covenants that barred a long list of ethnic and religious groups from buying or occupying real estate property.

These restrictions varied from place to place. In addition to blacks, various neighborhoods barred Jews, Catholics, Mexicans, Syrians, Armenians, Persians, Italians, and many others.

Since no most-favored-nation clause protected those minorities, racially restrictive covenants enjoyed support at all levels of the American judicial system. In 1926 the U.S. Supreme Court affirmed a District of Columbia court's decision to enforce a covenant against black buyers. In Maryland, local enforcement was strengthened when the Court of Appeals ruled in 1938 against a black man who had moved to a white Baltimore block a year earlier. The house was within a twenty-four-square-block area that white neighbors had protected with a 1926 covenant. Lawyers for Edward Meade, the black man, argued that the covenant had been rendered "ineffectual to accomplish" after blacks moved nearby. In *Meade v. Dennistone*, the court rejected that argument. It said that Meade knew about the racial restriction and should have obeyed it. Significantly, the court commented on the wider social context. "The large, almost sudden, emigration of negroes from the country to the cities, with the consequent congestion in colored centers, has created a situation about which all agree something ought to be done." While the Fourteenth Amendment precluded any "public action" from being taken to contain blacks and "to solve what has become a problem," the court found private covenants lawful and enforceable.

Baltimore enforced covenants without major violence. Chicago, by contrast, resorted to brute force. It was a chief destination of black migration from the Mississippi Delta, and attempts by blacks to move to white neighborhoods protected by covenants were repelled with violence. Jesse Binga, Chicago's leading black banker and real estate man, had his house bombed six times in a twelve-month period ending in 1920. He had "wormed his way into a white neighborhood," the *Property Owners' Journal* charged. (In 1945 the sociologists St. Clair Drake and Horace R. Cayton wrote a remarkable analysis of Chicago during the Great Migration, *Black Metropolis*.)

With Chicago leading the way, the nation's real estate industry took it upon itself to administer ethnic separation through covenants and other means of exclusion. In 1921 the Chicago Real Estate Board voted unanimously to expel any member who rented or sold property on a white block to blacks. Three years later the National Association of Real Estate Boards, of which the Baltimore board was a founding member, amended its code of ethics to forbid Realtors from introducing "members of any race or nationality" into neighborhoods where their "presence will clearly be detrimental to property values." Thirty-two states adopted "model real estate licensing acts" that authorized state commissions to revoke the licenses of agents who violated the NAREB's Code of Ethics.

Even before those actions, two Baltimore mayors led a search for additional segregation tools. James H. Preston was the first. America's local governments had not yet widely discovered condemnation as a land-acquisition tool, and none had used it to pursue racial goals. Preston was a pioneer on both counts. He presided over Baltimore's first government-sponsored Negro removal project, decades before post–World War II urban renewal. His target was the area north of the courthouse and City Hall.

After coming to power in a disputed 1911 election, Preston embraced a plan to widen St. Paul Street between Lexington and Centre streets downtown. St. Paul Street was a main artery leading to the new suburbs, but it became narrow and winding near downtown, causing terrible traffic congestion. Right in the shadows of the city's center of power, St. Paul Street cut through a largely black neighborhood, an embarrassment in the legally segregated city.

This neighborhood around today's Mercy Hospital had become a sought-after African-American area after the Civil War, when it housed an educational institute named after Frederick Douglass. The institute was deeded in the spring of 1865, while the Civil War still raged, to a group of white men for the simple reason that blacks could not own real estate. By the time Mayor Preston took over, blacks had enjoyed full property rights for decades. After Johns Hopkins University announced the relocation of its campus and new areas opened up for blacks, high-status families moved to Druid Hill Avenue and McCulloh Street. Nevertheless meeting halls of black organizations abounded around the courthouse, including several groups of Freemasons. They and African-American residents coexisted with a number of genteel old white families who still lived in dignified three-story rowhouses next to Gallows Hill, where public hangings had been staged in the city's early days. The offices of leading black lawyers and doctors stood next to modest hotels and rooming houses, even funeral parlors. Three powerful churches anchored the neighborhood. Bethel, with a twelve-hundred-seat sanctuary on Saratoga Street, was a national leader in the African Methodist Episcopal movement. Union Baptist on North Street was growing so quickly that it sent Baptist missionaries to other parts of Maryland under the dynamic Dr. Harvey Johnson, a founder of the Niagara Movement. St. Francis Xavier, occupying the corner of Calvert and Pleasant streets, was the nation's oldest Catholic church specifically catering to African Americans. Its white pastor was one Father Dennis, who addressed all black women as Mary and men as John, regardless of their age or standing in life. White communicants included Hugh (Ee-Yah) Jennings, the eccentric Orioles shortstop.

It is easy to imagine what went on in Mayor Preston's head. The courthouse area was going downhill. Unless stopped, low-class blacks might spill over to Mount Vernon, a high-class white neighborhood with its towering monument to the nation's first president, or to the fashionable shopping and residential blocks of Charles Street. All they had to do was to keep advancing east along Centre Street, an extension of Druid Hill Avenue. To prevent that from happening as the move of Johns Hopkins five blocks away produced a vacuum, Preston condemned the whole courthouse neighborhood. He copied a pioneering condemnation law that he had discovered while visiting London, and swiftly acquired the properties. The three churches were demolished—with Bethel and Union Baptist moving to Druid Hill Avenue—as were the old building of the *Afro-American* newspaper at 307 St. Paul Street and the rented law office of W. Ashbie Hawkins and George McMechen at 31 East Saratoga Street. The lawyer Harry S. Cummings was displaced at 219 Courtland Street; a Republican, in 1890 he had become the first black to be elected to the City Council. Evicted from 222 Courtland Street was the lawyer Warner T.

McGuinn, who would twice become a Republican City Council member. Mark Twain had met him and was so impressed by the young man's intellect that he took care of McGuinn's tuition at Yale, where the student was elected president of the University Law Club.

Preston's demolition plan went forward without a hitch. As renters, blacks had no say. At least one property owner sued, but the mayor disposed brusquely of legal challenges and then razed the buildings, most of them between 1914 and 1919. "He was a rough, tough fellow when he wanted to be," remembered the journalist Lou Azrael. "Politicians who opposed him were not eased out or mollified; they were kicked out with a bang. Reporters who opposed him too vigorously were barred from the City Hall. Businessmen who opposed him felt, and heard, his wrath."

A park was created in the middle of the bifurcated St. Paul Street. It was named after Preston. In 1917, when this Preston Gardens construction was still under way, he declared that health conditions justified the segregation and relocation of blacks on a vaster scale. "The mortality rate among negroes for all forms of tuberculosis is 260.4 per cent higher than that of the white race," he noted. Preston announced that he would introduce an ordinance to "set aside certain sections of the city, allowing ample room for expansion, and to compel the colored people to have homes only in those segregated areas." He would do this by invoking the city's police powers in order "to protect the health" of white citizens. Blacks would be quarantined. "They constitute a menace to the health of the white population," he advised.

Preston thereupon convened a blue-ribbon committee, which included several black members. When it proved unable to divide the city between the races, he forwarded a copy of a Chicago segregation plan to the Real Estate Board of Baltimore as an example of how things could be controlled. "No doubt a similar plan would be quite effective in Baltimore," the board replied. "We hope to be able to start something along the same line here in Baltimore." The Chicago plan relied on the use of the full weight of municipal enforcement machinery to implement bans against blacks. It was now put into practice in Baltimore. When the Real Estate Board got wind of a "threatened invasion" by blacks of property near the harbor, it sent an investigator to the scene. Louis Buckner, who owned the property, acknowledged that he intended to rent the second floor to blacks; the first and third floors had white tenants. "When asked if he did not feel that he was rather inconsiderate of the interest of the other people in the block, [Buckner] replied, 'They do not pay my way, I must look out for myself.'"

The Real Estate Board's investigator told the mayor that Buckner's house was not constructed to care for three families. "We believe a suggestion from you to the Building Inspector and the Health Department to inspect this property and insist upon the owner complying with all building and health regulations of the city will go a long way toward discouraging the owner from permitting negroes to occupy the property," the investigator wrote in the Real Estate Board's name. Preston did as asked. He sent city inspectors to hound Buckner. Faced with costly repairs and other headaches, Buckner came around. In a meeting with the Real Estate Board, he pledged not to rent to blacks.

Racial separation became a cornerstone of real estate activity. Even in neighborhoods without restrictive covenants, the board's standard real estate sales contract decreed that "at no time, shall the land included in said agreement or any part thereof, or any building erected thereon, be occupied by any negro or negroes, or persons of negro or African extraction or descent, in whole or in part."

Zoning provided further enforcement tools. Introduced in New York in 1916, the concept swept through progressive cities, which separated residential, industrial, and commercial areas from one another. "Most early zoning advocates believed in racial hierarchy, openly embraced racial exclusion, and saw zoning as a way to achieve it," writes the historian David M. P. Freund. Among them was Judge Charles W. Heuisler of the Baltimore Supreme Bench. In the early 1920s he repeatedly urged Mayor Howard W. Jackson to specifically include segregation in the zoning law. That approach would be constitutional, because the "welfare" of the city was at stake, the judge argued. He pointed to Richmond and Atlanta. Both had passed racial zoning laws that had received the blessings of Virginia's and Georgia's highest courts. But Jackson refused to try this approach, fearing that he would run afoul of the U.S. Supreme Court.

Segregation was a prime concern in Baltimore. Just how much time and effort were devoted to race separation is seen from Jackson's mayoral schedule for January 5, 1924. In a single day he met with three delegations. One consisted of white neighborhood associations alarmed by the "Negro invasion." A separate delegation from the Real Estate Board called on the mayor, as did a group of black ministers. "We will have to find some place for the Negro," said C. Philip Pitt, secretary of the Real Estate Board. One solution would be "to put the Negroes in a bag and throw them overboard," he said, according to the *Afro-American*. *The Sun* quoted him as saying that "we will have to care for those who are here and those who are continuing to pour into the city. No one builds houses for the Negroes and it is up to us to find a place for them."

Jackson's solution was to appoint a biracial committee to apportion the city among the races. After much publicity, the committee in 1924 proved unable to agree on securing more living space for blacks, just as a previous mayoral committee had failed in 1917 under Preston. This produced a stalemate. Despite increasing migration, Baltimore blacks continued to be corralled within shabby, overflowing slums.

Whites' unwillingness to relinquish any established blocks or vacant land made the creation of additional black residential areas nearly impossible. That led to steadily worsening social problems in overcrowded black districts. One densely packed alley off Pennsylvania Avenue carried a dreaded nickname, "Lung Block." The death rate there for tuberculosis was 958 per 100,000 of population as compared with a citywide rate of 131.9. Yet it was just around the corner from Druid Hill Avenue's elite black residences.

In 1934 the Joint Committee on Housing, convened by the Maryland advisory board of the Federal Emergency Administration of Public Works, proposed a cleanup. It urged the city to condemn three black neighborhoods with high tuberculosis and juvenile delinquency

A trim and young Howard Jackson, seen here in 1924 after testifying before a grand jury probing corruption, sought new ways to enforce race separation after the Supreme Court struck down residential segregation laws. *(Special Collections, University of Maryland Libraries)*

rates. They should be turned over to whites and rebuilt because the locations were desirable and public transportation good. The committee justified this proposal on hygienic grounds because "a large number of the domestic workers in private homes are drawn from these areas . . . a great deal of laundry work is done within them, and . . . a large proportion of those employed in handling the food supply of the city resides within their boundaries." The committee made no provision for the resettlement of the existing black residents or the improvement of their current or future sanitary conditions.

Because of Baltimore's three-tiered real estate market, the Real Estate Board did not generally accept Jews to membership. As a result, the board lacked capacity and will to enforce segregation in predominantly Jewish districts, which became transitional zones. The Seventeenth Ward, which included Pennsylvania Avenue, illustrated the inkblot effect of racial change. The ward's black population increased from 1,499 in 1900 to 12,738 in 1910 and then to 16,736 during the following decade. Meanwhile the number of whites fell from 18,926 to 10,946 and then to 3,900 persons. In other words, the ward's overall population remained relatively constant, but its complexion changed almost entirely within two decades.

In the neighboring Fourteenth Ward, which included McCulloh Street, the pace of racial change was no less striking. The white population declined from 18,264 in 1900 to 13,738 in 1910, and then dipped to 11,189 in 1920. More significantly, the black population, which was squeezed into only one part of the ward, exploded from 3,043 to 8,392 and then to 14,012. Ethnic rotation was evident to a visitor in 1925:

One has but to stroll through McCulloh Street and Madison Avenue . . . and observe the number of houses with "For Rent or Sale to Colored" signs to realize that this vacating of homes by whites and the moving in of Negroes is going steadily on. . . . In several blocks, the Negro now occupies the western side of this street while white families are still on the eastern side.

By that time blacks had moved farther up along McCulloh Street, taking over previously Jewish blocks near Druid Hill Park. Although the two-story rowhouses there were cramped, those blocks nearest to the park became magnets for strivers. Lawyers and educators moved there, as did leading caterers in charge of white high-society events— catering was dominated by blacks in those days—chauffeurs, waiters, bell captains, and postal workers. Rivers Chambers, the most sought-after bandleader at white weddings and cotillions, lived there. Other blacks began calling the area Sugar Hill after an upscale part of Harlem. The moniker stuck.

By contrast, the suburbs remained closed to blacks. Only five suburban developments, totaling fewer than one hundred houses, were built for blacks between the 1900s and World War II. The earliest of those developments was Cherry Heights. It was located outside the city along Belair Road in Fullerton, and was already under development by a group of investors who included W. Ashbie Hawkins when the McCulloh Street controversy erupted in 1910. Full-page ads in the *Afro-American Ledger* claimed that its lots were "equal to Roland Park in beauty." To make sure the development remained isolated, Baltimore County ordered streets built so that they all dead-ended and did not connect to surrounding white farms.

Nothing more strikingly illustrated the difficulties of expanding black living areas than the experience of Morgan College. The college had begun in 1867 as the white Methodist Episcopal church's outreach to "the colored people." It built a stern-looking, four-story stone edifice in a white west Baltimore neighborhood at Fulton and Edmondson avenues. Within a few decades it became clear to Morgan's president, John Oakley Spencer—who was white, as were the leading administrators at the time—that the site was inadequate. There was no money for expansion, but the college found a benefactor in Andrew Carnegie, the industrialist, who in a 1907 speech had contradicted the prevailing opinion of doom and declared at a conference in Scotland: "Never in the history of man has a race made such educational and material progress in forty years as the American

Negro." The school contacted Carnegie, challenging him to back his words with money. He agreed to give Morgan $50,000 for new buildings on the condition that the college raise a like amount (roughly $1.2 million in 2009 money). But a larger site needed to be found.

After scouting numerous alternatives, Morgan president Spencer located a site at Greenspring and Kelly avenues in northwest Baltimore. Surrounded by cabbage fields and fruit orchards, it contained a stone-built hunting lodge that had once belonged to Charles Carroll of Carrollton, the only Catholic to sign the Declaration of Independence. The site appeared ideal. Just a few hundred yards away was an old black hamlet dating back to slavery times. A small church existed there, and a handful of modern cottages were being built to be sold to middle-class blacks. Morgan's goal was to use half of the forty-three-acre parcel for the college and the rest "for the development of a first-class residential area."

Nearby was Mount Washington, one of Baltimore's earliest rail-commuting suburbs for well-to-do whites. Its residents learned of Morgan's plan in 1913, just as the City Council was considering another version of the segregation law. Racial tensions were high. "Not only is Mount Washington in danger from the invasion of this negro college. The entire community from York Road to Forest Park . . . is jeopardized," thundered a leader of the Mount Washington Improvement Association. Mayor Preston joined the dispute, even though the site was outside the city at the time. "I think it is quite clear that the settlement of a colored institution or school of learning at Mount Washington would have a depressing effect on the value of property," Preston said. As an alternative, he suggested that Morgan take over the buildings of a reform school for delinquent black boys in southwest Baltimore. The college rejected the idea.

During this squabble the *News* sent a reporter to the white neighborhood where the college had been located for more than thirty years, to find out how existing residents felt about Morgan. "We scarcely know it is a colored institution. I have asked people if they find it objectionable and have yet to hear the first person complain," the

Reverend Peter Ainslie told the paper. (He was identified as being "a native of Virginia and in close touch with anti-negro race feeling.")

Rebuffed in Mount Washington, Morgan continued its quest. In 1917 the college settled on a northeast Baltimore parcel, also outside the city's borders at the time. Morgan was in for a fight there too. Not far from the new site—previously occupied by a decrepit hotel and a beer garden of ill repute—were old estates and white villages. Those neighbors were most unhappy. Hoping to derail the project, they first offered to bribe Morgan's president. He refused. They then filed two lawsuits to prevent Morgan from going ahead with its plans, but were defeated in the courts. In a last-ditch effort the opponents sought to abrogate Morgan's charter through legislative action. More than fifty opponents, led by Edgar Allan Poe, the poet's grandnephew, chartered a special train to a hearing in Annapolis. President Spencer represented Morgan. For two hours the duo sparred.

Poe insisted that allowing Morgan to build in northeast Baltimore would engulf the community in racial conflict. Spencer demolished that argument by revealing that more than eighty black students already resided peacefully on the newly acquired property. The statement "seemed to surprise the opponents." The focus then shifted to Morgan's charter, the point of the proposed legislation. "Has Morgan ever violated its charter?" Spencer asked. There was no response. Spencer then asked each opponent the same question individually. In each instance the answer was negative. When it was all over, the House Judiciary Committee, by unanimous vote, determined that Morgan had operated within its charter. Nevertheless the opponents made three additional attempts to stop Morgan through legislation. All failed, including the final one that would have prohibited "colored persons from hereafter acquiring residences in Baltimore County" in the election district where the college planned to build its campus.

Considering the fierce opposition, it was somewhat ironic that another new black suburban community became located within a mile of Morgan's new home. Neighboring landowners there were no more tolerant of blacks, but prejudice against blacks was not their only prejudice. The farmland in question belonged to German Americans. Amid World War I jingoistic fever, patriotic white Americans wanted nothing to do with Germans, and the land languished on the market. This gave an opening to Harry O. Wilson, the city's leading black banker. He bought the land in 1917. It became known as Wilson Park, and modest cottages rose there.

These two suburbs were exceptions. Most of Baltimore's blacks lived caged inside three main districts. One, on the west side, was slowly expanding to marginal white blocks, like a smaller one on the east side. In addition to a third district, in south Baltimore, some twenty tiny "black spots" were scattered elsewhere. *The Evening Sun* coined a name for these segregated islands: "Baltimore's Negro Archipelago."

5

ЛЛЛЛЛЛЛЛ

Mapping Bigotry

AMERICA was in the grip of the Great Depression when President Franklin D. Roosevelt's administration initiated a process that further segregated blacks and ghettoized Jews. The government's Home Owners' Loan Corporation (HOLC) surreptitiously mapped 239 cities, dividing neighborhoods into various real estate risk categories. From Norfolk to San Diego, Miami to Seattle, Galveston to Duluth, HOLC assembled local working groups that rated every residential area, determining its market value and future prospects. While age and conditions of housing were prime considerations, also factored in were the race, ethnicity, class, religion, and economic status of residents, and their homogeneity.

These maps added a new cartographic dimension to the pathology of race in America, promoting residential segregation and fostering economic discrimination, which had been widely practiced by the lending and real estate industries for decades. The purpose of the maps was to prevent the federal government and financial institutions from exposure to risky loans; but the contents were not shared with the general public. Four colors were used to classify neighborhoods on the maps: green, blue, yellow, and red. Red, the universal color of alarm, smeared neighborhoods deemed to be "hazardous" and "dangerous," where banks had stopped issuing mortgages altogether or charged exorbitant fees and interest rates. A new and ominous real estate and banking term was coined: redlining.

Home Owners' Loan Corporation grew out of the Home Owners' Refinancing Act of 1933, a major piece of New Deal legislation that President Roosevelt introduced to bring the tottering nation's housing market back from the abyss of the depression. Mapping was just one of HOLC's tasks. In a few years of existence, the agency achieved two remarkable feats. It standardized an appraisal system for making mortgage loans, and it bailed out one million homeowners who faced losing their properties to foreclosure in the midst of the worsening economy.

Homer Hoyt set the tone at HOLC after becoming the affiliated Federal Housing Administration's chief economist in 1934. He wanted to improve the accuracy of real estate appraisals so that the federal government could avoid undue risks in insuring lenders against losses in the event of homeowners defaulting on mortgage loans. Hoyt had spent the preceding decade in Chicago as a real estate broker and consultant. He saw ethnicity as a key to predicting value. Using a hierarchy developed by John Usher Smyth, a veteran Chicago real estate man and zoning activist, Hoyt graded various nationalities in the order of their real estate desirability. Here is the comparative ranking that he first published in his 1933 Ph.D. dissertation at the University of Chicago, "One Hundred Years of Land Values in Chicago: The Relationship of the Growth of Chicago to the Rise of Its Land Values, 1830–1933":

(1)   English, Germans, Scots, Irish, Scandinavians;
(2)   North Italians;
(3)   Bohemians or Czechoslovakian;
(4)   Poles;
(5)   Lithuanians;
(6)   Greeks:
(7)   Russian Jews of the lower class;
(8)   South Italians;
(9)   Negroes,
(10) Mexicans

Hoyt allowed that many whites on the lower rungs could become less objectionable once they "conform to the American standard of living." Blacks and Mexicans, on the other hand, had no chance of overcoming "the opinion or prejudice" of the real estate market, even though such bigotry "may have no reasonable basis." That was just the way real estate operated, he wrote. "If the entrance of a colored family into a white neighborhood causes a general exodus of white people, such dislikes are reflected in property values."

Hoyt's list looked suspiciously like the hierarchical rankings that eugenicists had been publishing about various ethnic groups for decades. Since nothing in his background suggested any particular interest in eugenics, his adoption of the movement's assumptions showed how pervasive the influence of eugenics had grown. The University of Maryland professor Steven Selden, who surveyed high school and college biology texts from 1914 to 1948, found most of them carrying the eugenics message of selective breeding and racial betterment. "It is important to repeat that none of those texts reflected overt racial bias. The arguments were never made in terms of race. They were always made only in terms of biological merit," Selden writes.

Hoyt was also influenced by the Chicago School of pioneering sociologists who introduced the use of surveys and other modern methodologies to urban research. Robert E. Park, Ernest Burgess, Roderick D. McKenzie, and Louis Wirth—whose help Hoyt acknowledged in his book—used maps to demonstrate how alcoholism, juvenile delinquency, homicides, suicide, and poverty concentrated in certain areas. Mining census reports and housing and welfare records, they and their colleagues divided Chicago into square-mile blocks and cartographically correlated social phenomena and problems with the race, ethnicity, age, and gender of the population. They burned shoe leather to make on-the-spot observations. They argued that a system of concentric circles radiated from the center of the city, giving each sector a different function. Residential neighborhoods within such circles were in constant flux, with lower socioeconomic groups succeeding higher ones as the latter kept moving to the suburbs.

The influence of eugenics was evident in HOLC's uniform instructions to mapmakers in various cities. Those instructions never mentioned Charles Lindbergh by name or religion, but "American business and professional men" of the aviator's Nordic type and Episcopalian faith were held up as ideal residents. They made the perfect score. Any deviation from that norm, whether by race, religion, ethnic background, recent immigration, or economic status, lowered the score. The instructions reflected the belief that blacks and Jews damaged property values and should be confined within their own areas.

The real estate industry shared this bigotry. Appraisal manuals continued to repeat Hoyt's hierarchy until the 1960s, coloring assessors' views and implying that the groups lowest on the ladder were detrimental to housing values and undesirable as neighbors. Manuals also repeated HOLC and FHA recommendations that all neighborhoods should have covenants.

*

Lenders had long been preoccupied with race, class, and religion. After the deadly 1919 race riots in Chicago, that city's leading bankers adopted a blanket provision not to make loans "on property in changing or depreciated districts." In 1932 the Mortgage Conference of New York, the coordinating body of the thirty-seven biggest lenders, prepared block-by-block maps and encouraged members to avoid loans in areas with concentrations of blacks. Even color-coding had been tried before. In 1934 J. M. Brewer, owner of a property services company, pinpointed those areas in Philadelphia where various ethnic groups lived, using green for Italians, red-orange for blacks, blue for Jews, and boxes with name tags for other "conspicuous" nationalities. Price information was included. Brewer also used letter grades. A denoted "highest class," B "upper class," C "middle class," and D "lower class." E described a population group the map called "decadent." HOLC's signal innovation was to map racial, religious, and class concentrations in various cities according to criteria that were uniform throughout the nation.

In Baltimore, HOLC entrusted the supervision of map preparation to fourteen white men—eleven real estate brokers, a male economics professor from Goucher College for women, and two federal
banking officials. Aided by appraisers, they began their work shortly
after the opening of HOLC's Baltimore office on July 24, 1933. The
day was long remembered. Some five hundred desperate applicants
showed up seeking relief from foreclosure. "They were solid-looking
citizens, most of them having run into difficulties through unemployment or salary cuts," a newspaper reported. One man said that he
was about to lose a $3,000 property because he was unable to make
payments on the remaining $300 balance. Formerly of means, he had
lost his savings in two bank failures. He was jobless. HOLC was his
last hope.

Another applicant was an African-American minister, whose home
was to be auctioned off that very afternoon. HOLC intervened. Rac-
ing the clock, the agency won a reluctant last-minute reprieve from
the building and loan association holding the mortgage. Yet another
applicant was a woman who was told that HOLC could do nothing
about her situation. She would not take "no" for an answer. Clutch-
ing two letters from President Roosevelt in which he assured her of
help, she vowed to write FDR again. She knew that her president
would help her, she told a startled official.

Statistics from 1931 showed that one in five persons in the Baltimore workforce was without a job, with blacks in the worst position. By Christmas 1933 one family in six in the city was on relief.
The unemployed mobbed soup kitchens, relief services, police stations, and even City Hall in search of money, food, or advice. HOLC's
Baltimore office said that three-quarters of homeowners applying for
federal intervention—usually refinancing—were desperate, on the
verge of insanity or suicide, and without food. A week before that
bleak Christmas, Thomas T. Hammond opened the gas jets in his
kitchen near Johns Hopkins University. Next to the body of the sixty-
one-year-old real estate broker police found a note addressed to his
wife. It was mostly indecipherable. All that detectives could say with
certainty was that Hammond had died a mental and material victim

of the economic collapse: he had owned the apartment house where he died but had lost it.

Amid such acts of desperation, HOLC worried about panic. It recognized that the nation's economic ruin had eroded housing values to the point where untold numbers of homeowners held titles to worthless properties. That's why the redlining of maps had to be kept secret from the public, an agency document said in tortuous language. If "hundreds of thousands of home owners, who today believe that their properties are safe from that urban disease which has gradually destroyed the savings of so many other thousands, examine these maps, they would be dismayed to realize that the ultimate loss of their equities is inevitable, unless prompt, concerted action to save them is undertaken."

Baltimore escaped the ravages of truly epidemic foreclosures that devastated other cities. It was a homeowner town, with 71,070 "native white" and 22,589 "foreign-born" families living in houses they owned or were buying. So were 3,793 black families. By 1936, when the worst of the depression was over, local financial institutions had taken back 7,375 properties. HOLC intervention saved well over 10,300 other homes from foreclosure.

The city's estimated 700 building and loan associations—they were so unregulated that no one knew the exact number—repossessed 45 percent of foreclosed homes. The Safe Deposit and Trust Company held another 38 percent in its portfolio, but the firm was in sound financial shape. The remaining defaulted properties were widely dispersed among mutual savings banks, insurance companies, and liquidators. Those felt so little need to sell at depressed prices that only 456 foreclosed houses were resold in 1935 and 1936. "There is no large concentration of distressed housing, and consequently no active campaigns have been undertaken to dispose of such houses," HOLC observed at the time. Instead lenders rented them out in a housing market that was incredibly tight. "With the exception of some of the 'hazardous' areas, all sections report today either practically 100% occupancy or an actual shortage," HOLC noted. That shortage was due to the continued influx of outsiders to Baltimore that even the depression had not halted. Hard times put the brakes on housing construction, though. Only 119 housing starts were recorded in 1934, a far cry from 4,871 in 1926.

HOLC's guidelines to mapmakers reflected Homer Hoyt's ranking of races and nationalities. The agency sternly admonished appraisers to document "infiltrations of lower-grade population or different racial groups"; the latter definition included Jews. Instructions advised appraisers to be precise. "What is the general type of occupation, i.e. *executives, business men, retired professional, clerical, skilled mechanics* or *factory workers, laborers, etc?* Indicate predominating nationalities, *estimate* percentage of foreign-born families to total. *Estimate* percentage of Negro families to total number of families. Any threat of infiltration of foreign born, Negro or lower grade population? If so, indicate these by *nationality* and *rate of infiltration* like this: 'Negro—rapid.' If a considerable number of families are on relief, indicate as 'few' or 'many.' Indicate rate as 'rapidly' or 'slowly.'"

On HOLC maps, the "best," or grade A, neighborhoods were colored green. These were "hot spots; they are not yet fully built up," so desirable that mortgages were available there at liberal terms even in the depths of the depression. A dozen Baltimore neighborhoods won this top ranking in the map that HOLC completed May 1, 1937. They included three communities developed by the Roland Park Company—the recently built Homeland, the much grander and somewhat older Guilford, and Northwood, a more modest neighborhood still under construction. By contrast, Roland Park itself merited only a blue-colored B rating of "still desirable." Appraisers regarded its houses, by then as old as forty-five years, as timeworn. Forest Park, Roland Park's onetime archrival for bragging rights as the city's most exclusive neighborhood, shared a B rating. Not only were houses in Forest Park also several decades old but restrictive covenants there had broken down, allowing Jews to move in and rowhouses and duplexes to be built, some containing rental units to provide income for homeowners. Regarding areas like Roland Park and Forest Park, HOLC wrote in 1937: "They are like a 1935 automobile—still good, but not what the people are buying today who can afford a new one."

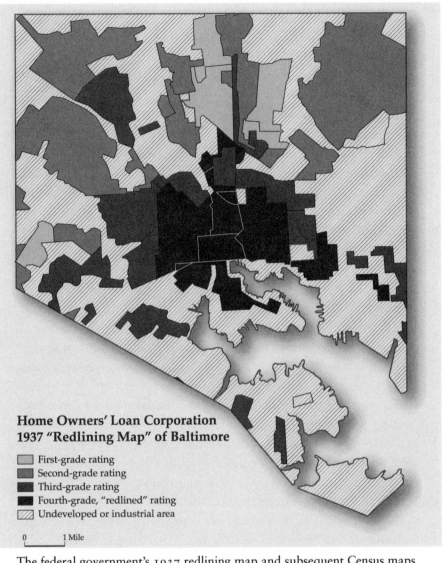

**Home Owners' Loan Corporation
1937 "Redlining Map" of Baltimore**

☐ First-grade rating
▨ Second-grade rating
■ Third-grade rating
▧ Fourth-grade, "redlined" rating
▨ Undeveloped or industrial area

0 _____ 1 Mile

The federal government's 1937 redlining map and subsequent Census maps
(on page 69) show how real estate discrimination and bigoted lending
determined the expansion of black residential areas.

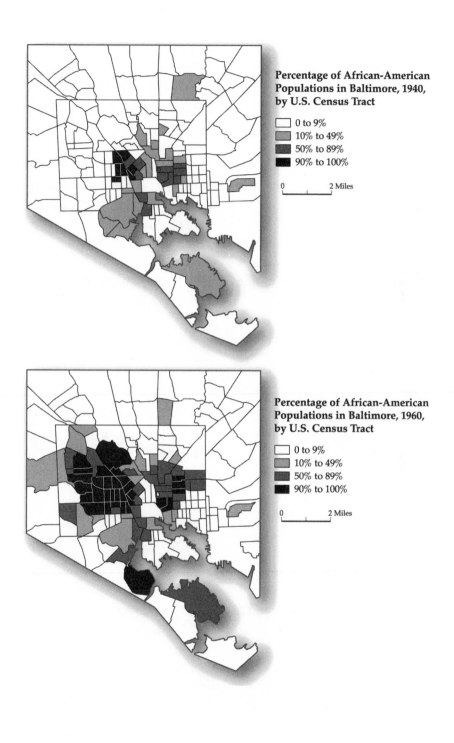

Percentage of African-American
Populations in Baltimore, 1940,
by U.S. Census Tract

☐ 0 to 9%
▨ 10% to 49%
▧ 50% to 89%
■ 90% to 100%

0   2 Miles

Percentage of African-American
Populations in Baltimore, 1960,
by U.S. Census Tract

☐ 0 to 9%
▨ 10% to 49%
▧ 50% to 89%
■ 90% to 100%

0   2 Miles

HOLC regarded newness of construction and design—accompanied by requisite restrictive covenants—as supremely important. Among HOLC's key assumptions was that once the cycle of racial or economic succession began in a neighborhood, conditions would inevitably worsen. Large swaths of Baltimore's traditional white working-class rowhouse blocks earned a marginal C grade of "definitely declining," colored yellow on the map. Lenders were advised to exercise caution in issuing mortgages in such neighborhoods, which were "characterized by age, obsolescence and change of style; expiring restrictions or lack of them, infiltration of lower-grade population. Generally, these areas have reached the transition period." Their eventual fate was to be redlined, HOLC proclaimed. Indeed, the agency explained that the red color given to "hazardous" areas "represents those neighborhoods in which things that are now taking place in C neighborhoods, have already happened."

The neighborhoods colored red, then, evidenced "detrimental influences in a pronounced degree, undesirable population or an infiltration of it." Because of such trends, "some mortgage lenders may refuse to make loans in these neighborhoods and others will lend on a conservative basis." By redlining, HOLC said, "we do not mean to imply that good mortgages do not exist or cannot be made in the Third and Fourth grade areas, but we do think they should be made and serviced on a different basis than in the First and Second grade areas." A lasting stigma became attached to such areas. A two-tier lending industry was born. Banks served well-to-do white areas; blacks had to get their financing from speculators at harsh terms.

Most of Baltimore's city core—stretching a mile and a half north and south of City Hall and some two miles east and west—was redlined as too "hazardous" for conventional lending. The determining criteria were the age and condition of housing, along with residents' race, national origin, religion, and economic and immigration status. Such considerations produced intriguing results. The McCulloh Street rowhouses, by then almost entirely occupied by blacks, were within the borders of a stigmatized area, but so were the fading mansions on Eutaw Place, which continued to be white but frequently were no longer occupied by members of the elite. Bolton Hill also was red. HOLC saw little future for them. "In most of the 'hazardous' or 'red' areas it is difficult to see how any improvement can take place," the agency suggested.

Hundreds of yellowing block-by-block worksheets, stored at the National Archives, show the appraisers' meticulousness. As required, their reports predicted future trends—"upward," "downward," or "static"—and included other observations. "Good residential area of homogeneous character," a 1937 Baltimore assessment said of a "white-collar class" neighborhood with "very few" foreign-born residents and no Jews or blacks. The area was graded B. Another neighborhood of fifty-year-old rowhouses was redlined as D. It had good transportation and central location, the appraiser acknowledged, but those qualities could not compensate for its twin handicaps— "obsolescence" of housing and increasing "Negro concentration."

Yet another worksheet contained a rare rebuke to the anti-immigrant instructions. It noted that one entire area of tidy east Baltimore rowhouses "is populated principally by persons of Polish extraction who have considerable pride of the appearance of their property." These were the rowhouses with quintessential white marble steps that were scrubbed every week. Nevertheless the appraiser gave the neighborhood a marginal C because of "Negro and Italian infiltration."

The Columbia University historian Kenneth T. Jackson was the first scholar to look into HOLC redlining records. His 1985 book *Crabgrass Frontier* categorically declared that "Jewish neighborhoods or even those with an 'infiltration of Jews' could not possibly be considered 'Best' any more than they would be considered 'American.' This was not true in Baltimore, where one Jewish neighborhood received an A grade. It was Dumbarton, a highly restricted small enclave near Pikesville, where downtown department store owners and other patricians of German origin built their suburban mansions. Dumbarton clearly met the HOLC criteria of "homogeneous character." Its residents were close-knit and conscious of their social rank. In addition to written covenants against blacks, a gentlemen's agreement prohibited Jews of Eastern European origin. The Suburban Club, another bastion of this social self-selectivity, was located right across from Dumbarton along Park Heights Avenue. It excluded Jews of Eastern European lineage, who thus founded Woodholme, a rival country club a few miles farther out.

All black neighborhoods were redlined, with two exceptions. One was Wilson Park, where the lawyer W. Ashbey Hawkins lived; the other was Morgan Park. The two small enclaves, within a mile of each other, shared the B, or "still desirable," rating of the surrounding white area. Tiny Morgan Park splendidly satisfied HOLC's prejudices. It was new and still under development; its residents were restricted to educated blacks—W. E. B. DuBois lived there between 1939 and 1950—and its covenants prohibited "inharmonious" elements: whites.

The redlined maps were HOLC's last hurrah. By the time the nationwide mapping process was completed in the late 1930s, the agency was being dismantled, its functions transferred to other federal bureaucracies. Many of HOLC's tasks were taken up by the Federal Housing Administration, which had a more direct impact on the American people between the depression and the end of the twentieth century than probably any other federal agency.

HOLC had handled emergency refinancing to bail out homeowners facing foreclosure. The FHA set up a permanent system that guaranteed loans by private lenders for creditworthy borrowers who might not otherwise have been able to obtain financing. It made homeownership an achievable American dream. In effect it invented the modern mortgage system, which brought modest down payments and thirty-year terms within the reach of millions of buyers. This was nothing short of a revolution. Up to that time lenders had routinely demanded a 50 to 60 percent down payment on a house and full repayment of the loan within one to three years, necessitating frequent refinancing of balloons, which was difficult or outright impossible in adverse economic conditions. But the revolution carried a price tag: the FHA became the government's leading practitioner of ethnic, religious, and economic discrimination. Under policies that carried on

HOLC's legacy and lasted until at least the 1960s, the FHA promoted homeownership in new—and primarily suburban—neighborhoods so long as they were white and not ethnically or economically diverse. This encouraged further redlining by banks, insurance companies, and other businesses, thereby dooming older city neighborhoods to advancing decay, particularly if they were black or mixed race.

"FHA did more to institutionalize redlining than any other agency by categorizing mortgages according to their risk levels and encouraging private lenders who wanted insurance for their mortgages to do the same," writes Professor Amy E. Hillier, of the University of Pennsylvania.

The FHA's adherence to covenants was so fundamental that the agency tried to enforce restrictions even after they expired. A case in point was Sidney Salzman. In 1941 Salzman, a court stenographer, wanted to buy one of seven foreclosed houses in Hunting Ridge, a grade A neighborhood off Edmondson Avenue in west Baltimore, where the homeowners' covenant against Jews had expired one year earlier. The Salzmans—he was Jewish, his wife Christian—had "always lived in Gentile neighborhoods," he wrote to the FHA in justifying his interest in Hunting Ridge. Federal bureaucrats were not impressed, and Salzman got a runaround.

He repeatedly offered purchase prices verbally suggested by FHA officials, proposing to put nearly half the money down. He was rejected each time, even though he had been preapproved for a mortgage. Finally one official, "with evident embarrassment . . . gave as reason for the turning down of my offer the fact of my Jewish extraction, that it was thought best not to sell one of these properties in a restricted neighborhood to me, that it might affect the sale of other properties, and that the Steffey Co. real estate brokers handling the properties strenuously objected to such sale to me, on the same grounds."

Salzman complained of religious discrimination and charged that the FHA engaged in "a needless credit investigation, which with attendant circumstances had led personal friends and acquaintances to doubt my credit standing in the community." The FHA's state director denied those charges. "Frankly, I was amazed to read the document," he responded to Salzman's letter. "There is no religious discrimination on the part of any one in the Federal Housing Administration."

In the end, Salzman's tenacity paid off. After he threatened to take the matter to Maryland's two U.S. senators—"for whatever action they deem proper"—the FHA's deputy administrator in Washington fixed a definite price on the property. Salzman met the price, got the title to the house in 1941, and lived there the rest of his life.

In April 1941, as Salzman was still battling the FHA, W. Ashbie Hawkins died, six years after the demise of his nemesis, William L. Marbury. Hawkins had been a trailblazer, and not only as an attorney for the NAACP and the *Afro-American*, where he owned stock. He was the first black to seek a U.S. Senate seat from Maryland, running a protest campaign as an independent in 1920. He did not win, receiving only a few thousand votes. H. L. Mencken, always an iconoclast, cast his vote "with joy" for Hawkins, he wrote in *The Evening Sun* on November 1, 1920. "This Hawkins I do not know, and have never knowingly witnessed. My decision to vote for him has been reached by pure reason. He at least has an intelligent platform; justice and self-determination for our fellow-Christians of the darker side of the moon." Until his death, Hawkins's main efforts remained the fighting of restrictive covenants. Despite partial victories, covenants persisted. Courts upheld their legality, and the real estate industry helped the FHA enforce them.

Baltimore had a strong real estate board, and discipline was easy to maintain. The board owned a multiple list service that was reserved to member firms, which thus tended to trade among one another. A handful of big, old-line firms ruled, including the Roland Park Company. Banks, all run by non-Jews, followed the federal government's recommendation and made sure that mortgages were not issued to buyers seen as "inharmonious."

6

⊓⊔⊓⊔⊓⊔⊓⊔⊓

The Good War

THE JAPANESE ATTACK on Pearl Harbor came as a surprise to Baltimoreans on December 7, 1941, but war did not. Much of the city's industry had been gearing up for war ever since Hitler unleashed his blitzkrieg on Europe in 1939. As war clouds gathered, Baltimore burst with new vigor and purpose every day. In the six months *before* Pearl Harbor, the city's electricity demand rose by one-third, water usage exceeded previous records, and railroad freight traffic increased by 25 percent. After Pearl Harbor, Baltimore became a twenty-four-hour city, living according to the peculiar rhythms of shift work.

An avalanche of changes in the life of the city followed. People began dressing less formally. Streetcars, operated by "motormisses," became the transport mode of necessity after the government limited gasoline purchases to three gallons a week for "nonessential" drivers and imposed tire rationing. Meat disappeared from stores; items like coffee and sugar could be obtained only with ration coupons.

Twenty-eighth in population, Maryland ranked as the twelfth state in the value of its war contracts. Its factories produced huge numbers of ships, aircraft, iron and magnesium castings, radar and communications gear, x-ray machines, rockets, shells, cartridge cases, fuses, cannon, powder, piston rings, railroad brake shoes, steel, chemicals, cotton duck, and heavy-duty tires. Bethlehem Steel mills and shipyards employed 58,000 men and women in Baltimore, Glenn L. Martin's aircraft factories another 53,000. The state's agricultural output was considerable. In 1942 the federal government requisitioned 100 percent of carrots canned in Maryland and substantial percentages of spinach, asparagus, and peas.

Maryland's largest city did not become a war production center by accident. The foundation had been laid in 1890 when a steel mill was erected in the Sparrows Point peninsula in Baltimore County, a few miles outside the port. Under Bethlehem Steel ownership the plant grew until it had no rival in the world. In 1928 the entrepreneur Glenn L. Martin bought twelve hundred sandy tidewater acres in Middle River, not far from Sparrows Point, claiming that the land was for a New York hunting club. Instead he built a visionary airplane testing and manufacturing complex. For a while in the mid-1930s it seemed that Baltimore would outrank New York as a global aviation gateway. Most anyone flying to Europe first had to travel to Baltimore because flying boat operators believed that Maryland winters were milder than New York's and winds were gentler. From Baltimore, Pan American World Airways' seaplanes darted to Bermuda, then to the Azores, and finally to Portugal or Ireland. It was an arduous journey. Britain's Imperial Airways used the same route. Germans did not wish to be left behind: they planned to make Baltimore the North American landing site for their helium-filled Zeppelin dirigibles.

In 1937 the swastika-decorated airship *Hindenburg*, returning from Europe, exploded while docking in New Jersey, killing thirty-five of the ninety-seven people on board. That ended the use of dirigibles in passenger traffic. About the same time the inevitability of a European land war convinced Martin and other manufacturers that the future of aviation lay in the perfection of aircraft using land-based runways. Martin concentrated on developing and manufacturing bombers. The era of flying boats was cut short, and so were Baltimore's aviation dreams.

Just one day before the Pearl Harbor attack, Bethlehem's big shipyard launched a boxy freighter with the traditional smashing of a champagne bottle against its prow. The SS *Roger B. Taney* was the fifth in what was to become a huge fleet of freighters riveted and welded together at conveyor-belt speed. Baltimore was one of the biggest production centers of Liberty ships, of which 2,751 were launched. It took an average of 42 days to build a Liberty ship, though one was completed in a publicity stunt in four days and 15½ hours after the keel was laid. Nicknamed "Ugly Ducklings," the ships became the workhorses of wartime convoys, carrying men and materiel through U-boat-infested seas.

The *SS Roger B. Taney* honored the U.S. Supreme Court chief justice from Maryland, who in the 1857 *Dred Scott* decision ruled that blacks—free men as well as slaves—were not and could not be citizens of the United States, and that Congress had no authority to deprive slaveowners of their property. His ruling had been long discarded, but such were racial attitudes at the beginning of America's involvement in World War II that the Red Cross, on orders from the military, turned away black blood donors nationally at an emergency blood drive. This was such an insult to Dr. Charles R. Drew that he resigned from the Red Cross in disgust. The former athletic director of Baltimore's Morgan College had invented the Red Cross blood bank; he was black.

Despite such incidents, America was changing. Six months before the Japanese attack, President Roosevelt ordered defense contractors to halt racial discrimination at plants, even though the armed forces remained segregated. Companies operating in Jim Crow cities were not happy; their white workers took the mandate as an insult. When Bethlehem Steel announced that it would train blacks as welders and riveters but then retracted in face of a white uproar, six hundred black shipyard workers walked out. After the company again changed its mind, some seven thousand whites walked out in anger, protesting that blacks were unqualified for the job. Unqualified? In 1918, before suffocating segregation forced him out of Baltimore to seek work in New Jersey shipyards, a black man named Charlie Knight snatched the coveted riveters' crown in a Bethlehem company contest, outperforming all white rivals.

Later generations would call World War II "the good war." It certainly was good for many who worked on the home front. Millions were employed for the first time since the depression and made more

money than they ever imagined was possible. Moreover labor shortages forced plants to hire population groups that never had made
much money to begin with. White mountain folk streamed to industrial cities. They came by train and bus, in battered pickup trucks and
limping cars from Appalachian hamlets with names straight out of
bluegrass songs—Bald Knob and Granny Dismal. By the time the war
ended, 250,000 "hillbillies," mostly from Virginia, West Virginia, and
Tennessee, had found jobs in Baltimore, helping the city briefly break
the one-million-population mark. At plants and shipyards, loudspeak-
ers blared country music; certain residential sections were known as
"Kentucky Colony" and "Hillbilly Heaven."

Women's entry into well-paying defense jobs went smoothly. Rosie
the Riveter and her sisters would keep these jobs only for the duration
of the war, or so it was thought before it turned out that women actually preferred the drudgery of well-paying shift work to the drudgery
of unpaid household duties. African Americans from the South also
arrived in numbers. An estimated 25,000 blacks, mostly men, were
hired for jobs in the city's war industries. Some responded to recruit-
ers' calls from Bethlehem Steel, which preferred malleable, out-of-
town black workers for its shipyards, blast furnaces, and rolling mills,
instead of those already living in Baltimore. Others were lured by the
siren songs of the *Afro-American*, a newspaper that in those days
circulated in the South. Since 1939 the paper had argued that a war
would benefit blacks because it would increase migration from the
South to the Northern industrial states. "Come North Now!" urged
one editorial. "Somehow word must be gotten to them. There are jobs
and freedom in the North. Now is the time to move this way. They
may never again have such a golden opportunity. They have nothing
to lose and everything to gain." Another editorial demanded "We
Must Have War" more than two years before Pearl Harbor. "War
is the most hateful and horrible thing in the world, yet it is our only
agency which can bring us a more abundant life."

The war indeed produced a bonanza. "There are jobs for everyone—at good wages," reported the city's welfare director. "Wages,
in fact, are probably higher than at any other time in the City's long

history. The grim spector [sic] of unemployment whose shadow fell on so many Baltimore families during the thirties—temporarily, at least—has vanished. More nutritious food is being consumed by low-income groups and better clothes and shoes are being worn. . . . The insecurity that wrecked so many families has been replaced by a virtual spending spree." Few could have anticipated that the feeble initial steps toward equality in factories during the war would one day spawn a civil rights movement that changed America.

Housing had been tight throughout the depression, and the war worsened the shortage. Eutaw Place's elegant residences were cut up into warrenlike rooming units. Working-class families with a house of their own routinely took in roomers. Every unused space—from chicken coops to trailers—was turned into rooming for war workers. Ten men, working and sleeping in shifts, sometimes shared five "hot beds" in one room. Men slept on cots in coal cellars. If all else failed, one might try to catch some shut-eye at downtown newsreel houses that operated around the clock.

Baltimore recorded no black residential vacancies. Nevertheless in 1941, six months before Pearl Harbor was attacked, Mayor Jackson went to Washington to testify before a congressional panel that the city was experiencing no housing shortage. Jackson's statement was demonstrably false, and Dr. Abel Wolman, chairman of the state planning commission, said so as diplomatically as he could. The city lacked at least 9,000 housing units in the lower-income brackets, he testified. And those lucky enough to find a roof above their heads often lived in scandalous circumstances. A 1942 spot-check by the city health department found 590 persons—45 percent of them out-of-town war workers—sharing 121 rooms on a block near the shipyards. Officials counted only 53 bathtubs for those units, many of which depended solely on outhouses.

Despite the obvious housing emergency, Baltimore officials insisted to the Roosevelt administration that the city did not need federally financed housing. Leading politicians expressed fears that with all the strangers streaming in, the city's stability would be threatened once the war was over and the jobs disappeared. "Today I talked to two of the representatives of the biggest employers of Negro labor, and they tell me that they need them but the kind that is coming won't work," Congressman Harry Streett Baldwin told a public hearing. "They offer them jobs, they work a day and leave. What do you think is going to happen when this war is over and that type of people have no jobs, because they will be the first ones laid off. They are going to remain in those houses, rent free, and the people in the State of Maryland and the City of Baltimore will keep them on relief." Elected officials and civic and business leaders made no attempt to hide their biases. "They are going to bring in here from North and South Carolina, Negro workers. They are going to send us scum," warned Cleveland Bealmear, chairman of the Baltimore Housing Authority, who had twice served as president of the Real Estate Board and who doubled as treasurer of the Episcopal diocese. Senator Millard E. Tydings and Representative Baldwin called for formal restrictions to stem the inflow of blacks. "If more Negroes are brought here," Baldwin told a public meeting, "they should be housed in trailers so that they can be easily moved out after the war is over." *The Sun* agreed. "Keeping unneeded and unwanted Negroes out of Baltimore in a time like this is a national problem," the newspaper wrote in an editorial.

Such sentiments reflected not only the racial bigotry of Baltimore's decision-makers but also their hostility toward President Roosevelt. Jackson was an example. A champion of states' rights, he served as Baltimore's Democratic mayor from 1923 to 1927 and again from 1931 to 1943. During the depression years of that second span, he grew bitterly critical of Roosevelt's policies, endorsing Thomas E. Dewey, the Republican presidential candidate, in 1944. Jackson was not the only Democratic Roosevelt foe. Senator Tydings voted against so many crucial New Deal measures that the president tried to engineer the fellow Democrat's defeat but embarrassingly failed. *The Sun*, often dubious about the New Deal, supported Tydings. "*The Sun* stands for competitive capitalism," the newspaper editorialized. "It is a system which most effectively uproots the unfit, the unworthy, the lazy. It is the system which gives place to the vigorous, the competent, the purposeful."

"Hillbillies" were among "the unfit, the unworthy." Many Baltimoreans felt nothing but scorn toward Appalachians who, according to the stereotype of the time, cherished marshmallow and chocolate MoonPies with sugary RC Cola in their lunch pails; thought bathtubs were for growing corn; and kept partying at all hours in "bucket of blood" taverns. Stereotyping didn't end there. When a celebrated cast-iron fountain was removed from Eutaw Place, presumably to be scrapped for war needs, neighbors insisted that the real reason was that the city had grown tired of hillbillies bathing and washing their clothes in it. The pent-up bitterness burst into the open in 1943, when a reader sent to *The Evening Sun* a set of verses titled "Beloved Baltimore, Maryland."

> Baltimore, oh Baltimore, you moth-eaten town,
> Your brick row houses should all be torn down.
> Your winters are cold and your summers are hot,
> The air is so foul with mildew and rot,
> The land of bad cold and sore throats and flu,
> Of stiff aching muscles and pneumonia, too.

The rhyme went on for five stanzas, calling the locals dim-witted, poking fun at their pronunciation of English, and castigating them for price gouging. It then reached a crescendo finish:

> You're not worth this paper, you're not worth this ink,
> You can take it from us: Baltimore—YOU STINK!

The criticism struck a raw nerve. *The Evening Sun* editorial office was buried under a mountain of more than thirteen hundred missives from readers. Most gave back as good as they got. "I'd like to know how those stump jumpers and ridge runners lived back in the hills," asked one reader. Another sneered, "Baltimore is a dirty city but not until a bunch of plow jockeys came here from other States." Summarizing the letters, *The Evening Sun* wrote, "Chump, Jerk, Okie, Arkie, goof, half-wit, hillbilly, windbag, slacker etc. figure prominently among the invectives."

The poem's author remained unknown. A Westinghouse Electric Company employee, James R. Cater, was the obvious suspect because he had given the poem to *The Evening Sun*. When that was disclosed, he felt the ire of the locals. A laundry refused to serve him; someone sent him the picture of a Baptist church with the accompanying text: "I have been a member of this Beloved Baptist Church in Beloved Baltimore for more than 53 years. Come and worship with us."

Cater also received this poem, one of many:

Do not look for filth and rodents
In strange cities where you dwell
As you measure for your neighbor
He will measure you back as well.

Another Westinghouse worker, Maurice Geipi, of New Orleans, also had a hand in the creative process. He had found a similar poem about Charleston, South Carolina, and was inspired to do a local version. This revelation earned him so much grief that he publicly apologized and told newspapers that he would make amends by marrying a Baltimore girl, a registered nurse. Resentment toward out-of-town workers was so strong that one protest letter came from a Baltimore soldier in New Guinea. At home, people made sure that elected officials knew just how they felt. "If it is a social experiment that is being tried all over the country, please, preserve us from this trial," the president of the Ladies' Harford Road Democratic Association wrote to Mayor McKeldin. A leading insurance man wrote, "The vast majority of white citizens plus the majority of the decent colored people of Baltimore do not want these whites and Negroes as permanent residents of this city because most of them are white and black trash. The decent Negroes of the South have the same contempt for what they style 'po white trash' as the decent northern Negroes have for both 'poor white and black trash.'"

Some officials took their prejudices to ridiculous lengths. Senator Tydings proposed an employment census of blacks as a way to determine whether the defense industry really needed to import out-of-town workers. City Solicitor F. Murray Benson did his own tabulation. By eyeballing passersby along Pennsylvania Avenue's black shopping district, he concluded that the streets "are literally swarming with able-bodied men and women who apparently have nothing to do but to roam the streets and indulge in social pleasantry," he told the top municipal officials in a formal meeting. Stung by Benson's accusations, the *Afro-American* sent reporters to interview 550 black men and women "swarming" the streets between 11 A.M. and 3 P.M. It concluded that 505 were gainfully employed but working in evening or midnight shifts; others were either married homemakers or between jobs. "I get up at 8 A.M. and walk around in the afternoon until work time—a fellow must have some recreation," one worker said.

Amid these ethnic and class tensions, City Hall continued to battle the federal government. Washington wanted more defense housing; Baltimore's officials opposed it. A particular bone of contention was the federal government's insistence that housing for blacks be built close to large defense plants on the east side. The proposed sites consisted of isolated expanses of vacant land, whose closest neighbors were white. The residents held protest meetings, bombarded officials with petitions to stop the scheme, and ran ads in the newspapers. "It is a notorious fact that vile social diseases, tuberculosis, juvenile delinquency and mental ailments prevail to an alarming extent in slum areas," one protest ad said. "Our school children and people should not and must not be subject to the dangers of a slum housing project in our community. These slum families will of necessity use the same public transportation facilities—street cars and buses—as other residents of the northeastern section—and the same public schools."

Ultimately several separate public housing projects for whites and blacks were built. Each triggered controversy. None was as explosive politically and emotionally as a plan initiated in 1939 to construct seven hundred units of public housing on vacant land near a lazy stream called Herring Run and Philadelphia Road, a meandering onetime wagon trail leading to Pennsylvania. Perhaps Washington did not care, but the city housing authority did not wish to create a colony of blacks near white working-class families.

The Herring Run project was still in limbo in March 1943 when the Governor's Commission on Problems Affecting the Negro Population issued a report. The housing crunch was bad and getting worse, the panel concluded. With some three thousand additional blacks arriving in the city each month, overcrowding had become alarming. "Where one family lived a few years ago, there now live three or four." The commission made several recommendations. It urged the authorities "at least temporarily to control the unregulated migration of both whites and Negroes." Dormitories for black men and women should be created inside large buildings, including churches, and temporary barracks erected in public parks reserved for blacks. The panel also proposed that, in an effort to free up living space for war workers, families not engaged in war work be evacuated from neighborhoods closest to defense plants and their housing turned over to workers.

Then came the kicker. The governor's commission pointedly urged that

> Undeveloped areas in and adjacent to the City of Baltimore must be made available for Negro housing to take care of the present overcrowded situation and for future development. Sites selected for this temporary housing should have in mind future permanent building after the emergency has passed. This might go far to solve not only the present emergency but the long term program.

To anyone knowing the racial reality and customs of Baltimore, the meaning of the coded wording was clear: the commission advocated that new black neighborhoods be created on the city's eastern and southwestern fringes, near white working-class bastions. In other words, the Herring Run project was just the beginning.

About this time a new mayor, Theodore R. McKeldin, came to office. As soon as he reached City Hall, McKeldin began punching holes in the segregationist superstructure that his Democratic predecessors had established over the previous half-century.

During his campaign McKeldin had stressed the urgency of "breaking the deadlock between City officials in the matter of Negro housing." Now he declared, "While it is not my function to determine where these houses shall be built, it is my duty, as Mayor, to insist that the officials charged with the immediate responsibility shall act, and that the various City bodies shall no longer continue in a stalemate."

As a practical matter, McKeldin could not disregard the threat of a backlash. He agreed with those who recommended Herring Run, but he wanted more political cover. He appointed an interracial commission to look into the matter; that handpicked group too recommended the Herring Run site. Only the city housing authority opposed the location. Meanwhile Senator Tydings and Representative Baldwin continued their agitation against Herring Run with the help of northeast Baltimore's Democratic bosses. They got ammunition from rumors— "with some basis of fact," McKeldin acknowledged—that the new housing would be reserved for workers to be recruited from Alabama and Mississippi rather than for existing city residents.

Trying to play it safe, McKeldin made no recommendation of his own in the matter. He simply sent to Washington all the favorable recommendations he had received from various groups and agencies. He also included the city housing authority's singular vote against the Herring Run site. The mayor then departed on a fishing vacation to Maine, expecting the Federal Public Housing Authority (FPHA) to select Herring Run in his absence and take the political heat. McKeldin had hardly left town before Democrats staged a palace coup. Senators Tydings and George Radcliffe as well as Representatives Baldwin and Thomas J. D'Alesandro, Jr., demanded to see the FPHA commissioner in Washington. Acting Mayor James F. Arthur, president of the all-white, all-Democrat City Council, joined the revolt. Exercising his temporary powers, Arthur ordered the city solicitor to be present at the Washington meeting "in order that the City might be fully protected against encroachment by the Federal Government on its rights and prerogatives in connection with the housing situation and to see that all laws are obeyed and respected by the Washington authorities."

FPHA caved under the pressure and decided against Herring Run. By the time McKeldin returned from vacation, the mayor could do nothing more than send a bitter protest letter, which his aides toned down. McKeldin was a realist. "Herring Run is as dead as the dodo," he declared. Instead the federal government selected Cherry Hill for permanent black housing. It was an isolated locale of farms and dense woods near the municipal incinerator in south Baltimore. Three existing black communities in Baltimore County, close to defense plants, were chosen to provide temporary housing for blacks.

The Cherry Hill site selection set a precedent. For decades to come, politicians would find it easier to concentrate public housing projects in black areas or wastelands than to disperse them throughout the city. One result was a public housing program that would aggravate poverty and disease.

Although blacks constituted roughly a fifth of the city's population during the war, they accounted for 33 percent of meningitis cases. Half the deaths from infectious and parasitic diseases occurred among the black population. These were consequences of abysmal sanitary conditions and overcrowding. In January 1944 the city housing authority reported that Baltimore would need to replace or rehabilitate at least 26,000 existing dwellings and construct 6,814 new units to house the black population.

The Citizens Planning and Housing Association also studied the situation. This progressive advocacy group "strongly urged that more space be allotted to the existing black population and no Negro labor be recruited from outside Baltimore" until the housing situation was alleviated. "Where numerous White vacancies exist in neighborhoods already partially occupied by Negroes, it is suggested that these vacancies, upon renovation, be turned over for Negro occupancy," the association's report said. "This would appear to be a matter of convincing the general public of its interest in such a step, which will be taken eventually and is important now."

Black residential areas would have to be expanded, one way or another.

Part Two: 1944–1968

BLACKS NEXT DOOR

Get down
Gainin' on ya!
Movin' in and on ya
Gainin' on ya!
Can't you feel my breath, heh.
—The psychedelic rock band Parliament

7

⊓⊔⊓⊔⊓⊔⊓⊔

Crossing Fulton Avenue

BLACKS BROKE THROUGH the Fulton Avenue barrier during the Christmas holidays in 1944. Ever since the City Council's first 1910 segregation law, that thoroughfare had marked the far end of west Baltimore's black district. One side of the street was black, the opposite was white. For thirty-four years the demarcation line held, with blacks staying on "their side" and peering across a nicely landscaped median strip. On the white side, tidy rows extended as far as the eye could see. Rowhouses there had porches and lawns. Big single-family frame houses occupied tree-lined streets farther northwest. "It could have been the Moon," remembered the historian Louis S. Diggs, who grew up on the overcrowded black side. "I recall many days looking far up, wondering what it was like up there."

How the first black family came to cross to the west side is not known. Perhaps someone figured that it was all right to sell to blacks because white homeowners had let the restrictive covenants lapse two years earlier. Or a feud provoked someone to swear revenge and let a black occupant slip in. Or someone simply calculated that it was more profitable to sell to a black. It did not matter how it happened. Once the first black crossed Fulton Avenue, whites were on the run. They would run for more than three decades. Neighborhoods would be devastated and the entire metropolitan area redefined.

The prestigious rowhouses of Fulton Avenue in the 1880s. Three decades later the avenue became a racial demarcation line, with whites living on one side and blacks on the other. After blacks broke through in 1944, the median was removed and the street designated as a truck route. *(Maryland Historical Society)*

Leon Sachs was among the first to learn what had happened. On the morning after New Year's Day in 1945, the executive director of the Baltimore Jewish Council rushed into his office and fired off letters to nineteen Jewish real estate operators active along Fulton Avenue. "There is an urgent matter involving a real estate situation that has been brought to my attention," he wrote. Sachs feared that Jewish involvement in home sales to blacks would trigger anti-Semitism. His fears materialized two weeks later when an agitated crowd packed St. Martin's Roman Catholic Church hall, where the chairman of the meeting charged that Jewish real estate people were "taking advantage" of their blue-collar neighborhood. A shout was heard from the audience: Before anything was done about blacks, something should be done about Jews. The next meeting was as ugly. "If we can't get any justice, I am sure that the Ku Klux Klan can take this matter in their hands," a man in the crowd yelled.

Prominent advertisements appeared repeatedly in *The Sun* and *The Evening Sun*:

WARNING

TO REAL ESTATE DEALERS, SPECULATORS, PROPERTY-OWNERS AND THEIR AGENTS, BUILDING ASSOCIATIONS—AND ALL OTHERS CONCERNED:

We, the members of Fulton Improvement Association, property-owners, and residents of North Fulton Avenue and adjacent streets, members of neighboring Churches, supported by our Pastors, Clergy and Trustees, do hereby serve notice that we are strongly organized—and determined to RESIST by all legal, moral and persuasive means, the efforts of certain unscrupulous dealers, money-lenders, selfish property-owners, and their agents, to intimidate or force us to move from our homes, in which we are happy and content.

These "Homes" and "The Right to Live in the Manner We Choose" are the very things for which our boys are fighting; and when our boys come back—God willing—we want them to enjoy the comforts and pleasures of the only "HOME" they have known—with its FOND MEMORIES, ASSOCIATIONS, AND ENDEARMENTS.

FULTON IMPROVEMENT ASSN. INC.
MEMBERS OF ST. MARTIN'S R.C. CHURCH
MEMBERS OF FULTON AVE. BAPTIST CHURCH
MEMBERS OF GARRETT PARK M.E. CHURCH
MEMBERS OF FRANKLIN STREET MEMORIAL CHURCH
MEMBERS OF FULLER MEMORIAL BAPTIST CHURCH
PROPERTY-OWNERS OF NORTH FULTON AVENUE

Whites demanded that Mayor McKeldin declare a sixty-day moratorium to prevent further sales and rentals to blacks. The mayor rejected the idea out of hand. In his letters to constituents he played the role of a teacher, patiently trying to make pupils grasp the root causes of a thorny problem—"the enormous inflow of warworkers" and "the extraordinary migration of colored people." These were unspeakably complicated matters, McKeldin wrote. At City Hall he himself had asked 250 Fulton Avenue protesters for solutions, "and none of them had any suggestions, not even the members of the State Legislature and City Councilmen who brought them there."

"The colored people of the City have outgrown their quarters and now have reached the overflow point and they must go somewhere," he wrote. "If anyone has the wisdom to suggest an available place where colored homes could be built, it would undoubtedly help a great deal. In the meantime, they follow the lines of least resistance and purchase homes adjoining the neighborhoods in which they already live. It seems to me that this is the crux of the subject." McKeldin appealed for calm. "I want to assure you that I have the profoundest sympathy for everybody involved. I can see the problem from the standpoint of both the white people and the colored people and am frank to say that in the interest of peace and good will in Baltimore City everyone must be patient and as reasonable as possible until the housing situation is eased up enough to enable people to become adjusted according to their wishes and not forced by circumstances to live where they have no desire to live. It seems to me that everyone by now should know that the Mayor of Baltimore City is legally powerless to do anything at all."

This was not what whites wanted to hear. "Who said anything about legal action anyhow?" one letter writer told McKeldin. "What those white home owners and white residents there want is action, whether legal or otherwise. Action to keep out the 'jiggs.'"

No leader in Baltimore better understood the city's anxieties than Theodore Roosevelt McKeldin. Born in 1900, he had grown up in a white working-class neighborhood in south Baltimore. Even so, McKeldin also understood the aspirations of blacks. More powerfully than any other elected official in Maryland's history, he advocated equal rights, even at times when he did not necessarily have to do so. The following were among his achievements during his first term, from 1943 to 1947: he selected black staff members and hired a black secretary for himself; he named the first black assistant city solicitor and the first black school board member. McKeldin ordered that race be removed from applications for city jobs; he even tried to

Theodore R. McKeldin, shown here after his election in 1943, tried to calm emotions when blockbusting began the next year. He had a speech impediment but overcame it by practicing with pebbles in his mouth. *(Special Collections, University of Maryland Libraries)*

secure jobs for freed convicts. Some questioned his sincerity, for he was nothing if not solicitous. At one event he gave a Jew a *yarmulke*, a Catholic a rosary, and a Protestant a copy of the New Testament. "McKeldin was vilified, McKeldin was loved," remembered Solomon Liss, a Democratic city councilman who became a judge. "McKeldin was an unusual man. He loved all people—black and white, Jews and Gentiles."

McKeldin's father was a semi-illiterate stonecutter of Scotch-Irish ancestry who sired a brood of eleven and drank so heavily before sobering up and becoming a policeman that the son swore off liquor for life. From his mother he got his deep Christian faith and sense of duty. At fourteen, McKeldin quit school and took a job in a bank. He spent his evenings studying for a high school diploma; on weekends he earned extra money as a gravedigger. That money he spent on mail-order courses in public speaking by Dale Carnegie, who would become a household name a few years later when he wrote the wildly popular *How to Win Friends and Influence People*. Teddy McKeldin suffered from a bad childhood speech impediment, and public speaking initially was an ordeal for him. He overcame that handicap by practicing speaking with pebbles in his mouth. McKeldin was determined to be somebody. When he graduated from an evening law school at twenty-five, his mother, who was of German origin, got him a job as secretary to William Broening, the Republican mayor. Teddy McKeldin was on his way.

He triumphed in politics through sheer willpower and stubbornness. In 1939 he unsuccessfully challenged the incumbent Democratic mayor, Howard W. Jackson. In 1942 he almost beat the Democratic Governor Herbert R. (for Romulus) O'Conor. The next year he again ran for mayor against Jackson, who was seeking a fifth term and was feuding with the state party, headed by O'Conor. This time McKeldin won handily, attracting a strong crossover vote.

McKeldin was a forward-looking moderate. In 1952 he stirringly nominated Dwight D. Eisenhower for president at the Republican National Convention, yet twelve years later he rejected his party's right-wing choice, Barry M. Goldwater, and instead endorsed the reelection of the Democrat Lyndon B. Johnson. The Texan showed his gratitude by helicoptering to Baltimore to thank McKeldin, whom he wanted to make the first mayor of the District of Columbia. A lot of Baltimore's major infrastructure projects began under McKeldin, who served as mayor on two separate occasions and was elected to two terms as governor. The rebirth of Baltimore's Inner Harbor, tunnels underneath, a new airport, and a massive highway construction program that included the Baltimore Beltway—all those projects were conceived on his watch.

That was yet to come when the Fulton Avenue controversy erupted in early 1945. It soon became evident that despite all the commotion, white residents would not fight. They could not even muster the required signatures to renew the lapsed restrictive covenants against blacks. One woman sold her house after her husband, who had signed the covenant and subsequent petitions to restore it, died and she needed the money. We know all this because Maurice C. Sturm continued to send McKeldin and Sachs updates on the situation, and many have survived. He also sent copies of letters that he wrote to various real estate speculators, and their replies. Sturm, a manufacturer of sash pulleys, screen wire, nails, and tacks, was president of the Fulton Avenue Improvement Association and headed St. Martin's Holy Name Society. The church was the center of segregationist agitation, and its pastor, Monsignor Louis O'Donovan, was a leader.

Sturm's reports indicated that public auctions were among the initial methods through which speculators acquired properties that they then flipped to blacks at exorbitant profits. Such auctions were numerous because during the depression years and the war the neighborhoods had deteriorated, and many houses experienced serious heating and plumbing problems. In late 1944, after Appalachian war workers began returning home, vacancies proved difficult to fill. "Under normal conditions it is likely that the former white occupants would have kept up their homes. But the restrictions on building materials, occasioned by the war, as well as the scarcity and cost of skilled labor and materials, were prohibitive," wrote the Morgan State sociologist Clifton R. Jones.

Because Fulton Avenue was the first white neighborhood to open up beyond west Baltimore's traditional black district, it attracted members of the elite. Better educated than indigenous blacks, they probably also had more schooling than the fleeing working-class whites. "In fully 35 percent of the families the husband or father is engaged in one of the professions, in business, or is a white collar worker. Their occupational status implies academic training at the college level or above," Jones wrote after interviewing 203 black families. Many of the achievers were out-of-towners attracted to Baltimore by wartime opportunities.

When Dr. Gilbert Banfield bought 806 North Fulton on January 30, 1945, the three-story rowhouse had gone from one speculator to another three times within two months. Victor Posner first acquired it and then sold it to L. Warnken, who then sold it to Laura Moran. It was Moran, a busy speculator, who sold the house to the Banfields for an undisclosed amount. It appears that Dr. Banfield, too, quickly sold the house, because a year later the family lived at 722 Fulton Avenue. He also bought 724, moving his parents from New York to the first floor and renting out the other two floors. Dr. Banfield, a native of Barbados, was an anesthesiologist at Provident, Baltimore's black hospital; his wife, Marion, was a social worker. The family of the dental surgeon Dr. Bruce Alleyne moved to the same block. They were big socialites, whose comings and goings the *Afro-American* covered and who would move to a better neighborhood as soon as one opened up. By 1958 the Banfields also were gone, even though Dr. Banfield kept his medical office on Fulton Avenue until he retired in 1986. Another prominent resident was the Reverend Hiram E. Smith, a Baptist leader who ran a real estate business. From his rowhouse on Fulton Avenue he sold houses to other blacks, buying listings from white speculators.

Although speculators came in many faiths, the *Afro-American* reported threats against Jewish real estate men. The Baltimore Jewish Council's Sachs, in a message marked "urgent" and "confidential," summoned speculators to another emergency meeting. He spoke of a "dangerous real estate situation" but made no headway. That was not surprising. The Fulton Avenue wheeler-dealers included the city's most unscrupulous cutthroats. They were quickly nicknamed "blockbusters" after the huge Allied bombs that rained ruin on German cities in World War II.

The early blockbusters' corporate names—including the Maryland State Housing Corporation and Victory Holding—could not hide the sleaziness of their operations. Owners included the formidable Esther "Mama" Kirsner and her lawyer-son Milton. Piles of violation notices established them as the city's worst slumlords. Herbert Kaufman, a reckless high-stakes gambler, would go to jail a couple of times before losing his empire of nearly a thousand rowhouses, apartment buildings, and single-family homes for taxes on gambling profits that he owed to the Internal Revenue Service. Victor Posner also was in the mix. He was to become a notorious Wall Street corporate raider in the 1980s. He got his start by ousting his own parents from the family's ma-and-pa grocery store. He then liquidated it, using the money to buy rundown houses. He hired his father as the office gofer, barking orders to the old man and working him like a slave.

The blockbusters were in a hurry. Even as the Battle of the Bulge raged in Europe, they knew that Hitler was kaput. They anticipated the end of the war and the big changes that were sure to come. The housing stock in much of old Baltimore was in deplorable shape, having deteriorated first during the depression, when it was redlined, and then during the war. Sanitation was a joke. The 1940 Census listed 34,166 dwelling units without private flushing toilets and 6,889 with those conveniences but no bath. The next Census, in 1950, showed that despite the return to peacetime, the situation had actually worsened: 45,187 dwelling units were without a private bath, and 17,711 had no running water. There was a logical explanation for the increase: during the war, landlords yanked tubs out of bathrooms, which did not produce rent revenue, and converted them into rentable sleeping spaces. What business residents needed to conduct could be done in outhouses known as crappers.

Blockbusters did not need to be told what this presaged. As soon as peace came, the authorities would order stinking backyard outhouses razed and plumbing installed. The costs of retrofitting would be enormous. The city was already making noises about tightening codes and enforcement. It was no empty talk, either. The housing court had hit the Kirsners with record fines. They had illegally subdivided dwellings into large numbers of sleeping rooms, where inspectors found flimsy partitions, furnaces without fire protection, defective electrical wiring, dense overcrowding, and insufficient stairways. Rats swarmed in the backyards, where uncovered pails of garbage invited their inroads. In some cases rats overran the inside of the houses as well. Ominously, a new ordinance gave the health commissioner broad powers to correct plumbing, sewage, drainage, and light or ventilation deficiencies at the landlord's expense if the landlord failed to do so within ten days.

Statistics from 1950 underscored the magnitude of the problem—42.1 percent of 49,472 black housing units lacked private baths, and 22.4 percent had no running water. Speculators saw gold amid this misery. Fortunes could be made through the acquisition of dirt-cheap substandard houses, which then could be unloaded on unsuspecting buyers. Blacks would buy them, first paying dearly and then ending up shouldering all future modernization liabilities. This kind of racially targeted disposal began on a large scale. The goal of unloading substandard properties was so obvious that leading speculators were called Standard Liquidators, Inc. and Straw Man, Inc.

Such unloading went on unnoticed during the early years of the war in areas east of Fulton and west of Broadway, the heart of the city that the federal government redlined in the mid-1930s. While there were still many substandard houses to dispose of and white pockets to conquer, by 1952 big operators like Milton Kirsner were no longer interested in trading there. The houses presented just too many problems. Fantastic profits could be reaped without headaches in newly broken neighborhoods. Fulton Avenue set the standard: according to a survey by the Baltimore Urban League in 1946, blacks bought houses there for "an average of 170 percent over prewar levels" and "at least 75 percent above the present market value."

In order to obtain a foothold on a new block, blockbusters typically cast lures by offering good cash prices to the first whites agreeing to sell. Someone was always happy to oblige because the unavailability of conventional financing due to redlining made houses difficult to sell. The more glutted the market became, the less blockbusters offered. Then they turned around and sold to blacks at a steep premium. Blacks had little choice in the matter because the speculators were the only game in town. Banks did not lend to blacks. They also denied loans to any whites trying to place blacks on all-white blocks.

Real estate agents had to submit letters with the address of another house on the block that was already occupied by blacks.

Blockbusters didn't bother with these lending constraints. They were financed by syndicates of private investors, often headed by lawyers, who all believed that manna from heaven would rain when substandard houses sold at high prices. Among other sources of capital were unregulated building and loan associations, which blockbusters and their associates controlled or owned outright. With that money, blockbusters provided 100 percent financing to blacks. Of course, there would be carrying charges and incidentals.

The sales mechanism that blockbusters used was a rent-to-buy arrangement known as a land-installment contract. Such contracts were hocus pocus on pieces of paper, amounting to tentative sales at best. They were not recorded, no deed changed hands, and there was no settlement. That enabled purchasers to move in right away, if need be, instead of waiting for closing, as in regular sales. No appraisal was conducted, either. No conventional valuations thus constrained the speculator, who could demand as much as he thought the market would bear.

Principal, taxes, insurance, and fees were all rolled into unitemized weekly payments, which were made to suit a purchaser's pocketbook by adjusting the redemption period. The receipts looked like ordinary rent receipts. For the seller, the risks were minimal. The title remained in his name until the purchaser accrued enough equity, usually 40 percent, to qualify for a mortgage. Often that day never came. If a contract buyer failed to make payments on time, the seller could simply evict the deadbeat and offer the property to the next family, perhaps at a higher price.

The land-installment concept had been around for as long as anyone could remember. As early as 1899 the *Afro-American* advertised six-room houses for sale on a rent-to-buy basis. "Come to see us. Bring in your references. We must have sober, industrious families. No loafers fed by hard-working wives," one ad said. "Stop renting and buy now." The method became the rage during World War II as a dodge against rent control, which remained in force until 1956.

By simply converting renters into rent-to-buy contract buyers, land-lords performed a magic trick that enabled them to jack up payments without having to fear interference from the federal Office of Price Administration (OPA). Renters who declined could simply be put out on the street. In 1943 the OPA sued Herbert Kaufman after he evicted thirteen renters who refused to be converted into land-installment-contract occupants. Several other landlords were caught playing hard-ball with tenants because they wanted to get rid of their liabilities.

Victor Posner argued in court that once a prospective buyer signed a land installment contract, it was the buyer and not the seller who was responsible for major repairs. A succession of judges rejected that interpretation, ruling that sellers as titleholders were responsible. Nevertheless many sellers figured that they satisfied this legal inter-pretation by issuing work orders for plumbing, electrical repairs, and other costly overhaul and then simply adding the costs to the contract buyers' mounting debts. Some sellers were not beyond double bill-ing for extensive work that the contract buyer had already paid for. (In his 1954 novel about that period, *The City of Anger*, the future historian William Manchester described how fly-by-night operators squeezed every penny out of black buyers until they lost their houses. While working on the book—he was a cub reporter for *The Evening Sun*—Manchester moved to Eutaw Place, just around the corner from the black district. He frequented a Turkish bath where speculators swapped stories about their daily exploits.)

Roughly fifteen particularly unscrupulous blockbusters became known as the "Forty Thieves." The Kirsners, Kaufman, and Posner were charter members. With others they formed a brazen cartel that rigged trustees' home auctions. To do so, they picked one designated bidder who, accompanied by straw buyers, had strict instructions on how high to bid. Competitors learned not to tamper with the Forty Thieves, who were able to acquire homes at rock-bottom prices. A few minutes after the rigged public auction ended, cartel members reconvened for a separate private sale among themselves to deter-mine who would actually get the property. To keep that latter bid-ding within bounds, any profit over the price paid at the first auction was divided among members. Profit splitting kept the Forty Thieves happy. Everything went smoothly until one day in the 1950s a judge, deciding that widows and orphans had been defrauded, put an end to rigging, according to Aaron Baer, a lawyer and Fulton Avenue speculator who became a judge himself.

The Forty Thieves and their gofers hung out at Bickford's, a smoky downtown cafeteria of modest culinary achievements. Bickford's was convenient to many seats of power—City Hall and other municipal buildings, lawyers' and speculative investors' offices, even the Democratic party headquarters. There they waited for auctions to begin at the courthouse steps, just a block away, while they swapped real estate listings and contracts. Politicians were well represented among the habitués. Some wisecracker nicknamed Bickford's No. 10 Downing Street after the British prime minister's residence, and that's how it became known.

Operators like the Forty Thieves flourished in a regulatory twilight zone where few rules existed. Some had a license from the Maryland Real Estate Commission, which was reputed never to have rejected an applicant if proper consideration—in cash—changed hands. But many did not bother even with that technicality. As long as they acquired and sold properties in their own name, they did not need a license, they argued. They were not members of the Real Estate Board. Thus they could ignore the board when, three months into the Fulton Avenue blockbusting controversy, it asked brokers, dealers, investors, and owners to "forgo participation in any real-estate transactions likely to encourage ill-will or disturbances between any group of local people."

Over the next several years racial change spread deeper into west Baltimore. In Goose Hill, white residents felt spooked even though railroad tracks and a long bridge separated the neighborhood from Fulton Avenue, five blocks away. In the 1940s Goose Hill was a world unto itself. Farmhouses with chickens and small animals still survived. Geese paraded around in a field where the Ringling Bros. and Barnum & Bailey Circus erected its tents. The special train of the "The Greatest Show on Earth" was parked and off-loaded at a rail siding a few blocks away, and the exotic animals marched through the neighbor-hood. On the developed blocks close to Bentalou Street, rowhouses accommodated the families of a used-car salesman, mechanics, insur-ance agents, bill collectors, and bread-truck drivers of German, Irish, Italian, Lithuanian, and Jewish extraction. One day in 1947 a polite stranger appeared, wearing a suit and carrying a stack of signs that declared, "THIS HOUSE IS NOT FOR SALE." No one knew who he was. The visitor went from door to door—as he would later be seen doing in other neighborhoods—offering signs to residents. No blacks had crossed the bridge yet, but after the sign man's visit the neighbor-hood spoke about little else than them coming any day now.

Among Goose Hill residents was the Cripps family. Benjamin F. Cripps, the breadwinner, had been reared in a German orphans' home, where he met his future wife, Marian, a dutiful *hausfrau*. De-spite his outward conservatism, Cripps exhibited unusual curiosity about blacks. He read the *Afro-American* and on occasions took his son, Thomas, through black neighborhoods, pointing to well-kept houses or a black-owned pharmacy. He seemed to suggest that racial change did not have to result in deterioration. At his office at the gas and electric company, he once introduced Tom to a black janitor. "He is a college man," Ben Cripps whispered with a tinge of awe in his voice, because he himself had only an eighth-grade education.

Ben Cripps did not take a lawn sign. He suspected that those signs were a blockbusters' ploy to sow uncertainty and fear before they attacked the all-white Goose Hill, a neighborhood now known as Rosemont. But what was he to do? He had exceeded his dreams. From the orphanage he had risen to become an ironworker, a job that enabled him and his wife to buy a fourteen-foot-wide Goose Hill rowhouse in the middle of the Great Depression for a measly $400, which they financed from a nonbank source. What clinched the deal was that a German had built the house at 2323 Mosher Street. "They were only two years away from the orphanage where German was the first language," his son recalled. From the steel mills, Ben Cripps graduated to truck driver for the gas and electric company, as steady and respected a company as existed. During the depression the utility said that if he wanted to keep a job, he would have to become a bill collector. Wearing a white shirt and tie, Cripps made his rounds carrying a huge accounts book. As to Frau Cripps, she worked as a waitress and apprentice chocolate dipper in a busy ice cream parlor sandwiched between two downtown movie theaters.

In 1947, without telling the family, Cripps contracted to buy a house yet to be built near Memorial Stadium, which would be inaugurated three years later. "We're moving," he finally disclosed in 1949 without tolerating any discussion, even though the new house was not ready. Next came a visit by a black man, Ellsworth F. Davage, who was a teacher in Baltimore County, as was his wife, Elizabeth. Tom, sixteen at the time, felt that he had a right to know what was going on, but his father banished him to the basement, where he could only hear the rising and lowering cadences of the adult voices. How did father know Davage, Tom wondered? In the end, a deal was struck. Tom wanted his father to explain the sale, which seemed at odds with his benign attitude toward blacks. Ben Cripps refused. With a tone of finality in his voice, he announced at the dinner table that he was selling because "I'm not going to be a pioneer."

He was the first homeowner on his Mosher Street block to sell to a black.

The legal murkiness of the unrecorded land-installment contracts invited all kinds of problems. Some contract buyers lost the property on which they had been making payments when liens were placed against the titleholder, who defaulted or went bankrupt. It was a system rife with abuse and with little recourse for the buyers. Yet because of the critical housing shortage, landlords could force renters to sign land-installment contracts.

Speculators counted on buyers' ignorance. In some instances, buyers, not knowing any better, overpaid on the purchase price. But sellers, instead of giving the title to the house, kept demanding more weekly payments. One purchaser, having overpaid a substantial amount, had enough sense to turn to the Legal Aid Bureau. He sought help after receiving the following dunning notice from the seller: "You are eleven weeks in the back please send money I need it for Drs and medicine. I was always nice to you and your wife. Your friend, Mr Z——."

Maryland law restricted the interest rate on land-installment contracts to 6 percent, but 6 percent of what? The law did not specify. By flipping properties and offering them at inflated prices, speculators could achieve a high interest rate that rendered the legally sanctioned maximum meaningless. So if a speculator acquired a house for $5,000 and then flipped it for $7,000, he was well ahead of the game. He not only pocketed the $2,000 difference but could also charge 6 percent on the higher price. Seldom counseled by lawyers, thousands of black families assumed contractual obligations that they could not afford and did not understand. One elderly couple signed a contract that would take seventy-five years to pay off. Few had the means or foresight to hire legal help. "I was almost like a person blindfolded when I bought," one woman lamented. "I don't know any law."

Many purchasers were oblivious to fiscal realities. Some contract buyers spent 60 percent or more of their income on house payments. That left little money for repairs. In desperation, many took in renters to help with costs, but that seldom worked out. Neither did debt consolidators and other assorted vultures ready to descend on a struggling buyer. *The Evening Sun* recorded the story of a woman and her elderly mother who scraped together enough money to buy a home on a land-installment contract. But after the daughter lost her well-paying job, she could not keep up with gas and electricity payments. With power cut off, her renters left. In order to make payments, she sold most of her household furniture and even pawned her television set. Nothing helped. In the end, she and her mother were evicted. Yet she continued to visit a small loan office each Saturday to make a weekly payment on a new gas furnace that by then provided heat for the next sucker. Similarly, contract buyers who had installed a club basement or a new roof lost their investment if they fell behind in payments.

Much of Baltimore's subsequent urban decay can be traced to the exploitative practices that blockbusters introduced along Fulton Avenue.

8

ЛЛЛЛЛЛ

Covenants Crumble

FULTON AVENUE was in racial turmoil in 1948 when the U.S. Supreme Court considered the legality of covenants that barred certain races, nationalities, and religions from neighborhoods throughout the country. Behind the scenes the drama of American race relations played out even before the arguments began. Three of the nine justices asked to be recused, meaning that the Court was able to convene with a bare quorum. Justices Robert H. Jackson, Stanley Reed, and Wiley B. Rutledge offered no explanation, and none was requested; it was known that they all lived in Washington, D.C., and Virginia neighborhoods where discriminatory covenants barred blacks, Jews, Armenians, and Syrians.

The landmark case, an amalgamation of several suits from different parts of the country, became known as *Shelley v. Kraemer*. Its origins were in St. Louis, Missouri, where J. D. Shelley and his wife, Ethel Lee, had acquired a yellow-brick house on a tree-shaded street. A few days after they settled in the fall of 1945, the Shelleys received a summons to appear in court. Louis and Fern Kraemer, who owned property in the neighborhood but did not live there, alleged that the Shelleys had violated a covenant prohibiting "people of the Negro or Mongolian race" from living on the block.

Baltimore had been a forerunner in the use of restrictive covenants, and a remarkable number of people with Baltimore roots made
arguments before the Supreme Court in the *Shelley* case. Chief among
them was Philip B. Perlman, onetime city editor of *The Evening Sun,*
who had switched careers and risen to be U.S. solicitor general. As
Baltimore's city solicitor he had advocated racially restrictive covenants and other forms of segregation, but in his federal role he opposed them as "a friend of the court"—and of the Shelleys. President
Harry S Truman wanted it that way. "We must make the Federal
Government a friendly vigilant defender of the rights and equalities
of all Americans. Our National Government must show the way," the
president declared.

Truman's attitude marked quite a departure. Since the mid-1930s
eugenics-influenced government policies had promoted racially restrictive covenants as necessary bulwarks against "inharmonious elements." Now the Missourian sought to open America's neighborhoods to blacks and Jews and Mexicans and, and, and . . .

Thurgood Marshall appeared on behalf of the National Association for the Advancement of Colored People. Framing the issue as a
constitutional fight, he contended that covenants violated Americans'
right to equal protection under the law. For him, this was also a personal fight. Marshall knew the hurt and cruelty of such restrictions
from his childhood in Baltimore when covenants had determined
where his family could live. The wounds cut deep, and Marshall seldom had anything good to say about his native city.

Alger Hiss represented the American Association for the United
Nations. He had lived just a few blocks from Marshall in the white
Bolton Hill neighborhood. Hiss had been a rising star in the State Department and secretary general of the San Francisco conference that
gave birth to the United Nations. He argued that racially restrictive
covenants violated basic human rights.

Two of Hiss's erstwhile neighbors from Bolton Hill also submitted
a brief. Thomas F. Cadwalader and Carlyle Barton *favored* covenants.
Cadwalader epitomized the inner contradiction of many a Southern
Progressive: he had organized the Maryland Legal Aid Bureau in 1911

to offer free legal assistance to immigrants and other poor people, but he also was a white supremacist, as had been his law partner, William L. Marbury. As the Supreme Court heard the case, Cadwalader was running the Maryland campaign of Senator Strom Thurmond, the segregationist States' Rights Democratic party's presidential candidate. Carlyle Barton, for his part, was the epitome of establishment respectability. He was chancellor of the Episcopal Diocese of Maryland and president of Johns Hopkins University's board of trustees, a position he held for seventeen years.

Barton and Cadwalader represented the Mount Royal Protective Association, which Marbury had established to keep blacks out in the aftermath of the 1910 McCulloh Street controversy. They freely admitted that racial objective and explained to the Court how the goal had been achieved through a network of block captains and lieutenants. "The restriction has been kept in force, and attempted violations have been quashed by threatened suits or by injunctions obtained from local equity courts, with the result that the properties covered by the covenant have been completely restricted in fact to occupancy by white people." The brief further stated: "Should such covenants be held invalid for constitutional reasons, the effects on the social life and economy of the City of Baltimore would be extremely serious."

Many other briefs were filed. A dozen supported the outlawing of discriminatory covenants, including those by the American Jewish Congress and the American Jewish Committee. Only two other briefs were submitted favoring racial covenants. One was from the National Association of Real Estate Boards.

The Supreme Court announced its unanimous decision on May 3, 1948: the enforcement of racially restrictive covenants was contrary to public policy. Chief Justice Fred M. Vinson qualified the ruling. "The restrictive agreements standing alone cannot be regarded as a violation of any rights guaranteed by the Fourteenth Amendment," he said. In other words, the Supreme Court outlawed the *enforcement* of racially restrictive covenants by the courts, but not the private contracts as such. Even so, the ruling prompted jubilation around the nation among groups that had been victimized by racially restrictive covenants. In Baltimore the *Jewish Times* editorialized that "the most important prop of the ghetto system" against Jews had been dealt a blow. The *Afro-American* was cautious, placing the decision in a wider racial context: "As important as this victory is, let us not lose sight of the fact that the forces of prejudice have only had a temporary setback and are just as strong and vicious today as they were yesterday, and are only looking for a loophole to circumvent the ruling of the Court."

More important than the editorial was the *Afro-American*'s news story, banner-headlined across the front page: "WISE HOME-BUYING URGED WITH OUTLAWING OF RESTRICTIVE COVENANTS." Readers were warned against looking for homes along Eutaw Place, in Bolton Hill, or elsewhere in the Mount Royal district, where "150-year-old barn-like houses standing under leaky roofs, containing weak floors and lacking heating plants, have little to offer." Instead the newspaper urged blacks to "make the wise choice" and move into neighborhoods northwest of Fulton and North avenues. Purchase prices there were more reasonable, and houses modern and desirable, the *Afro-American* wrote. "Many of these properties, marked with 'for sale' signs, have porches, garage space and 186-feet rear lots which can be used for flower or vegetable gardens. The little side-street houses are particularly attractive, tree-shaded and well kept."

Those areas were largely Jewish. The *Afro-American* saw this as an advantage. Since the end of the war, "Jewish persons" had helped blacks expand to previously white blocks, the newspaper wrote. "Among these were the real estate dealers who arranged the negotiations, homeowners who were willing to sell their property and residents who accepted the newcomers without questions." The story went on to quote a number of real estate agents, white and black. They all advised blacks to seek houses beyond Fulton Avenue. Thus real estate firms, with help from the *Afro-American*, determined the direction of black expansion. Those firms were the newspaper's largest advertisers.

Over the previous four decades much of the Jewish community had abandoned its historical home in east Baltimore's slums and trekked deeper and deeper into the northwest side. An internal census showed that in 1947, the year before the covenant ruling, 51 percent of Baltimore's 74,991 Jews lived in the suburban sections of the city beyond Fulton and North avenues, the very area that the *Afro-American* recommended for black expansion. An additional 29 percent rented or owned modest rowhouses on streets in the general vicinity of North and Fulton avenues. Already largely abandoned by non-Jews around the time that W. Ashbie Hawkins bought 1834 McCulloh Street in 1910, those neighborhoods had become perceived as Jewish. Since the mid-1930s, redlining had marked them as too risky for conventional mortgage lending. Houses could be sold only in all-cash transactions. As a consequence, the area had the city's highest concentration of aged Jews, often renters, though in the years before World War II, Jewish organizations tried to rejuvenate it by settling there some 3,000 refugees from Hitler's Germany. Still, 43 percent of the population was not Jewish but consisted of a mixture of other white ethnicities, including a high number of Appalachian renters.

Beginning in 1944 those war workers began returning home. At the time of the Supreme Court's *Shelley* ruling, 55 percent of Baltimore's out-of-town defense workers had gone back to their homes. Even though the overall housing shortage continued to be acute, non-Jewish whites, under Baltimore's three-tiered real estate market system, did not wish to rent or buy in neighborhoods perceived as Jewish if they had a choice. To blockbusters, North and Fulton avenues became irresistible. In the absence of white home demand, blacks kept advancing. Those neighborhoods became early black expansion and infill areas.

While *Shelley v. Kraemer* did not explicitly endorse desegregation, the ruling opened previously restricted neighborhoods to the possibility of legal racial change. In 1953, one year before the Supreme Court's school desegregation ruling in *Brown v. Board of Education*, the Federal Housing Administration concluded that the ethnic redrawing of west and northwest Baltimore after World War II "represents one of the most rapid and extensive shifts in racial occupancy that has occurred in any city." Thanks to land-installment contracts, the rate of black homeownership exploded by 194 percent between 1940 and 1950, compared to a 58.8 percent rise among whites.

Racial transition was surprisingly free of violence but not totally devoid of it. In 1948 a black family, including a five-month-old baby, narrowly escaped after nighttime arsonists set their newly acquired Fulton Avenue home on fire. Real estate agents were harassed. In 1952 one hostile flour company salesman threatened to kill Samuel Rosenthal as he was showing houses to blacks along Fulton Avenue, then called Rosenthal "a son of a bitch" and twice spat in his face. The attacker was arrested. A judge let him go after residents testified that they saw nothing.

Easterwood Park was among the early Fulton Avenue neighborhoods that blacks penetrated. Bordering on North Avenue, it had been colored yellow, or transitional, in the 1937 redlining map. That meant that few insured mortgages were available to buyers. In any case, many rowhouses were only fourteen feet wide and would never qualify because they fell two feet shy of the FHA minimum requirement. Easterwood Park was the domain of *zaydas* and *bubbes*— grandpas and grandmas—originally from Eastern Europe, whose children prospered in business or professions, bought homes in Forest Park, Arlington, and Upper Park Heights, all desirable suburbs, and who then forgot the old ways and couldn't even speak Yiddish. This was the milieu of Barry Levinson's cinematic valentines to Baltimore, *Avalon* and *Liberty Heights*.

Mendel Glaser and his wife, Sora Chaya, gravitated to Easterwood Park in 1922, settling in a good-sized rowhouse at 1730 Ruxton Avenue. He was from Lithuania, a tailor by training but also a skilled carpenter who could do roofing and metalwork. She was a dark-complexioned woman from Latvia. After he declared his affection for her, she sputtered in Yiddish, "Why do you like me? I look like a *Schwarzer*!" He won her heart by replying, "Black poppy seeds are the sweetest!" In keeping with Orthodox traditions, a full week of celebrations followed their marriage. On the morning after the wedding, the bride was mortified when her new mother-in-law stormed

The Glaser family in 1915, before it moved to Easterwood Park. From left, Henry, Esther, Nathan, Zelda, Ida Sara (mother), Mike (father), Ethel, Benjamin, and Milton. *(Courtesy of Robert A. Steinberg)*

into the bedroom to inspect the sheets. She wanted to make sure Sora Chaya was a virgin.

Mendel became Mike; Sora Chaya mutated to Ida Sara. Two things did not change: every day, when Mike returned from work, she was waiting at the door to welcome him home with a glass of milk. Also, the *Forward*, the Yiddish newspaper from New York, remained their reading of choice. Mike believed in socialist ideas and in the garment workers' union. Many of his neighbors also worked in the needle trades.

One of the Glasers' seven children, the third-born son named Milton, married a girl whose father ran Baltimore's biggest bootlegger. Milton brought a brother, Henry, to the business. A sister's husband, Al Steinberg, was the office manager and kept the books. The office was located above a grocery store along Pennsylvania Avenue, near where the white area ended and the black district began. One day someone climbed up the creaky stairs, knocked on the door, and claimed he was aware of "what's going on." The visitor threatened to squeal if he didn't "get cut in on the action." Sure. The bootleggers summoned their iceman. He knocked out the intruder and dragged him to the sidewalk to be "never heard from again," according to the Glaser family's history.

The enforcer was James H. "Jack" Pollack, an orphan from east Baltimore's slums and a onetime prizefighter who had killed a man and attempted to shoot a police officer, or so it was said. His police rap sheet was long and varied—consisting mostly of prohibition violations—but except for minor fines he was never convicted. After prohibition ended in 1933, he recast himself. Starting as a lieutenant of the Irish-dominated organization of Willie Curran, he rose to become one of the city's most influential Democratic bosses of the 1940s and early 1950s, a man who wielded nearly absolute control over the Jewish vote. He made mayors, city councilmen, and judges; rigged elections; manipulated liquor inspectors; directed housing-code enforcers; and ran the zoning board. If money changed hands, it could be channeled as legitimate expenses through an insurance company that he owned or lawyers who were part of his organization. "His entry into public life gave Baltimore's unorganized Jewish population a sense of political identity and a powerful vehicle for winning recognition in government," Laurence Stern wrote in the *Washington Post.* Race was part of that identity. "Exclusion of the Negro from the Pollock [sic] organization became one of its keystones—one of its strongest cohesive forces," observed the historian Harvey Wheeler. "Many lower-class Jews regarded Pollock as virtually their only stronghold against a frightening ethnic invasion."

Pollack derived his power from alliances with high non-Jewish officials. He was close to Thomas J. D'Alesandro, Jr., who capped his long political career as Baltimore's mayor from 1947 to 1959. In 1953, when D'Alesandro's twenty-year-old son, Franklin Roosevelt, was arrested and charged with raping two underage girls with fourteen other sons of leading Little Italy citizens, Pollack got so involved that he was charged with obstruction of justice. "Roosie" was acquitted, and so was Pollack.

Pollack was a practical man dealing with other practical men. One day he was on the telephone with D'Alesandro, talking about some *schmo* who needed a job.

"What can he do?" the mayor asked.

"Well, he really can't do anything," Pollack replied.

"Good," D'Alesandro said. "Then we don't need to break him in."

Pollack lived in a better rowhouse neighborhood some distance away, but he was a regular in Easterwood Park, a seven-acre spread of greenery just one block from the Glaser house. Since 1927 the park had been the home of a highly competitive softball league whose players started in their early teens and continued into their twenties. Thanks to Pollack's clout at City Hall, the park's diamond was the city's finest. The neighborhood was poor, and ballplaying was free. Enthusiastic shouts and the crack of the bat could be heard from the diamond from dawn to dusk, with players responding to such wonderful nicknames as Coddie, Dodgie, Bince, Moocher, Beezer, Phil the Fumbler, Boffer, Cocky, Boogie, Schnickles, and Yoodle. Local businesses and clubs sponsored teams. The Glasers' team was Steinberg Liquors, owned by Al Steinberg, the in-law. Mike and Ida Sara's grandsons played on that team. Pollack's team carried the name and colors of his Trenton Democratic Club. The team was his pride, and it frequently competed with considerable success in other East Coast cities, winning favorable newspaper mentions. Although the players were supposed to be amateurs, Pollack saw to it that they were rewarded. Some received cash, others got a job at the courthouse. If a kid didn't need it, there was always a father, brother, or uncle to consider.

Not everyone in the park was Jewish, but all were white. The only exception was Rap Wheatley, who was occasionally invited to practice. He could "pitch, run and hit the hell out of a ball," remembered Milton Bates, an outfielder for the Mohawk and Phoenix teams.

The political boss Jack Pollack at bat in Druid Hill Park. Nearby
Easterwood Park was home to his Trenton Democratic Club softball team.
(Special Collections, University of Maryland Libraries)

But when Ginny Paul, a Trenton Club star, wanted to recruit the
African-American kid, the supervisor from the city's Playground Athletic League told him, "You can sign him up, but he ain't gonna play.
And not only that, I'll see that you never play again." (The city enforced the all-white park rule for several years even after blacks began
moving to the neighborhood.)

When Easterwood Park boys returned from the war, they used
their onetime veteran's mortgage to buy homes in the suburbs where
they started families. They became lawyers, doctors, accountants,
teachers, home-improvement contractors, and entrepreneurs, thanks

to the GI Bill. Without kids, Easterwood Park became just another aging rowhouse neighborhood fearful of its fate.

The Glasers moved out in 1948. Blacks were already on their brick-paved two-block stretch thanks to an enterprising real estate agent, Daniel W. Spaulding. He was light-skinned enough—due to his ancestors' shared Scottish heritage—to wander around at will in white neighborhoods. One evening he was strolling on the Glasers' street and struck up a conversation with a homeowner. They had a good talk, and Spaulding left Easterwood Park with a listing in his pocket. He sold the house to a recognizably black family the next day. The transaction was extraordinary. As a rule, black agents could not get exclusive white listings, which meant that white agents did the initial blockbusting. The sale generated anxiety but also produced more listings for Spaulding, who could provide financing to a select clientele of educators, government employees, and Pullman porters through the North Carolina Mutual Life Insurance Company. It was the nation's biggest black-owned business, and Spaulding's relatives in Durham, North Carolina, controlled it.

A few weeks before the *Shelley v. Kraemer* ruling the city designated Druid Hill Avenue and McCulloh Street as one-way thoroughfares to ease growing commuter traffic to and from the suburbs. Much of Baltimore's black elite lived on those two streets, but no residents were consulted. When the rumble of one-way traffic was added to streetcar screeches, residents reported that cracks appeared in the plaster walls of their houses. They protested vigorously, but to no avail. Clarence M. Mitchell, Jr., the NAACP's lobbyist in Washington and a resident of Druid Hill Avenue, sued the city. He said the traffic decision "might be all right if we had a decent American community where people could move to the outlying sections of the city. But no matter how much money these people have, they cannot move to the outlying districts. We must live where we live now."

Shelley v. Kraemer changed everything.

The first African Americans to move to an entirely white suburb were William and Victorine Adams. In July 1949 they quietly abandoned their third-floor apartment over Little Willie's Tavern on

Druid Hill Avenue and relocated to the fringes of Forest Park with his daughter from a teenage romance, Gertrude. The neighborhood was heavily Jewish. With a Jewish friend arranging the sale, Adams acquired a nearly new red-brick home at 3103 Carlisle Avenue, near Lake Ashburton. Neighbors were not happy. If Adams was bothered, it did not show.

William Lloyd Adams was a mirror image of Jack Pollack, who built a political machine after a career as a strong-arming bootlegger. Adams, for his part, rose from an operator of illegal lotteries, which thrived in many cities until New Hampshire in 1964 set up a legal lottery as a revenue source and more than forty states followed suit. In Chicago the racket was known as policy; in Baltimore it was called numbers. Every day hundreds of thousands bought betting slips at newsstands, barbershops, corner stores, and dry cleaners for as little as two cents, dreaming of a "hit." Pimlico Race Track results determined the winning three-number combinations. Adams gained a reputation as a man who always paid out. He eventually became the first truly important African-American businessman in Baltimore's history. His story illustrates the speed of neighborhood change and its political consequences. It also further documents the sprawling roots of corruption in Baltimore.

He was born in 1914 in Zebulon, North Carolina, near Winston-Salem. In his hometown he earned a reputation as a kid who was never idle. He delivered newspapers; he also repaired bicycles. Math was his favorite subject in school. He also became known for stinginess: while others spent, Willie saved. He was fifteen when he moved to Baltimore in the depression year of 1929, living initially with an uncle on the east side. He went to Dunbar High School for a while, worked in a rag factory, tinkered with bicycles, and found a lucrative sideline delivering betting slips. One day a numbers boss rejected the slips Adams brought in, saying they came in too late. Since he had to find a way to cover those bets personally anyway, Adams went solo and got a "book" of his own, undoubtedly backed by some unknown sponsor. He was sixteen.

Adams entered the racket at a time when the long career of a legend, Thomas R. Smith, was coming to an end. Born in southern

Maryland, Smith did not know his exact age and could hardly read or write, but his wit was quick and he mastered exceptional skills that had their uses, including tampering with ballot boxes after the votes were cast. The Democratic machine hired him to suppress the Republican vote in the disastrous 1895 election. He did his best. Oral tradition held that "the notorious Negro"—as Frank Kent, the foremost political writer of the era, called him—was caught in the very act of tampering and went to jail, taking the rap for a white politician. Whatever happened, the Democratic machine was grateful. It gave him a numbers franchise. Smith became the city's richest and most powerful African American. Whenever he called the Western District police station and a desk sergeant asked who was on the line, Tom simply announced: "Demparty." According to the *New York Times*, he was known as "The Black King."

Smith owned a twenty-six-room hotel, where a life-size photo of Joe Gans, the great lightweight boxer and Baltimore native, adorned the lobby. Pictures of Smith's patrons—the white Democratic bosses John S. "Frank" Kelly, John J. "Sonny" Mahon, and Senator Millard Tydings—occupied places of honor on each side. Completing the shrine was a bust of boss Kelly, nicknamed "Slot Machine" and "King of the Underworld."

Tom Smith's access to money and power gave him a unique standing in the black community, which by and large was deprived of both. His illegal activities did not seem to taint him. Evidence of this was the creation in 1921 of the Smith Realty Company, whose first acquisition was an eighteen-room office building on L Street, N.W., in Washington, D.C. Its board members included the Reverend Dr. Ernest Lyon. He was a respected national symbol, having served as the U.S. minister to Liberia from 1903 to 1911 under presidents Theodore Roosevelt and William H. Taft.

Real estate was a natural place for numbers kingpins to channel their profits, and Smith had substantial holdings in his own name. His money also likely financed William L. Fitzgerald, a leading lawyer, real estate man, and insurance broker, who was married to a sister of Smith's wife. A Republican, Fitzgerald served on the Baltimore City

Council from 1927 until 1931. He then joined several other prominent African Americans in defecting to the Democratic camp. Soon
thereafter he concluded a curious transaction: he merged his insurance company with Riall-Jackson. It was the largest in the city, for
a reason. Its owner was Howard W. Jackson, the once and future
Democratic mayor, who kept the city's cash in his firm's account,
awarded the huge municipal fire insurance policy to himself, and who
practically extorted city contractors to win their business. "Jackson
was a smooth-talking, hard-drinking thief when he first moved to
City Hall," the journalist Mark Bowden wrote in a 1979 examination
of boss rule in Baltimore.

By 1938 new rivals were squeezing Tom Smith. A white associate,
Charlie Gaither, was found dead in a cornfield with a bullet hole in
his head. That same year Smith died of natural causes, and segregated
Maryland's top white Democratic leaders assembled to pay their respects at a funeral attended by four thousand mourners. Fitzgerald
was appointed executor of the estate. Tom's brother Wallace took
over the numbers operation, but two out-of-town hoodlums gunned
him down inside his base, a Druid Hill Avenue Democratic club, while
he was tabulating numbers profits. He died; his killers were executed.
Meanwhile white Philadelphia mobsters dynamited Adams's tavern.
He repulsed the takeover attempt, living up to his nickname, "Little
Willie." It had been inspired by the 1931 gangster movie *Little Caesar*. Was Adams like the film's merciless Rico, masterfully played by
Edward G. Robinson? "Willie is an unmeddling man," an associate
replied. "You don't meddle with him, he don't meddle with you."

Adams became a multi-millionaire. In a city where banks did
not lend money to blacks, many a budding black entrepreneur came
knocking on his door. If he agreed to participate, his condition was a
51 percent stake, regardless of how small his investment was. Adams
ended up controlling a bewildering array of businesses, ranging from
beauty parlors to funeral homes. He ran a tight ship. Hardly a black-
owned tavern in west Baltimore was not part of his empire or did
not have his vending machines, jukeboxes, and pinball machines. All
bought their liquor from his liquor wholesale business. All his proper-

William L. "Little Willie" Adams, an avid golfer, rose from a numbers boss to become Baltimore's first important African-American businessman. *(Special Collections, University of Maryland Libraries)*

ties were listed in someone else's name. Operators of his nightclubs and taverns always signed an undated license transfer application just in case things did not work out. Adams installed relatives of numbers lieutenants as licensees. Thus drinks fueled numbers, and vice versa.

Adams also owned Carr's Beach, the segregation era's most popular black amusement park, which overlooked the Chesapeake Bay near Annapolis. His boxer friend Joe Louis occasionally trained there.

Each weekend tens of thousands headed to Carr's from Washington, D.C., and Baltimore to swim and cavort and to hear top entertainers, whose performances were broadcast live on WANN radio. Between acts they could gamble on one-armed bandits, which were legal in Anne Arundel County.

Adams Realty Company was run by Maurice "Mo" Lipman, a white operator, who also fronted as the for-the-record owner of a Pennsylvania Avenue nightclub. The firm concentrated on rental properties and painstakingly refrained from being mixed up with obvious blockbusting. Adams's cardinal rule was to avoid doing anything that would call attention to him. He drove Buicks instead of flashier cars, and ordered his lieutenants to do the same. But in moving to Forest Park he violated his cardinal rule. He crossed the line and paid the price. Bribes and payoffs suddenly failed to protect him. Four months after his move in 1949 he was arrested and charged with numbers violations. He was acquitted, though he was clearly guilty as charged. That single November day's take: $391,515 in 2009 dollars. The *Afro-American*, for one, saw a connection between his arrest and his disregard of accepted racial borders.

In 1951 Adams went legitimate. He was subpoenaed to testify in a closed-door hearing before the U.S. Senate's Kefauver Committee probing organized crime. Unlike many others, he answered senators' questions and, under oath, said his daily take was $8,000 in 2009 money. Back in Baltimore, a grand jury indicted him. He was convicted, but the U.S. Supreme Court overturned his conviction, ruling that Adams had testified under a grant of immunity. He negotiated a settlement on his back taxes. Based on the lowball estimate he gave to the Kefauver Committee, he ended up paying the equivalent of $357,000 in 2009 dollars against claims totaling $5.8 million after convincing the Internal Revenue Service that not all was profit but that he had suffered considerable losses as well.

After Adams recast himself as a legitimate businessman—without having spent a single night in jail—even those in the black community who had regarded him with disdain afforded him a measure of respect. Their attitude had begun changing in 1946. That year Victorine

Adams launched the Colored Women's Democratic Club, Maryland's first political organization for black women. Willie quietly financed desegregation lawsuits, including one involving municipal golf courses for he was an avid golfer. The following year he opened the Charm Center, an upscale fashion shop on Pennsylvania Avenue, near buildings that housed his other businesses. The wives, daughters, and girlfriends of doctors, dentists, ministers, and lawyers could now try on the latest fashions right in Baltimore. Until then, one had to travel to Philadelphia or New York to buy them because Baltimore's segregated department stores denied blacks the feminine necessity of trying them on in front of a mirror and admiring eyes. At the Charm Center, Victorine, a soft-spoken former schoolteacher, taught social graces to adults and children, forming a base of support that eventually vaulted her first to the Maryland legislature and then in 1967 to the Baltimore City Council as its first elected woman member of any race. Her political group trained a bevy of history-making elected officials.

The Adamses' Forest Park home was decorated with Japanese touches. It was comfortable but looked so unremarkable—giving the impression of a duplex—that in later decades people found it difficult to believe that such a wealthy man lived so modestly. At 3,100 square feet, it was uncommonly large for the time. The *Afro-American* described the two-story house on a quarter-acre lot as an "estate." When Victorine's friends from her other clubs, the Martiniques and Charmettes, saw it, they told their husbands that it was time for them too to move to white neighborhoods. The *Afro-American's* gossip columnist could soon print a list of "local yokels forsaking the ghettoes and moving into swankier maisons." But, for about three years, Adams was the only one living in a white suburb; others had to contend with previously white rowhouse neighborhoods.

Streets northeast of the Adamses' house near Lake Ashburton had been marked "blue" in the 1937 redlining map, or "still desirable," and thus eligible for insured mortgage loans. They remained white. In the opposite direction, the number of blacks rapidly increased in areas that the map had classified as "yellow," or transitional. There stretches of 1920s rowhouses became blockbusters' first targets; they then zeroed in on modern rowhouses that had been constructed on previously vacant land for the Jewish market after World War II. New sections were still rising when the Supreme Court delivered the 1954 *Brown v. Board of Education* decision. It jolted the city like an earthquake. While most other cities dragged their feet, Baltimore became the first major city not only to desegregate schools promptly but citywide.

Because schools reflected their segregated neighborhoods, little racial change was recorded in classrooms that September. Among a handful of exceptions was the elementary school closest to the Adamses' home. At Gwynns Falls Parkway Elementary School, the student population went from all white to 44.5 percent black. A stampede ensued. A sixth of the school's white pupils withdrew during that academic year, resulting in a student body that was 77.4 percent black the very next year. Across the street from the school was the construction site for Mondawmin, the city's first shopping mall. When it opened in 1956, its coffee shop, the White Coffee Pot, did not serve blacks. By that time Gwynns Falls Parkway Elementary School had become 92.8 percent black, with the black enrollment to rise to 96.1 percent in 1957. Such a transformation in just three years scared away white shoppers, who never materialized at Mondawmin in projected numbers. Many out-of-town retailers quickly terminated their leases.

A powerful political aftershock followed school desegregation just two months later. In the November elections a bipartisan coalition of blacks caught Pollack's political machine napping. Their action spoke volumes about the extent of racial change in the Fourth District, which included the once Jewish but increasingly African-American North Avenue, as well as the no-man's-land on the way to the still all-white neighborhoods northwest of the Adamses' home. Emboldened by the Supreme Court's school desegregation decision, African Americans united behind Harry B. Cole, a well-regarded lawyer who was running as a Republican for state senator in the overwhelmingly Democratic district. With the help of white Pollack foes, the organizing of black women by Victorine Adams, and some financial support from Willie Adams, Cole beat the machine incumbent by thirty-seven votes, becoming the first black state senator in Maryland history. Two other blacks—one Republican, the other Democrat—won seats in the House of Delegates.

So eager was Pollack to regain power that his machine put a black, Walter Dixon, on the ticket in 1955. Dixon was well known for running the Cortez Peters business school, which graduated the best black secretaries who were beginning to find jobs in the federal bureaucracy. He became the first African American to win a City Council seat in three decades and the first black Democrat ever. In the next legislative election, Pollack even recaptured the Senate seat—with a black candidate. The machine also retook two of the three delegates' seats. But only one of the winners was Jewish. One of the "strongest cohesive forces" was falling apart.

In the midst of this political upheaval, Pollack began buying houses from fleeing Jewish owners and renting them to other Jews at subsidized rates, hoping to slow racial change and stop the erosion of his political base. After buying four houses, he realized the futility of it all. He moved his political club to the neighboring Fifth District, where the Jewish population was still growing due to relocations from desegregating areas. Religious and educational institutions also moved. The exception was Pollack's synagogue, Shaarei Tfiloh, which overlooks Druid Hill Park. It considered dismantling its majestic sanctuary and carting the stones and the huge dome to some spot in the suburbs. But cost estimates were shockingly high and Shaarei Tfiloh stayed put, even after it became difficult to achieve a minyan of ten men for prayers.

Pollack's Jewish political base had been solid. By contrast, African-American politicians were so fractious that Adams never gained total control of the district. Yet his clout was unmistakable. He had his appointees on the planning commission, the liquor board, and the zoning board (administered for forty-nine years until 1996 by Pollack's one-time driver, Gilbert V. Rubin, a lawyer). Adams's ability to secure patronage was great, thanks to two white friendships that were as rare as they were personal.

One friend was Irvin Kovens, who was as close to a brother as Willie had. They had grown up together in east Baltimore, where Irv's parents operated a grocery store. As both thrived, they became business partners in many ventures. Other members of their families also invested together. The cigar-puffing Kovens's bread and butter was an installment-sales furniture store on West Baltimore Street, but that was the least of his interests. He acquired a stake in Caesar's Palace gambling casino in Las Vegas and owned racetracks. In the 1960s he became Maryland's most influential political godfather. From his office "the furniture man" ran a fund-raising and patronage juggernaut that launched governors, mayors, and county executives, reaping plenty of spoils after they won. Kovens mostly backed Democrats, but in 1966 he shook the money tree to bankroll the gubernatorial election of Spiro T. Agnew, who was a Republican but less noxious than his segregationist Democratic opponent. Kovens was the godfather behind Marvin Mandel, the speaker of the House of Delegates who became Maryland's first Jewish governor in 1969, when Agnew went to Washington as Richard M. Nixon's vice president. Kovens also masterminded the career of William Donald Schaefer, a briefless lawyer who first went to the City Council, then served multiple terms as mayor and governor and, ultimately, state comptroller. When patronage was distributed, Adams got his share. In 1991, when Maryland established a state lottery, Adams's expertise was recognized and he was hired as a consultant.

Adams's empire grew, though not everything he touched turned to gold. Among flops was his early attempt to exploit the name and fame of his boxing champion friend by marketing a soft drink called Joe Louis Punch. It fizzled. Other ventures did better. Adams bankrolled Parks Sausage Company, which made history in 1969 by becoming one of the first African-American corporations to go public. He backed a local grocery that grew to become the nation's biggest black-owned supermarket chain, and he branched out into construction, specializing in building market-rate apartments and senior citizen complexes. He obtained a high school degree and took business courses at the Johns Hopkins night school. Like the nearly illiterate

Black King Tom Smith—who surrounded himself with smart, educated men—Adams recognized his limitations. In the mid-1970s he
hired Theo C. Rodgers to run a new real estate company, A & R
Development Corporation—as in Adams and Rodgers. Rodgers was
in his early thirties, a then rare African-American Harvard Business
School graduate, who had previously worked for General Motors as
well as a data processing company before becoming the corporate
secretary of Parks Sausage. Eventually many came to believe, incor-
rectly, that they were father and son.

Adams avoided publicity. He networked through go-betweens.
Victorine took care of the hereafter as an important donor to Catholic
causes and as the founder of a wintertime emergency energy program
for the needy. The daughter, Gertrude Venable, also gave generously
and eventually moved to Emmitsburg to live with nuns. A cousin of
Victorine's, Allen T. Quille, became the black ambassador to the Jewish community. Frequently honored as one of the biggest local fund-
raisers of any faith for Israel, he also raised money for the United
Negro College Fund. Quille was president of Club Casino Corporation, one of the nightclubs owned by Adams, who set up Quille as a
big-time parking lot operator, the only black one in the city. In the
1980s Quille could be seen dragging bags of coins—revenue from
his parking lots—to Carrollton Bank at opening time. Nothing in
his appearance or demeanor suggested that he was a man of consequence, or that he, a high school dropout with a stutter, was the only
black board member of this conservatively run white bank founded
by Germans.

Adams's other close white friendship was struck at the height of
the 1938 gangland war over the control of numbers, when he was
doing his regular banking at Equitable Trust. Somehow he and the
new North Avenue branch manager, John Luetkemeyer, got chatting.
The two began talking frequently. One day Luetkemeyer was raving
about the benefits of newly introduced consumer credit, a pet idea of
his. Adams said, "You know, Equitable and others don't lend to us."
But instead of belaboring the point, he offered a solution. He handed
$40,000 in cash to Luetkemeyer—more than $600,000 in 2009

John A. Luetkemeyer, a banker and state treasurer, was one of Maryland's true power brokers. *(Courtesy of John A. Luetkemeyer, Jr.)*

dollars—and instructed the banker to put the money into a safe deposit box and keep the key. That way, Adams explained, no one would have to worry about risks. Luetkemeyer could only shake his head in amazement. He realized that Adams had just figured out a way to become the first African American with a line of credit at a Baltimore bank.

Luetkemeyer, an orphan, had been raised in Cleveland, Ohio, by his German immigrant grandparents. "I spoke German before I spoke English," he remembered. He went to Harvard University on a partial scholarship, graduating with honors. He then completed a year at Harvard Law School but left because "I didn't like the fine print." The Harvey family of Baltimore secured him a job in banking. Part of the Quaker merchant Johns Hopkins's rich legacy through a marriage, the family owned Maryland National Bank, the state's No. 1

bank. Luetkemeyer had tutored the family's sons for five summers. He was hired help; the Harveys sent him to their biggest rival.

In World War II, Luetkemeyer, a Marine, spent a year in the Philippine jungles with anti-Japanese guerrillas. He returned a swashbuckling hero with two Purple Hearts to his name. He rose to head Equitable and became one of the Maryland's two or three ultimate power brokers. He was a force in Democratic politics, thrice elected by members of the General Assembly to be state treasurer, Maryland's No. 3 official. Luetkemeyer voted on all state contracts, all the while heading Equitable, which had an interest in many deals. His improbable friendship with Adams continued to be shrouded in secrecy. He served as a director of the Adams-bankrolled sausage company while it was still private. In 1967, when the Real Estate Board was about to reject Adams's membership application, ostensibly because of his criminal past, Charles F. "Buck" Morrison intervened. He was Equitable's powerful vice president for mortgage lending, a man whose cooperation every broker needed. He startled the board meeting by asking to be recognized. He then firmly advised that Adams was a valued longtime customer of Equitable and that a positive outcome of his membership application would be much appreciated. Adams was voted in.

Luetkemeyer died in 1998. Hundreds of Maryland's most influential attended his funeral. They were stunned to see Little Willie Adams among the pallbearers. Most had no idea that the two even knew each other.

9

.ⅎⅎⅎⅎⅎⅎⅎⅎ.

Fighting Anti-Semitism

> "Having grown up in a largely Jewish
> neighborhood in Boston, the anti-Semitism
> of Maryland came as a puzzling surprise,
> soon displaced by fear and, ultimately,
> defiance. I was frequently harassed
> and taunted—'Jew Boy,' 'kike'—and
> occasionally beaten up by older boys."
> —Richard N. Goodwin,
> *Remembering America*

THE RAPID racial change in Baltimore's northwest neighborhoods would not have been possible without the massive suburban home-building boom that followed World War II. Fueled by federal subsidies, it provided whites of various ethnic backgrounds, social classes, and income levels with plenty of alternatives whenever blacks began encroaching on old neighborhoods. The Supreme Court's 1948 rejection of racially restrictive covenants made such opportunities increasingly available to Jews.

Jews had journeyed a long road to first-class citizenship. Maryland's historic 1649 Toleration Act had excluded them, limiting tolerance to Catholics and Puritans. The colony made the denial of Jesus as Son of

God a crime of blasphemy punishable by death. In 1658 that charge was lodged against a physician, Jacob Lumbrozo, a Sephardic immigrant from Portugal. Arguing with a proselytizing Quaker, "Ye Jew Doctor," as he was called in charging documents, denied that Jesus was the Messiah, ascribed the New Testament's miracles to "ye Art of magic," and said that "necromancy or sorcery" explained the Resurrection. Lumbrozo was convicted and sentenced to death, but he won a pardon from the royal governor and became a respected member of the colony. "So it would seem that the Jews who found their way to Colonial Maryland, could become Land Owners, undertake trade ventures, and, with certain restrictions, become citizens," wrote A. D. Glushakow, the author of books about the Jewish community.

Once Jews won the right to vote and hold public office in 1826, several made a name for themselves in politics. They were not liberals on race. Solomon Etting, an American-born merchant who was among the first Jews to be elected to the City Council, served as a director of the Maryland State Colonization Society. "The colonization of the free people of color, of the United States, on the coast of Africa, will not only promote their own temporal freedom and happiness, but be the means of spreading the light of civilization and the Gospel in Africa," the society resolved.

A political milestone occurred in 1886 when Isidor Rayner was elected to the U.S. House of Representatives. He later became the state's attorney general. In 1904 Democratic fellow legislators voted him a U.S. senator, the first Jew from Maryland to be so elected. He campaigned to disfranchise blacks. "The race issue is not a political one, but in this State a question of self-preservation," he said. Another Jewish attorney general, Isaac Lobe Straus, wrote a constitutional amendment to disfranchise African Americans, which voters defeated in 1909.

Even though Jews advanced in many fields, social and employment discrimination persisted. Throughout the 1940s, anti-Semitism was so ingrained that one store was named Schaefer's Gentile Furniture Company. It was located amid Jewish-owned businesses on Greenmount Avenue and "did not want to be mixed up with kikes," the owner said. That may have been an extreme case. But the Baltimore Jewish Council's 1942 survey of employment ads in the *Sunpapers* found 2,242 ads requiring job applicants to be "gentile"—or, sometimes, Jewish or black. Several blacks seeking employment as domestics, cooks, and butlers specified in their ads that they would not work for Jews.

Most membership clubs barred Jews, not only such selective bastions of Anglo-Saxon hegemony as the Maryland Club but also private beaches and swim clubs. Among "restricted" white resorts, Beverley Beach, near Annapolis, was typical. "Membership limited to gentiles only," a big sign declared at the entrance gate. "Positively NO DOGS permitted." Such juxtaposition—documented in several old photographs at the Jewish Historical Museum of Maryland—was so common that people later claimed to remember that signs at Beverley Beach and elsewhere had actually said "No Jews, no dogs." Jews were not the only excluded group. Italians also were among those not desired. "Our restrictions are more extensive than against the Jewish people only, and include gentiles of South European, African, Asiatic and Indian ancestry, again not because of any feeling of superiority but merely because of a desire for congeniality," Beverley Beach club manager Edgar R. Kalb explained.

At least one Anne Arundel County beach admitted Jews, but mostly the community retreated to its own facilities. A caste system prevailed. The elite consisted of German Jews, whose social organizations generally rejected membership applicants of Polish and Russian heritage until the 1960s. Eastern European Jews clustered in their own clubs; intermarriages between the two groups were frowned upon. The dividing issues were not only national origin and social status but also ideology and attitude toward religion and Zionism. German Jews were more assimilationist and not enthusiastic Zionists. Even though a big step in 1921 had brought together parallel German and Eastern European benefit organizations, merging them into the Associated Jewish Charities, a caste system persisted. "The Baltimore Jewish community was divided between East and West," observed Marion Freyer Wolff, who arrived in 1940 from Germany. "There was a country club for the people from Minsk, Pinsk and Cracow, and then there was a country club for people coming from Germany. I thought that was very strange."

During all that time, the Jewish community continued to fight the bigotry of the larger American society. Discrimination was widespread, starting with the leading universities.

After World War I, Harvard, Yale, and Princeton were among the schools that adopted quotas to limit Jewish admissions. World War II intensified anti-Semitism on Ivy League campuses, despite gruesome revelations about Hitler's Final Solution. Even though it was not Ivy League, Johns Hopkins University entertained pretensions to elite status. As the flood of applications from Jews swelled after the war, officials expressed concern that if action were not taken, Hopkins would soon be viewed as another City College of New York, a school bursting with Eastern European Jews. Popular doggerel suggested that such a reputation would be hard to shake off and would dry up contributions from alumni:

> Oh, Harvard's run by millionaires,
> And Yale is run by booze,
> Cornell is run by farmers' sons,
> Columbia's run by Jews.

In fact Columbia limited the number of Jewish admissions. One day in the mid-1940s, Johns Hopkins dean Wilson Shaffer informed the Baltimore Jewish Council that Hopkins too "felt it necessary to impose some sort of restrictive practice on Jewish applications."

It was the task of Leon Sachs, born in 1907, to combat such discrimination. He was the Baltimore Jewish Council's executive director, one of the five sons of an immigrant from Latvia who had become a thriving wholesale grocer. Sachs went to City College, Baltimore's foremost public high school for boys. He graduated from Johns Hopkins, where he was elected Phi Beta Kappa, and received his law degree from the University of Maryland. He spent the summer of 1927 at the University of Geneva in Switzerland improving his French, hoping for a career in the State Department. That was not to be. In 1941

Leon Sachs had wanted to become a diplomat. He employed his mediation
skills as the Baltimore Jewish Council's executive director. *(Courtesy of
Stephen Sachs)*

he joined the Baltimore Jewish Council as its executive director, a
post he held until 1975. He was a bridge builder by nature, much in
demand as a mediator. He settled labor-management disputes at the
Baltimore Symphony Orchestra, in the garment industry, and among
tugboat operators and municipal and state employees. Sachs's Baltimore Jewish Council files from those years fill thirty-four boxes at the
Jewish Museum of Maryland. They contain letters, memos, meeting
minutes, transcripts, citizens' complaints, reports, research papers,
and articles that offer unusual insights into Baltimore during World
War II and the most crucial postwar years of the civil rights struggle.
The material also shows how it pained Sachs that his alma mater
practiced anti-Semitism; above all he wanted to be known as a Johns
Hopkins man.

   In founding a German-inspired graduate university, the Quaker
merchant Johns Hopkins stipulated that neither race nor creed should

bar anyone from admission to its academic programs or its hospital. When Kelly Miller, in 1887, became the first black student, trustees viewed him as an exceptional case. Subsequent black student admissions were so rare that no quota was needed. Jews were another story. Sachs was told that 75 percent of Hopkins applicants were Jewish, mostly City College students seeking premed slots. So when Hopkins established a ceiling for Jews, it was formal and deliberate. The quota initially limited Jewish academic and medical admissions to 10 percent each year; the ceiling later was raised to 14 percent, then to 17 percent.

Hopkins maintained that it did not discriminate against Jews. "There is no 'quota system' at Johns Hopkins, nor has there ever been," President Isaiah Bowman insisted in a 1948 letter. That was not true. In 1951 the university negotiated a deal with the Baltimore Jewish Council. The university agreed to drop a question concerning religion from application forms—which it had used to screen out Jews in case the applicant's name did not reveal ethnicity—and the Baltimore Jewish Council, with "resignation and concern," agreed to "try to disperse the Jewish pre-med applications from City College" to other institutions. But Hopkins was still worried, according to Sachs's notes. "After a trial of several years, if Hopkins finds the City College aspect of the problem still acute, they want the privilege of coming back to us to discuss the matter again," he wrote.

All this was handled without publicity. When the student newspaper, *The News-Letter*, learned about Hopkins's decision to drop religion from application forms, William F. Logan, the admissions director, said the university had asked about applicants' religion merely "to protect the cosmopolitan character of the Hopkins, including the prevention of dominance by any one religious group."

Across the city, at the University of Maryland medical school, the Jewish ceiling was set at 14 percent in 1936. In order to limit the number of Jews, the state university accepted abnormally few local applicants, according to the *Journal of the American Medical Association*. Commenting on that finding, the medical school's dean said, "We take all acceptable students from Maryland who apply." Harry

C. "Curley" Byrd, the university's segregationist president, also denied discrimination. "The laws of the United States and the State of
Maryland make it obligatory that the University of Maryland shall
not, in the admission of students, discriminate in any sense because
of religious creed," he wrote. That too was sophistry. In 1949 the
incoming and outgoing Student Government Association presidents,
neither of whom was Jewish, in Byrd's presence and at a public ceremony criticized the university's practice of anti-Semitism. The matter
was partially resolved in 1950 after President Byrd pledged to raise
the medical school's local admissions from about 50 percent to 70
percent and said the university would discontinue asking about religion on application forms.

This progress galvanized the Baltimore Jewish Council, and in
1953 it embarked on a new mission. Surmounting considerable fears
that public action might trigger a backlash, the council exposed the
anti-Semitic practices of George R. Morris, a leading builder who had
on two occasions headed the Real Estate Board and was a scoutmas-
ter and elder at his Presbyterian church. The showdown took place
in a public hearing before the City Council, which was considering
Morris's reappointment to a redevelopment commission.

The Baltimore Jewish Council and the community had never before resorted to a public shaming, and it had made repeated efforts to
avoid this one. But because Morris refused to end discrimination, a
showdown before the City Council was chosen. In hours of testimony,
civic and religious leaders detailed how Morris had barred Jews from
neighborhoods that he built, such as Ashburton and Hunting Ridge;
from his many apartment houses in Roland Park and Guilford, and in
the heavily Jewish Forest Park; from his Bonnie View golf club; and
from his Five Oaks and Meadowbrook swim clubs. "PRIVILEGES OF
THE SWIMMING POOL ARE EXTENDED ONLY TO APPROVED GENTILES,"
a sign declared at the entrance to Meadowbrook. The policy was
stringently enforced. During World War II, Captain Harold Greenstein, wearing a U.S. Army Corps of Engineers uniform, was denied
admission. He was among a group of out-of-town non-Jews seeking
to take a dip, and he complained. "Who in this city, that gave us that

phrase 'the land of the free and the home of the brave,' is possessed of such bigotry and intolerance as to set himself up, in defiance of the words of Christ, as a judge upon his fellow-men? Where is the conscience of this city?" he wrote in a letter to *The Sun*'s editor.

Denying that he was personally anti-Semitic, Morris said in response to the Baltimore Jewish Council's charges that he excluded Jews only for business reasons. He indeed may have adopted his discriminatory practices after learning how bigotry ruled the real estate business in Baltimore. In 1909, when he was newly arrived from his native Pennsylvania, he offered his services in the *Jewish Social Directory*. "Beautiful Suburban Homes Built especially for you," his ad said. It disappeared from later editions.

At the City Council hearing, a councilman asked Morris how his manager knew that a prospective swim club visitor was Jewish. "I guess by racial characteristics," he answered, but acknowledged that "Gentiles" were sometimes also excluded by mistake. Certainly no blacks had been admitted, Morris assured. During an intermission Leon Sachs found himself standing at a urinal next to an Italian-American councilman. "I'm starting to think he didn't like wops, either," said the councilman. "Christ," responded Sachs, "I've been trying to tell you that."

The City Council rejected Morris's reappointment by a vote of nineteen to one.

The Jewish community had a dirty little secret of its own. In preparation for the Morris confrontation, the Baltimore Jewish Council had spent the previous four years in tense, delicate negotiations with leading Jewish developers, trying to persuade them to end *their* discrimination against fellow Jews. "Time and time again in our discussions with non-Jews we became aware of the necessity of putting our own house in order before we could hope to make any effective representations to non-Jews," an internal memorandum said.

The situation came to a head in 1948. On April 29, a week before the Supreme Court's *Shelley v. Kraemer* decision outlawed the enforcement of racially restrictive covenants, a simple proposal was made: the Baltimore Jewish Council, the Associated Jewish Charities, and the Jewish Welfare Fund should exclude from their boards "any person of the Jewish faith guilty of restrictive real estate policies." The motion carried unanimously. A letter signed by the presidents of eight major Jewish organizations was sent to the community. It recounted how the Roland Park Company had systemized anti-Semitism in housing in 1913 and how, "like a cancer in our midst, it grew—to such extent, in fact, that we are reliably informed that today, Baltimore is probably one of the worst cities in the country insofar as anti-Jewish residential restrictions are concerned."

A glance at the map of Baltimore will graphically demonstrate the extent to which the Jewish community has been circumscribed in its residential opportunities. The suburban areas of this city from the northeast running counter-clockwise to the west are dotted with housing developments and apartment houses which are not open to Jews. Sandwiched in this area, like a veritable ghetto, is the northwest section of Baltimore which is now recognized as the section of Baltimore in which Jews have an unquestioned right to dwell.

The letter detailed how Jewish builders and apartment-house owners engaged in these discriminatory practices, and then said:

We feel, and we are certain that you will agree, that the conscience and the self-respect of the Jewish community can no longer tolerate such practices on the part of any Jew. We are willing to overlook the past, and we do not seek to punish or to ostracize. We do feel, however, that the Jewish community has a right to expect that all such anti-Jewish restrictive practices by Jewish realtors shall cease immediately, and that no Jewish home builder or apartment house owner shall ever engage in this practice in the future. The very least the Jewish community and Jewish organizations should insist upon as indispensable to their own dignity is that those who practice anti-Semitism shall not be permitted to act as their leaders or spokesmen.

The letter named no names. There was no need. Everyone knew about Joseph Meyerhoff, Morton Macht, and Samuel Hammerman, powerful builders and fund-raisers for Israel and Jewish causes, who nevertheless would not sell or rent to Jews. The most visible was Meyerhoff, who lived the American dream. He had been seven years old in 1906 when his parents fled Russia's pogroms with a retinue of six children in tow. *Goldene medina*, the land of gold, was good to him. He went to law school and rose to the top of the building industry, serving as founder and president of the National Association of Home Builders. His standing was such that President Truman invited him to the White House when postwar policies were promulgated. But Meyerhoff knew how quickly and painfully fortunes could change. In 1924 his brother, also a builder, had been forced into receivership. He himself had teetered on the brink.

When the confrontation with the Jewish community came in 1948, Meyerhoff, his brother, and their sons occupied a pivotal moral position. Everyone else, regardless of religion, said that if the Meyerhoffs could discriminate against Jews, so could they. The Meyerhoffs pointed out that they operated in a marketplace where non-Jews numbered 90 percent of customers. If they alone abandoned discrimination, without non-Jewish builders being forced to do the same, they could lose their customers and be ruined. This was the point that another Jewish builder made as well. He said that he wanted to comply with the council's request but could not commit himself "for fear that if and when he does build, and Gentile purchasers object to the non-discriminatory policy, he may have hundreds of thousands of dollars in jeopardy." He wanted a council guarantee against losses. The council refused.

Since before the depression, much of Meyerhoff's business had been with the Roland Park Company, which excluded blacks and Jews and set the discriminatory standard for the rest of the local real estate industry. He regretted the situation but said that his hands were tied. Meetings grew heated and confrontational. Meyerhoff once told the executive director of the Associated Jewish Charities that his Roland Park Company association was so important that if he "had to choose between his relations with [its president John McC.] Mowbray and the Baltimore Jewish Council, he would tell the Council to go to H——."

It was complicated and emotional. Meyerhoff probably had saved the Roland Park Company from bankruptcy during the depression's gloomiest days. But if the company owed him, he felt, so did he owe Mowbray, who in turn had saved him. What happened was that the company's founder, Edward Bouton, had grossly misjudged the severity and length of the depression. While others tried to stay afloat by liquidating or, at the very least, without taking new risks, he continued to buy, convinced that the economy had turned the corner. In 1931, two years into the economic collapse but before the worst of the depression, Bouton added 520 acres in Northwood to the 1,500 acres the company controlled in Roland Park, Guilford, and Homeland. This was sheer madness. Plenty of lots languished unsold in Homeland, and several properties had been repossessed because buyers had no money to make payments. Nevertheless Bouton insisted that Northwood was different, intended "for the man of average means." Such men were not buying homes, of course; they could hardly feed their families. As the depression showed no letup, the mighty Roland Park Company was about to go under, and so was Meyerhoff. By 1933 the situation had grown so dire that the company and its subsidiaries faced liquidation unless creditors gave them more time to pay.

During an earlier economic calamity, in the mid-1890s, Bouton had sold a handful of lots to Jews as a last resort before instituting the company policy against sales to them in 1913. This time he ruled out sales to Jews. "It must be recognized that the value of the properties of each Company depend primarily on the active operation, policies and restrictions of The Roland Park Company. Any weakening of these factors would be directly reflected in loss of prestige, confidence and values," he wrote.

Meyerhoff as a business relationship was a different matter. The Roland Park Company knew him and trusted him. A deal was struck. The company advanced land to him in hopes that he could build houses on them and sell them. "He was broke and we were broke, so the company let him *have* the land," Aurine B. Morsell, a longtime company sales agent told the writer James F. Waesche. "He built houses; then, after he sold them, he paid for the land. The com-

Joseph Meyerhoff, seen here in his Inner Harbor office, was a leading builder, philanthropist, and fund-raiser for Israel. Nevertheless he discriminated against Jewish buyers and renters. *(Special Collections, University of Maryland Libraries)*

pany had gotten really burned when they developed in Homeland. He saved it!"

In all, Meyerhoff took 350 lots in Homeland and Northwood. Whenever he signed a contract, the Roland Park Company, which controlled the subdivision plans and covenants, vetted the buyer, denying approval to Jews. That policy was part of his understanding with the Roland Park Company, Meyerhoff said, and he was not a man who broke his commitments. He accused the Baltimore Jewish Council of "blackmail," not once offering any reason to believe that he might be in a position to influence the Roland Park Company. He did repeatedly promise to talk to Mowbray, a polo-playing Johns Hopkins graduate and World War I artillery major who had risen from an accounting clerk to company president. Then he squirmed and recanted, protesting that any approach by him might be "misunderstood."

All this time the Baltimore Jewish Council was trying to end the anti-Semitic rental policies at apartment houses in the Johns Hopkins campus area, Roland Park, and Guilford, and in a neighborhood now known as Charles Village. Many of those apartment houses were not Jewish-owned. In 1949 the council tried to build pressure on unsympathetic apartment owners. It sought the aid of the larger non-Jewish civic and business community. A dinner meeting was convened, quite remarkably at the Maryland Club, which did not accept Jews as members until 1988. The Baltimore Jewish Council, if it expected help, was badly disappointed. The intended intermediaries turned out to share the wider community's prejudices about Jews. "The problem is very difficult," advised Luke Hopkins, a leading banker, according to Sachs's notes. "It is a fact, of course, that there are many Jews of an undesirable type who would not be desirable neighbors and consequently a very careful screening is necessary. Fortunately, people like [himself, Hopkins said] are in a position to contact their Jewish friends to make inquiry about prospective Jewish purchasers, but in other restricted developments, the Gentile residents may not have such excellent Jewish contacts for purposes of making similar inquiries."

Richard Cleveland then turned the tables. He was President Grover Cleveland's eldest son, a prominent downtown lawyer who headed the local Conference of Christians and Jews. He wanted to know "whether or not it was true that there are German-Jewish apartment houses that will not rent to Russian Jews." Sachs did not record the answer, if any. After the dinner, he summed up his impressions: "It was obvious to me that these people were very reluctant to lend their names to this movement. It was also obvious that some of them felt that the policy was justified, without, of course, their saying so in so many words. It seems that in their thinking there is a presumption that a Jewish purchaser would automatically be bad for the neighborhood." Sachs gauged the sentiment accurately. A year later the participants of that Maryland Club dinner said they wanted nothing more to do with the council's efforts. "Over the next five years it is quite likely that the so-called restricted areas will find themselves gradually becoming non-restrictive, and that a quiet unostentatious process is a wiser policy to adopt," they wrote.

The Roland Park Company's central role was underscored again in 1951 when the brand-new Marylander Apartments opened in an area of several restricted rental complexes on University Parkway, next to the exclusive Guilford. The Roland Park Company owned the parcel and had intended to develop it for apartments, a movie theater, and shops, but neighbors pressured the City Council to reject the plan. When the local builder, Victor Frenkil, said he could mollify the neighbors, the Roland Park Company gave its reluctant permission to him and his partner, Jacob H. Bodinger, a New York heating and ventilation contractor. After they constructed the 507-unit building, the Jewish owners turned over rentals to the Maryland Management Company, a firm set up jointly by the Roland Park Company and the mortgage bankers Hunter Moss and James W. Rouse, who had secured financing for the apartments. Even though the FHA guaranteed the Marylander's loan, the management company instituted a quota for Jews—three years after the Supreme Court's *Shelley* ruling. The quota called for a 12 percent ceiling on Jews until the building was 75 percent rented.

Moss and Rouse defended the quota, which created quite a controversy but never surfaced in the press. The Marylander was in a difficult spot, they said. All kinds of rumors were swirling, including a scurrilous whisper that the complex would rent to blacks. "The wise policy was a quiet cautious policy that would not stir up antagonism either by Guilford or the Jewish community," Moss told Sachs. As for Rouse, his feelings were hurt. "The simple fact is that a wholly non-Jewish management company has attempted to be effective in opening the doors of a previously closed community and the fruits of that effort are to be a public statement branding the owners of the apartment building and its managers as anti-semitic," Rouse protested to Sachs.

Rouse, who died in 1996, is remembered as a pioneering real estate developer, a visionary who was recognized on the cover of *Time* magazine at a time when that still was an ultimate mark of prestige.

He created cutting-edge shopping malls throughout the country. He also crafted new towns like Columbia, Maryland, which he bravely marketed in the 1960s as "The Next America," free of racial, religious, or economic discrimination. In 1951, though, Rouse was not yet a saint. He and Moss were vice presidents of the Northwood Company, headed by Mowbray. Like its parent, the Roland Park Company, the affiliate excluded blacks and Jews from residency without a murmur of protest from Rouse. In 1956, when Rouse opened Mondawmin Mall, it included stores that did not serve blacks.

The Marylander controversy divided the Jewish community. Some wanted confrontation; others warned that publicity would unleash anti-Semitism. The quota threatened to become a nationwide cause célèbre after the management first promised an apartment to a Johns Hopkins junior, then rejected him because the Jewish quota had been filled. That young man happened to be a nephew of David Sarnoff's, the Russian-born industrial titan, whose Radio Corporation of America supplied the world with television transmitters and sets to receive the pictures; refrigerators and washing machines; phonograph records that shaped America's tastes; and the NBC radio and television networks which he also owned. "How would you suggest that I answer this letter," Sachs asked Frenkil after the student's father complained. Frenkil's solution: the student was given an apartment forthwith. But the controversy persisted, to the distress of many. "Until now, the Jewish community has done a good job keeping quarrels among Jews out of the public," one unhappy developer warned in a long-distance telephone call from Atlantic City. "Once you start letting Jews 'bawl each other out' in public, there's no telling where it will stop."

Other apartment buildings near the Marylander excluded Jews altogether. The one great exception was the Broadview, a recent luxury complex whose owners were not Jewish. But after the Marylander opened, the Broadview too instituted a Jewish quota. Instead of getting better, the situation was growing worse. Ultimately, torturous negotiations produced an understanding the Baltimore Jewish Council could live with. Frenkil and his partners pledged to do their best in rentals. The council showed similar flexibility with Meyerhoff, allowing him to honor his commitment to the Roland Park Company as long as he promised not to discriminate against Jews elsewhere. The Roland Park Company's discriminatory policies continued unchanged, and no Jews were able to buy in its developments until years after the company was dissolved on December 30, 1959.

In general, progress in eradicating anti-Semitic real estate practices in Baltimore, as in the rest of the nation, was slow. When Sachs, soon after the Morris hearing, asked the Real Estate Board of Baltimore to "exert a great moral influence" and "take a definitive stand" against anti-Jewish discrimination, the answer was negative. E. Randolph Wootton, the board president, wrote:

> I am personally in accord with you in the hope that the greatest possible good might be achieved through a better and more understanding relationship between the Christian and Jewish faiths.
>
> Our directors felt, too, that racial restrictions eventually will disappear through a better understanding between all people, regardless of race or creed.
>
> We feel, though, that the attainment of such a goal cannot be practically accomplished through any prohibition against restrictions which might be included in any organization's ethical code or by-laws.

Many of the choicest residential neighborhoods would practice informal discrimination against Jews for years to come. But the suburban building boom created many alternatives in the aftermath of *Shelley v. Kraemer* and *Brown v. Board of Education.* So many new subdivisions sold to Jews that a separate "suburban" multiple listing was created to serve agents catering to that market along the northwestern rim of the city. It had nothing to do with the Real Estate Board, whose own multiple listing excluded neighborhoods perceived as Jewish. Existing in the 1970s, the separate multiple listings showed that Baltimore's three-tiered real estate market was alive and well.

10

⎍⎍⎍⎍⎍⎍⎍⎍

A Brotherhood of Profit

IF BLACKS wanted better housing, they had to buy from whites. That was the only way. While the home-building industry was working overtime to create new neighborhoods for whites whose trek to the suburbs was being subsidized by taxpayer-backed FHA loans and guarantees, hardly anyone was constructing housing for blacks. Building permits told the story. From 1950 through the first eight months of 1953, permits were issued for 53,161 units. Only 127 were for black occupancy. (Additionally, 3,427 public housing units for blacks were built, but that total was smaller than the number of dwelling units razed to enable their construction.)

Because the Real Estate Board of Baltimore did not accept African-American members until 1960, black agents established a separate organization, Real Estate Brokers of Baltimore. The former called its members "realtors," the latter "realtists." "Even the most respected realtors, knowing that sales to whites at this stage are out of the question, are found to have some people who, they say, are not in their company, but on whom they can call if forced with the necessity of selling to colored in a white area," one property owner wrote in 1957. For a 25 percent referral fee, a white broker would give a listing to a black agent, remembered Malcolm Sherman, a former president of the Real Estate Board. The end result was racial change, but the white firm could deny a direct role in it. "The way main-line, main-name real estate people operated always reminded me a little of the obstetrician who wouldn't perform an abortion but would tell you where to get one," reflected the civil rights activist Sidney Hollander, Jr.

Many so-called blockbusters never broke a block; they piled on only after someone else made the first sale. There was a reason for the relatively small number of actual blockbusters: while finding an initial white seller was not that difficult—if the offer was good enough or the property was bought at a public auction—not many blacks were ready for the scary experience of being the first to live among whites in a neighborhood being broken. To solve this problem, blockbusters sometimes planted black straw buyers to break a block. Since such impostors were hirelings, they were thought better able to withstand white neighbors' catcalls, vandalism, and occasional crosses burned as a threat. In fact, blacks were willing to pay the highest prices not when a neighborhood was being broken but when other blacks had moved in. Amid hostility there was safety in numbers.

The so-called blockbusters came from varying ethnic backgrounds. Jews predominated. Some operators were of Irish descent. One Italian brought an immigrant's gusto to the game, using his car's fender to write contracts. Another immigrant was Greek, yet another Polish. All were hungry guys eager to make a quick buck any way they could. There was room for everyone. Brokers hired cadres of part-time salesmen who worked on commission. Milkmen and mail carriers were much in demand. They were reliable, knew the neighborhood gossip, and had the white residents' trust. The number of black salesmen continued to grow.

In the early 1950s many operators got in the game quite accidentally. Richard Swirnow was a transplanted New Yorker in his early twenties, married with a child, and going to engineering school at Johns Hopkins University when he spotted a newspaper ad seeking part-time real estate salesmen. He had no real estate license and knew nothing about buying and selling houses. "I'll give it a try," decided Swirnow, who had a poor-paying civilian job with the U.S. Army Corps of Engineers. He was so new to Baltimore that he had to buy a street map to find Cold Spring Lane, a major east-west thoroughfare. But Swirnow had what it took—a willingness to burn shoe leather and knock on doors and plead and badger for listings. Getting a listing was the hard part in those early days; finding a black buyer was a piece of cake.

James W. Crockett was an army veteran of the Pacific theater. He had gone to a secretarial business school. He then ran a grocery store, drove Mayor McKeldin around to campaign events as a Republican volunteer, and was rewarded with a patronage job at the election board. When the Baltimore fire department desegregated in 1954, the call went out to blacks to make sure that the first fire academy classes would include black candidates. Crockett had no interest in becoming a firefighter, but he was able-bodied and a veteran and his arm was twisted. Real estate, initially, was a sideline.

Stanley Sugarman was a navy veteran with a degree from Brown University. He had worked as a mail carrier and taught science in his native Boston and in Washington. Once he moved to Baltimore, real estate became his full-time occupation. The more he sold, the more listings he got. A white seller would refer a friend or family member to Sugarman. The typical call in the early 1950s came from a white policeman: "Get me out of here." "Where is the nearest black family?" Sugarman would ask. "Two or three blocks away," came the answer. "But I don't want to be the last one to turn off the lights."

Most of the aggressive blockbusting in the 1950s and early 1960s took place on the west side, where Jewish neighborhoods adjoined existing black areas, providing room for expansion. After the first sale to a black, other homeowners were bombarded with solicitation cards and letters, telephone calls at all hours, and personal visits. Such tactics produced anxiety and a willingness to sell. Eventually agents began knocking on doors in east Baltimore as well, telling whites that a black takeover was a certainty and prices would never again be this good. Rumors flew. To some agents, no tactic was off-limits. "Did you hear about the rape?" they would ask—whether there had been a rape or not, just to drum up sales.

In contrast to the west side, east Baltimore was a tough sell. Many buyers were unfamiliar with that section of the city because the black district was quite small, less prestigious, and reputedly inhabited by hayseed transplants from the South. Except for Morgan College, all the black community's main institutions were located on the west side, where the elite lived. So any real estate agent hoping to sell on the east side needed to hustle. Until the 1960s, real estate agents routinely picked up prospective buyers and showed them around because few blacks owned cars. James Crockett remembered how he literally steered buyers to the east side. To put his west Baltimore prospects at ease, he did not take them straight across the city to strange surroundings. Instead he drove by familiar landmarks like Pimlico Race Course before crossing to the east side, where his first stop was Morgan, the state's foremost black institution of learning and the community's pride. They would get out of the car, stroll around the campus, and enjoy the sights. Many had never been there, and they felt welcome. With everyone feeling good, he then took the prospects to the first house. Crockett always showed three houses in this order: a so-so, a nicer one, and a showstopper. He talked about how negligible the price difference was to get the best.

The black expansion on the east side was slow. Arriving in 1956 from Pittsburgh to take over an economics professorship at Morgan, Homer Favor's was the first black family to buy on a block of decade-old rowhouses. The agent was white. "The lady next door was a public school teacher, another neighbor was a school teacher," Favor said. "All the rest of my neighbors worked at Sparrows Point, Martin Marietta, Western Electric, Westinghouse, Continental Can." Not many of them had cars either, but they found means to get out of Favor's block so quickly that racial transformation happened "almost overnight."

That Favor ended up moving to 1404 North Linwood Avenue, a working-class block, demonstrated the lack of choices in east Baltimore. On the west side he could have easily selected a more upscale neighborhood because properties were becoming readily available, including individual homes. The biggest blockbuster catering to the well-to-do niche was the Manning-Shaw Realty Company. While its rivals operated in rowhouse neighborhoods, Manning-Shaw found single-family homes in unbroken white areas for black lawyers, doctors, ministers, educators, and government bureaucrats.

"Manning" was Manuel Bernstein. A City College graduate, he had a business degree from the University of Baltimore; but after he returned from the war, his father's thriving wine and distillery business held no attraction for him. For a while Bernstein ran an Arthur Murray–type dance academy. That came to a bad end in 1948. The Veterans Administration determined that he had defrauded the government by overcharging for dance lessons, an educational benefit to demobilized soldiers under the GI Bill. He was sentenced to serve thirty days in a federal penitentiary.

Next Bernstein tried selling refrigerators and ovens door to door on the installment plan. One day he was playing tennis with a big landlord, who said: "Manny, you are wasting your time. Try real estate." The landlord paid his salesmen $300 for each signed land-installment contract. In the early 1950s that was good money for a couple of hours' work. Everything sounded so easy. "If they are doing this, why can't I?" Bernstein reasoned.

As a felon, he was ineligible for a real estate license. But who knew if he didn't tell? Bernstein chose not to tell. He had an idea. He could be different from everyone if he got an African-American partner. Looking around, Bernstein spotted Warren S. Shaw, who had come to Baltimore from California as one of the transit company's first black drivers. A born hustler, Shaw figured out in no time that much better money could be made in real estate. "He was so good that I knew that if I didn't hire him, someone else would," Bernstein said.

Manning-Shaw was a sensation. A black-and-white business partnership was unheard of when the company was formed in 1953, just as blockbusting was becoming a big issue and the Supreme Court was about to consider school desegregation. People found it even more incredible that Bernstein and Shaw were equal partners. In fact it was Shaw who was the public face of the company while Bernstein hovered in the background. With a tan, he looked like the light-skinned Shaw's brother.

Manning-Shaw's multi-ethnic sales force occupied a huge stone rowhouse at 1821 Eutaw Place, which retained heavy oak doors and expensive paneling from the better days. Eutaw Place had been broken in 1945 when a black dentist bought an apartment house at 1512, but hardly anyone knew about it because he kept white tenants in all twelve units. By contrast, Manning-Shaw made sure that everyone knew that racial change was on its agenda. The moment it got a new listing, an agent erected a bright-orange day-glo sign that screamed "SOLD." Such signs became the firm's calling card. Manning-Shaw never used "FOR SALE" signs, only "SOLD" signs. They broadcast to residents and passers-by that Manning-Shaw was in action and that racial change was an accomplished fact, even if it wasn't. The "SOLD" sign might remain in front of the house for months after the house was sold. That was against accepted trade practice, but Manning-Shaw did not care. The strategy worked. As the first black prospects inspected a property and new occupants moved in, white neighbors became agitated and anxious to sell. Some were so nervous that they counted the number of blacks just walking on their street. "Shaw was a sign fanatic. He fined any salesman $100 for a failure to put up a sign," recalled his agent Crockett.

Misrepresentation was another Manning-Shaw tactic, according to complaints to the Maryland Real Estate Commission. Aiming to break a neighborhood, a salesman would introduce himself to the homeowner as representing a totally different "honest and reputable" broker, denying any connection with Manning-Shaw and even denigrating the firm. What he did not disclose was that he was acting in the name of a Manning-Shaw subsidiary. Some sellers complained that Manning-Shaw agents disregarded specific instructions that the property was to be shown only to whites or falsely assured in writing that the block had already been broken.

Among neighborhoods that Manning-Shaw busted was Ashburton, where single-family homes ranged from expensive colonials and ranchers to modest cottages and Cape Cods. On the fringes were rowhouses, some Tudor style, along tree-shaded streets. When George R. Morris originally developed the neighborhood in the 1920s, he meant it for well-to-do Christians, as several imposing churches along Liberty Heights Avenue attested. Covenants barred Jews from residency. After that restriction expired in 1932 and influential Jews moved in, real estate agents began steering white Christians elsewhere.

In November 1954, six months after the Supreme Court's school desegregation order and on the heels of the first black electoral victory, an African-American physician, Dr. Barnett M. Rhetta, Jr., contracted to buy a white-columned redbrick showpiece colonial at 3247 Powhatan Avenue, a commanding site that overlooked a reservoir called Lake Ashburton. He came from a prominent family. His father, also a physician, had headed a black professional group, the Maryland Medical, Dental and Pharmaceutical Association, and had been among Mayor Jackson's appointees to the 1924 committee that failed to divide the city among the races. "The Rhettas are very fine intelligent young people who have traveled quite a bit. They have no children. Their complexion is quite light," one sympathetic social activist reported to the Baltimore Jewish Council.

That assessment omitted a crucial detail: Dr. Rhetta and his father were abortionists. Once that piece of information began to circulate, an impassioned all-Jewish delegation of "responsible citizens" from the Ashburton Improvement Association descended on the seller, Charles Rosenbaum, an innovator in constructing venetian blinds. The agitation reached such levels that the Baltimore Jewish Council's Leon Sachs recorded that he was "concerned" about "possible repercussions." He convened a meeting between the Jewish Council leadership and Ashburton firebrands. In the end the sale fell through. No one would give Dr. Rhetta a mortgage, even though he was willing to put down more than 50 percent.

Two years later, in 1956, an African-American high school principal broke the color barrier. But blocks in most sections of Ashburton stayed entirely white. Bernstein and Shaw knew that extraordinary measures were needed to bust the community wide open. In June 1958 Eutaw Realty, a Manning-Shaw subsidiary, acquired 3800

Grantley Road, a two-story stone-and-stucco home covered with ivy. There the company installed Joseph Carter, his wife, Audrey, and their eight children, who ranged in age from four months to twelve years. Manning-Shaw agents told curious neighbors that the Carters constituted a "pilot project."

The Carter family was dysfunctional, as a uniformed inspector discovered during an unannounced visit. She found Carter's wife and children huddled in the kitchenette, where a gas stove provided the only warmth because the family had no heating oil, despite freezing cold. There was no food; the children were hungry. They also had no shoes, though the oldest ones were supposed to walk six miles every day to and from a parochial school. Those were the observations of Sergeant Violet Hill Whyte, the first black woman on the police force, who was sent to investigate Carter's mistreatment complaint against her husband. "I couldn't believe all that I heard, that a family living at 3800 Grantley Road would be without heat and food," Whyte testified at a domestic court hearing, describing the section as "one of the finest in the city."

None of it made sense to Sergeant Whyte. She found the house clean and "extremely well furnished." Yet the refrigerator was empty. (Sergeant Whyte gave Carter a dollar so that she could buy milk for the children.) A monument to the family's helplessness stood in the basement. It was a washing machine they had brought with them; it had never been used in the six years that the Carters had owned it. Mrs. Carter washed baby clothes and diapers in the kitchen sink and dried them in the oven.

More puzzling details emerged in the domestic court case against fifty-nine-year-old Joseph Carter. Although he claimed to be a mechanic, he was employed by a car dealership as a janitor, whose duties included delivering mail and sweeping the premises. His average weekly earnings were $54.62. Yet he was paying $37 a week for 3800 Grantley Road and $20 a week for another property. "In other words, he can't really handle eight children and the house we live in," Mrs. Carter testified. The eight were not even all the children Carter had: he acknowledged to having fathered "seventeen head of children."

"I think the bottom dropped out of everything. I think the man has been used fraudulently," Sergeant Whyte testified. "Mr. Carter is not a malicious man. I cannot find anything that would add up to that. He is ill-advised and he is about broken-down physically because of the strain. At one time he said he was buying six houses. His ambition is to own property, which is fine, but I feel—this is my opinion—that he should take care of these children."

The domestic court judge thought so too. He gave Carter a suspended sentence of six months in the House of Correction.

A group of Ashburton homeowners thereupon lodged a complaint of improper practices against Manning-Shaw. Three days of hearings before the Maryland Real Estate Commission produced a transcript of more than seven hundred pages, plus numerous exhibits. Homeowners argued that Manning-Shaw had installed the wretched Carter family at 3800 Grantley Road as a scare tactic and that no sale had occurred. They voiced suspicions that the expensive furniture had never been used and that Manning-Shaw had supplied it only as a prop. The real estate firm denied the allegations. But Manning-Shaw's case was not helped when the firm supplied papers indicating that the sale was in fee, then claimed it was in fact a land-installment contract. As for Carter, he did not know how long the repayment period was. Neither did Warren Shaw. From fifteen to seventeen years, he guessed.

The Real Estate Commission had heard enough. It suspended the licenses of Bernstein and Shaw for three months. The two felt wronged. They asked a city court to overturn the Real Estate Commission's decision. Newspapers called it the city's first blockbusting trial, but the judge said that was not the legal issue at hand.

> We're not concerned with block-busting, as so far defined. If there is anything fraudulent in the way a listing is procured or a sale has been executed, that's what we want to hear. We are not going to rule, we're not going to be concerned with whether a house was sold to white or colored; that's besides the point. The question is whether it's properly represented or properly sold or the mechanics of the transaction were properly handled, regardless of whether it was between two white people, two colored people or between a white and a colored person.

So, now let's not get off on racial issues or even try to bring them into the case because we're not going to rule on them.

The judge quickly came to the conclusion that Manning-Shaw indeed had been involved in monkey business. He upheld the Real Estate Commission's action. The real estate men next took their case to the Maryland Court of Appeals. It too sustained the Real Estate Commission. Still, Bernstein and Shaw were not done. They appealed to the U.S. Supreme Court, which dismissed their petition. They then made a request for a rehearing, but the Supreme Court rejected that too. All these legal maneuvers cost a good deal of money, but Bernstein and Shaw paid gladly. "We thought what the Real Estate Commission did was not fair," Bernstein maintained. "Religiously or ethically we didn't do anything wrong. We advocated the cause of black people."

The victory over Manning-Shaw buoyed Ashburton residents, whose struggle against blockbusters and attempts to manage the integration of their community attracted national attention. One of the largest weekly magazines, the *Saturday Evening Post,* published a big spread, "When a Negro Moves Next Door," holding up Ashburton as an example of how communities throughout the nation could manage racial change. A dozen photographs depicted appealing homes or showed whites and blacks interacting with one another, adults amiably chatting on front steps and happy, integrated groups of boys and girls playing—separately—after school. But Ellsworth E. Rosen, the white Ashburton resident who wrote the article, was frank. "The color of my neighbor's skin does not bother me at all. His income and behavior are just about the same as mine. But the economic threat his presence has created for me, and for the entire community, is disturbing." That threat came from the real estate trade perception that Ashburton was headed for all-black occupancy. Agents no longer showed houses there to whites.

At the time, in 1959, approximately 110 black families lived on the "Gold Coast," as upwardly mobile blacks called the streets around Lake Ashburton. African Americans constituted a mere 5 percent of the neighborhood's 2,000 households. Yet even this small amount of racial mixing was unusual. That was the problem. "By normal Baltimore patterns a complete change-over should be only a question of two to five years, maybe a little longer if a recession intervenes," Rosen wrote. His prognosis was prescient.

One old-time resident, recalling the years when Ashburton barred Jews, gamely bragged to a Jewish neighbor that since "we survived the kikes, we'll survive the niggers, too." Such swagger was hooey. Eventually even the holdouts surrendered, people like Melvin J. Sykes and Judith Sykes. Both lawyers, they fought a losing battle to make integration work in Ashburton. As racial change quickened, they noticed, little by little, that theirs was no longer the same community. Shops and services they had taken for granted disappeared. When a neighboring church sold its building, the subsequent black congregation had no use for the basement bowling alley, which had given the Sykeses hours of pleasure each week. It was closed. In 1965 their Orthodox Jewish congregation, Beth Tfiloh, moved. All the reasons that had originally drawn them to Ashburton had vanished. They packed up and left. Another Sykes family would be living in Ashburton. Those Sykeses were black.

Warren Shaw lived at 3205 Carlisle Avenue, a side street near the reservoir but not technically in Ashburton. The wealthy William L. Adams lived across the street. Those who knew Shaw remembered him as an arrogant and crafty businessman who was likable and dependable to friends. Shaw possessed one additional quality that was as striking as it was unique: he was a civil rights activist who used blockbusting to further desegregation. Alone among all real estate brokers, black or white, he participated in sit-ins and demonstrated against segregation, and made sure that everyone knew. He arrived at protests at white downtown restaurants in his canary yellow Cadillac convertible. He was repeatedly arrested, sometimes with leading Black Power advocates like Stokely Carmichael. This gave Shaw a radical public profile. He demonstrated his militant streak in court when he accused the police of brutality and got so belligerent that he had to be restrained.

Shaw's mentor was the Reverend Logan Kearse, the first black preacher to buy airtime on local television. He was the Baltimorean closest to Martin Luther King, Jr., who visited frequently to raise funds for civil rights campaigns. Kearse was brazen and clever. "To call him flamboyant is an understatement," said the newspaper and television journalist George Collins, who recalled seeing Kearse arrive at sit-ins in a chauffeur-driven vintage Duesenberg. Once, knowing that he would be arrested, he wore a hand-tailored Italian silk suit, which he threw away after spending a night in a cockroach-infested cell that reeked of urine. In 1969 Kearse spotted a public auction involving a mansion in the lily-white Guilford community. He dragged a suitcase full of cash and outbid all others. He bought 203 Chancery Road in his church's name and invited his congregation over to sing, holler, and praise the Lord. Kearse had political ambitions too. Militant Morgan students wanted nothing to do with him. "He was too transparently slick," remembered the activist Walter Dean, Jr.

Manny Bernstein could not understand why Shaw ran around with Kearse, participating in civil rights confrontations and dabbling in politics, seeking unsuccessfully a nomination to the U.S. House of Representatives in the 1964 Democratic primary. Bernstein didn't think his partner's activities helped business, but he did not intervene. Baltimore was a conservative place, an NAACP town. Shaw himself defended blockbusting as a civil rights tool. "Were it not for blockbusting, colored people would be living three to a room, hopelessly mired in ghetto housing," he wrote in a letter to *The Sun*. He said his firm had helped "literally thousands of colored families" in their "struggle up from the ghetto."

> The constant attacks on me and my firm would make it appear as though I was a racist and that we made a concerted effort to panic individuals of a certain ethnic group to leave the city. The truth is that my motives have been just the reverse. I am a firm believer in the rather well-worn phrase "all men are brothers under the Father." Let history be corrected before the real racists create—with just such incomplete articles of this type—a more subtle yet far more devastating racism, contributing more sparks to the fires of blind hatred.

I have been an integrationist in that I have always believed in full social, economic and political brotherhood, and am sincerely convinced that daily we are coming closer to that goal, in spite of the flare-ups of either the subtle or the blatant extremists.

Warren Shaw had been born in Oberlin, an Ohio town that, despite a famous college founded by abolitionists, adopted segregation. The high school remained integrated, however, and Shaw played football there. During World War II, Shaw's father, the town's mailman, moved to California, and the son followed. Although Shaw had not gone to college, Baltimore's African-American elite embraced him. He was presentable and personable, and he had quite a story to tell, a story that was true. His grandfather, a slave in Louisiana, had walked to freedom, ending up in Berea, Ohio, with seventy cents in his pocket. The ancestor was so enterprising that he not only completed undergraduate studies at a local college but went on to receive a degree from Boston University. Eventually he was offered a professorship of bible studies at Howard University in Washington, D.C.

In 1953, when Shaw entered the real estate business, Baltimore's African-American middle class was so small that if families of a certain social standing did not go to church together, or belong to the same fraternities and sororities, they rubbed shoulders at the Sphinx Club, a select membership club on Pennsylvania Avenue catering to doctors, lawyers, educators, entrepreneurs, and postal and other federal employees. This middle class also included certain Bethlehem Steel and General Motors workers. They gained entry because their earning power made them attractive as mates to light-skinned, academically accomplished women, who did their best to refine them. "Everybody knew everyone else in those days," recalled Theodosia Johnson Stokes, who grew up among families belonging to the Talented Tenth, W. E. B. DuBois's term for the best and brightest African Americans. (Her father, a postal worker, played the cello and sang in a glee club.)

Segregation severely constrained Baltimore's African-American social milieu. Until the 1950s, Jim Crow was present even on Pennsylvania Avenue, the black retail and entertainment hub, where sev-

Warren S. Shaw regarded blockbusting as his civil rights mission. His black-and-white real estate partnership with Manuel Bernstein specialized in breaking upscale white neighborhoods. *(Afro-American Newspapers)*

eral restaurants served only white shopkeepers and shoppers; carry-out meals were sold to blacks at the back door. Since black hotel capacity for visitors was small and room quality somewhat doubtful, touring celebrities were hosted in private homes. Such visits became occasions for parties. Soon a relationship of mutual self-promotion formed between Shaw and Elizabeth M. Oliver, a niece of the *Afro-American* publisher Carl Murphy, who wrote a gossip column for the paper. Oliver got good items and gained social status by hosting parties for visiting celebrities such as the gospel singer Mahalia Jackson. Shaw, one of the *Afro-American*'s biggest advertisers, footed the bill. Such a party was arranged in 1957 when Shaw's Oberlin childhood chum, Howard Jones, became the first black to join evangelist Billy Graham's crusade team. The club basement of Shaw's home also was the scene of a 1961 party for Archie Moore, the light-heavyweight boxing champion. In a picture caption the *Afro-American* informed its readers that John H. Murphy, Jr., the publisher's nephew, was "a long-time friend of Archie's," as he shared the glory around Moore with Shaw, Bernstein, and Oliver.

The arrangement produced a steady stream of free publicity for Shaw. An example was a big 1957 spread in the *Afro-American*, with multiple photos. "How can you get a house and be certain to enjoy living in it without excessive payments and future trouble?" the story asked. Oliver, whose byline the article carried, answered, "You can go to Manning Shaw Realty Company, 1821 Eutaw Place, or call MAdison 3-6261." The article called Bernstein and Shaw "Baltimore's most progressive real estate brokers" and said they had sold $1.4 million worth of real estate in just four years of existence, a considerable amount at the time. Their reputation and business practices were praised. "They specialize not only in getting you the home of your dreams but they settle you in for a lifetime of comfort minus future hazards of steep payments and future losses. Their motto is 'Happiness comes to you in a Manning-Shaw home.'"

Happiness escaped Shaw. He left his wife and children for a white secretary from the office. The relationship did not last. His former wife sued him for being a deadbeat dad, garnering big headlines in the *Afro-American*. He refused to pay, and a judge sent him to jail for contempt. In 1970 Shaw was convicted of larceny. It was a minor case, involving his failure to return a $650 down payment to a client, and the main question was why he didn't resolve it amicably. Perhaps it was his hallmark arrogance. Perhaps he was broke. His health wrecked, he moved to Silver Spring, Maryland.

At the peak of blockbusting in the 1950s and 1960s, Shaw had been an African-American trailblazer. Fewer than twenty mourners came to his funeral in 1986—not Bernstein, not other agents, not anyone from the *Afro-American*. His relatives hardly knew him, but they embraced the prodigal son. Using their connections, they gave him a military burial in the Arlington National Cemetery, believing he had served in World War II. He had not; he had enlisted for one year after the war. That made no difference. In death, Shaw became a hero.

11

꟭꟭꟭꟭꟭꟭

Ordinary Lives

EDMONDSON VILLAGE was an ordinary place, inhabited by ordinary people. Largely German-descended and Catholic, it was a west Baltimore neighborhood of quintessential redbrick rowhouses, owned by fastidious families who bought cheap seats to Orioles games, rooted for the Colts, and during the summer months feasted on steamed crabs spiced with Old Bay seasoning. National Bohemian was their beer; local Pikesville Rye was their whiskey, if they had a choice. Breadwinners held white-collar jobs in the telephone and gas companies and banks, or worked as teachers and lawyers, plumbers and craftsmen, or as functionaries for the city or state government. Women, if they were employed, typically found jobs in department stores or as secretaries. Edmondson Village was so solid that the federal government's 1937 redlining map gave it the second-best grade, "still desirable."

Two decades later, blockbusters saw a different Edmondson Village: a stultified community whose solid façade hid unexpected fissures and surprising breaking points. After the first blacks penetrated in 1955, some two hundred blockbusters descended on Edmondson Village, warning residents to sell now instead of waiting until the neighborhood became all black. Whenever a house became available, they leapfrogged to streets where whites thought they were safe and still had time. That added to the frenzy and made the direction and speed of racial change impossible to predict. "Everybody was selling houses. The minute the street opened up, every broker was there," recalled Morris Goldseker, who single-handedly transferred hundreds of rowhouses from white to black. "The owners called them up. They wanted to get rid of the house."

Edmondson Village rowhouses and apartments offered opportunities to average working-class African-American homeowners and renters, unlike Ashburton, which drew upwardly mobile professionals. Rowhouses that sheltered single families when Edmondson Village was white soon were cut up into rental units. If blockbusters did not do that, new black home buyers did when they had difficulty making the payments. As overcrowding worsened and problems appeared, Goldseker got blamed, even if he had nothing to do with a particular case. He was the city's largest trader of rowhouses in changing neighborhoods. Wherever he plied his trade, the complexion of neighborhoods changed almost overnight. Within a single decade, Edmondson Village, the size of a small American town, transitioned from all white to nearly all black.

Until Goldseker appeared on the scene, one man, James Keelty, had molded Edmondson Village. Born in County Roscommon, Ireland, he was six years old when he came to America with big dreams. Beginning in 1916, he constructed hundreds of good-quality rowhouses in the hills three miles from downtown, offering a variety of architectural designs and amenities. Even his early homes featured front porches, and many had garages; later models came with club basements. Being two stories high, they were easy to heat in the winter. In the summer, a big central exhaust fan drew in night air that kept the houses comfortable.

Keelty, a stonemason, left a lasting mark on Edmondson Village. In 1929 he built a Roman Catholic sanctuary as a memorial to his deceased six-year-old daughter, Bernardine, and a separate parish was created. With a big parochial school, St. Bernardine's became the community's bedrock. On major feast days, Edmondson Avenue, the busy thoroughfare in front of the church's grey stone edifice, was closed to traffic, reaffirming the church's status and the standing of its pastor, Monsignor Louis C. Vaeth, who ran St. Bernardine's with an iron hand from 1945 to 1967.

In his prime Monsignor Vaeth was a perpetual-motion machine. He was in charge of the Boy Scouts throughout the archdiocese; he organized crusades for Catholic students. In 1930 fifty thousand students attended an outdoor mass. For almost forty years he ran the archdiocesan Society for the Propagation of the Faith. He was a superior recruiter: his efforts led to thirteen men from all parts of the city becoming archdiocesan priests; five others were ordained for the Jesuits, one received holy orders as a Passionist, and between forty and sixty women entered convents. He even had a hand in educating one white cardinal for Africa and three bishops. The Vatican recognized Vaeth's achievements: he rose to apostolic, the highest of three grades of monsignors, and was entitled to wear a black biretta with a red tuft and a cassock similar to a bishop's. He was properly addressed as the Most Reverend Monsignor.

On clear days many residents could stand on their front steps and see the spires of downtown buildings. That's where most worked, commuting by streetcar. Edmondson Village residents were so content that they seldom moved away. Although mortgages were available, the community was so remarkably devoid of normal real estate ownership rotation that in 1940, more than two decades after the first sections were built, wholly 62 percent of the residents consisted of the original owners while the rest had bought their homes from original owners. There were no third owners at all. Such false stability contained the seeds of disaster—the community was not rejuvenating itself. As early as 1946, St. Bernardine's baseball team, in an act tantamount to heresy, had to recruit non-Catholic players from outside the neighborhood because it had lost so much of its own young talent to the suburbs.

Over decades the James Keelty Company continued to accumulate land. It acquired old estates, subdivided them, and constructed rowhouses and apartment buildings. The population grew from 11,779 to 16,388. Residents smugly congratulated themselves in 1947 when Joseph Meyerhoff opened Baltimore's first regional shopping center there. It was fashioned after a retail village built a decade earlier in Colonial Williamsburg. A department store was now at Edmondson Village's doorstep, as was a car dealership. But one day in 1954, a decade after the founder's death, the James Keelty Company abruptly sold its remaining residential development lots in the village. Without an explanation, it transferred business to nearby Baltimore County, where the volume of home building for the first time outstripped that in the city. This decision was taken about the time when the U.S. Supreme Court's desegregation order sent the first African-American students to the local junior high school, followed the next year by black families moving to blocks near the school. Edmondson Village shopping center merchants tried to figure out what to do. Many did not serve blacks. Even those who allowed blacks denied them the use of public restrooms. The turning point came in 1960 when a popular variety store, Tommy Tucker, removed the race bar. By that time the number of white shoppers was in decline; instead they patronized rivals, such as Westview Mall, which Joseph Meyerhoff had opened in 1958 just a mile away across the county line near a soon-to-open Beltway interchange. Shoppers there were white.

Television took Baltimore by storm after the first station went on the air in 1947. Only 1,600 Baltimoreans had a set at the time, but in three years 252,226 sets were added, a number that more than doubled in the next four years. The impact was far-reaching. Like countless other communities throughout America, Edmondson Village began living according to the television schedule. Routines changed. Tuesdays were no longer good for bowling or bingo; that night belonged to Milton Berle, a comedian who was television's first superstar. Other nights had different must-see programs. The arrival of whirring room air-conditioning units further insulated neighbors. The result was that even on balmy evenings, fewer and fewer people walked around the neighborhood or sat on porches, listening to radio and gossiping, as they had done in the early years. Everyone was old in Edmondson Village, or so it seemed. "I remember seeing neighbors and thinking that even their front parlors smelled of death. There were no kids around," recalled the author Mark Reutter, who lived and went to elementary school there in 1958.

This is how racial change happened. In the decade after 1944, blacks continued to advance beyond Fulton Avenue. Many headed northwest toward Jewish neighborhoods. Others marched west, reaching predominantly Catholic neighborhoods, such as St. Edward's parish on Poplar Grove Street. Ultimately they came to the Gwynns Falls, a stream with a buffer of woods. A single bridge led across to Edmondson Village. "They will never cross the bridge," Monsignor Vaeth repeatedly assured from the pulpit. As it turned out, the first blacks did not cross that bridge. Instead, beginning in 1955, they penetrated from a flank, crossing another bridge near the recently desegregated Gwynns Falls Junior High School. At St. Martin's Roman Catholic Church on Fulton Avenue, a mile away, a priest could not restrain himself. Having been subjected to Monsignor Vaeth's endless harangues about how Edmondson Village was different, he sent the prelate a telegram consisting of just three words. *Alea iacta est,* it said in Latin, repeating Caesar's words at the Rubicon.

The die, indeed, was cast.

Lightning-speed racial change in Edmondson Village was due to a combination of many seemingly unconnected factors, small and large, local and national. The critical element was St. Bernardine's, where Monsignor Vaeth was losing it. He was incapable of handling race and always had been. In the early 1940s he had almost sabotaged Archbishop Michael J. Curley's outreach to blacks. The archbishop had invited members of black student mission clubs to remain after mass at the cathedral and told them they could sit anywhere in any church. He then sent them across the street to the communion breakfast at Calvert Hall High School, "much to the discomfort of the moderator, Monsignor Vaeth," according to the official archdiocesan history.

At St. Bernardine's the prelate assumed an uncompromising stance. His words and actions made it clear that he thought blacks to be inferior. But he also assailed departing white communicants, sneering at them as "yellow-bellies" and "cowards" who were betraying the parish and their white neighbors. "He said that there are three colors in this parish—white, black and yellow. White were the people who stayed, black were the people who were coming and yellow were the people who were running, selling out," said Father Paul Witthauer, who was assigned to the parish at that time. Some parishioners wanted to believe the monsignor; others felt offended by his attacks on fellow communicants in a time of crisis. Suspicion poisoned the community. Residents began bailing out on the sly without telling neighbors or relatives. Vera Johnson related the experience to the University of Maryland Baltimore County professor W. Edward Orser: "If you were depending on a certain number of neighbors to stick it out so you'd have white neighbors, forget it! Even my dear uncle—guess when we found out he was moving? The day the moving van pulled up! This was right next door, and he never told us one word about it."

This tumultuous period coincided with an upheaval within the Catholic church that produced the controversial reforms of the Second Vatican Council. Monsignor Vaeth fell from favor. His old ways became an embarrassment to the archdiocese, whose official weekly, the *Catholic Review*, had begun to oppose racial discrimination, advocate social responsibility, lambaste right-to-work laws, and support the United Nations—all revisionist positions that troubled many rank-and-file Catholics. But such was Monsignor Vaeth's hierarchical rank and support in the divided parish that when Lawrence J. Shehan, a social progressive, ascended to archbishop in 1961, he expressed his concerns to Monsignor Vaeth in a face-to-face meeting but did not take away the prelate's pastorate. St. Bernardine's became an unhappy place. "Nobody was doing anything. They didn't want to get involved, they didn't want to start something and not finish it," recalled Father Witthauer. Church buildings deteriorated.

School desegregation and the growth in the size of black families hastened change. Two decades earlier, the sociologist Ira De A. Reid had reported that an average black family in Baltimore consisted of 2.8 persons while a typical white family consisted of 3.36. By the time

Monsignor Louis Vaeth, seen in 1931, fought from the pulpit to keep blacks out of Edmondson Village, which blockbusters found attractive because of its aging population. *(Associated Archives at St. Mary's Seminary and University)*

African Americans began moving to Edmondson Village, black families tended to have more school-age children than whites, particularly among the lower socioeconomic strata. Public schools thus formed the earliest concentrations of blacks, a situation aggravated by the overall shortage of white children. St. Bernardine's parochial school was slow to desegregate, thanks to Monsignor Vaeth. The school was open to everyone, he explained, but in the interest of maintaining discipline, students could be admitted only if they started from the first grade. Just before Monsignor Vaeth's retirement, an arsonist hit the school. A further blow came in 1970 when racial transition was nearly complete. The sisters, Servants of the Immaculate Heart of

Mary, withdrew nuns from the parochial elementary school which they had staffed since 1928.

Some Edmondson Village diehards vowed to stay, but economic fears got the best of them. "Their life savings were in those homes," Father Witthauer said. "The idea was: today we can get out, tomorrow the bottom is going to drop off." Inevitably there were scuffles between whites and incoming black kids; there were thefts, purse snatchings, and worse. St. Bernardine's kept losing members. Some of the new black arrivals were Catholics, of course, and they came to mass. But even there they could not escape raw hostility. When one young African-American woman, occupying an end seat, went up to receive communion in the early 1960s, whites filling the rest of the pew would not let her back in. She walked out of St. Bernardine's and never came back.

This was the scene onto which Goldseker strode. He was a self-made man who spoke with a heavy Eastern European accent and had scant formal education. He was self-conscious about his modest five-feet-seven frame, which he tried to boost with the aid of elevator shoes. He never married but was famous for his voracious appetite for one-night-stand ladies whom he paid to leave. Tennis was another passion. But mostly Goldseker worked. He was the *Afro-American*'s largest advertiser, so important that sometimes the press run was delayed when his pages of advertising were not ready. Despite operating real estate companies under fifty different names, he maintained a low public profile. To customers he introduced himself as "Mr. Lane" instead of using his real name.

Goldseker prospered because he was tough and smart. Speaking no English, he had left Poland at the age of sixteen. He sailed on a German steamer, a crossing that took two weeks because of tensions in Europe. Joining a sister who sent the ticket, he landed in east Baltimore's slums. He worked in a sweatshop, then in an uncle's grocery store. Seven years after arriving in America, he partnered with a cousin and bought a grocery store. More important, the budding capitalist began acquiring rowhouses as an investment. He became adept at leveraging, using the houses he was already buying as collat-

Tough and smart but also insecure, Morris Goldseker rose from a Polish immigrant to become a leading trader of rowhouses for blacks in white neighborhoods. *(Courtesy of Sheldon Goldseker)*

eral for new debt. When the Great Depression struck, he was forced to forfeit his properties. But he made sure that no one who dealt with him lost money. As a result, Goldseker established a name for himself as a man who kept his word.

His reputation paid off. At the height of the depression, in 1934 he got a big break: The Home Owners' Loan Corporation hired him to manage 1,400 defaulted properties. Goldseker soon made a proposal: Wouldn't it be better for everyone concerned if he took some of the troubled properties off their hands? Yes, he would need financing for the deal to work.

Initially Goldseker dealt with both white and black customers. But after World War II he realized that more and more blacks were making good money and could afford to buy a home. So he started systematically acquiring houses from whites. A member of the Forty Thieves cartel, though someone else represented him, he bought rowhouses at auctions or from individuals. He also bought in bulk, taking over rival companies in order to replenish his stock. Resales to blacks became his market niche. Of course, banks were not making mortgages to blacks at the time. There was not even a way for blacks to establish credit, because department stores neither wanted their business nor sold them anything on time purchases. That was no problem for Goldseker. He conducted his own credit checks, reviewing wage records, rent remittances, electricity and telephone bills, and installment payments on stoves and refrigerators. If the results satisfied him, he sold a house for little money down and weekly payments. He was strict: "A man that doesn't have a good job doesn't have means to pay for a house. He cannot afford to buy a house. He may have all good intentions . . . but, if he can't make it, he can't make it."

Goldseker became a necessary middleman for lending institutions that had never dealt with blacks and did not want to begin doing so. He processed the applications, borrowed money in his own name, and then relent it to buyers whom he deemed deserving. He took a handsome profit each time. He sold thousands of houses that way in various parts of the city. Banks made money, Goldseker made money, and blacks got houses they might not otherwise have been able to acquire.

For Goldseker, the prevalent sales instrument was the land-installment contract. Many blacks were completely naive about buying a house; they were easily persuaded to sign anything. A typewritten clause added to a 1963 Goldseker land-installment contract showed the potential for abuse. Its sweeping language stipulated: "It is understood and agreed that the seller shall have the right at any time during the life of the contract to do any repairs or improvements now or hereafter required by law and add the cost of such repairs and improvements to the purchase price stated in this contract."

Among methods that Goldseker used were one-year leases with an option to buy. What sense such an option made was a mystery in a city where the stock of homes for sale to blacks was steadily increasing. It was also a mystery why people agreed to put money down on options that could be exercised "only during the last forty-five (45) days of the term of this Lease and only by notice in writing from the Tenants to the Landlord." The contract further mandated that settlement "shall be consummated on or before the last day of the term thereof, time being of the essence," perhaps implying that Goldseker would arrange for permanent financing. Using that method, Goldseker made lots of sales.

Tenants who exercised an option to buy typically became land-installment contract buyers. The successful ones eventually built enough equity to be given permanent financing with two mortgages and payments that came due on different days. This is how the arrangement worked. Suppose Goldseker bought a house from a fleeing white family for $6,500 and resold it to Leroy Johnson and his wife, Hattie, for $13,000. He took the black family to a savings and loan association of his choosing. It gave the Johnsons an $8,500 first mortgage, that being the approximate fair-market value of the house they had bought. This enabled Goldseker to cash out his acquisition price and take a $2,000 profit. But since a $4,500 gap still existed, Goldseker had the Johnsons sign a second mortgage to him. Then he would take a personal loan in that amount. In order to get it, he usually used hypothecation—a banking practice nearly unknown now—which required him to make a cash deposit, perhaps $1,500, to the bank as his collateral. After several years, Goldseker would ask the Johnsons to combine the two mortgages through refinancing at a savings and loan of his choice. That allowed Goldseker to cash out the rest of his profits while the Johnsons took on more debt and accrued new fees. Goldseker guaranteed all his sales, whether they worked out or failed. "No building and loan lost a penny due to Goldseker," one competitor recalled.

Using a Maryland peculiarity akin to Britain's ninety-nine-year leases, Goldseker always kept the land underneath the house. As a result, house purchasers paid him a user's fee, known as ground rent, twice a year in addition to regular payments. The point of Goldseker accumulating ground rents was that Maryland courts ruled that the landowner's rights superseded even the rights of the holder of the first mortgage. So if a mortgage holder missed the paltry ground-rent payment, ground-rent owners were within their legal rights to seize the house. Goldseker made sure that he established ground rents on all properties he sold, even if they previously did not have one.

To Goldseker, a contract was a contract. Perhaps other real estate people were lenient or understanding. Not Goldseker. Anyone who failed to make a payment on time deserved to be put out. If that happened, those buying from him (and other speculators) lost whatever money they had paid and whatever improvements they had made. About 30 percent of Goldseker's land-installment buyers failed, in the judgment of Stanley Sugarman, a competitor. But the rest managed to become permanent homeowners.

Goldseker's unforgiving attitude earned him a reputation as a hard man. Still, blacks came to him because he offered quality. He did not show houses that were in a derelict condition; he had radio-dispatched crews that did nothing but repairs. So when a black couple entered a Goldseker house, it was clean and had a nice kitchen and a sparkling bathroom. It smelled good and had freshly washed windows and gleaming floors that were shielded with protective covering similar to new show houses in the suburbs. To black buyers, who were shut off from the suburban market of brand-new homes, a Goldseker house was the next best thing, a place that one could show to friends with pride. As a rule, Goldseker houses cost more. Human nature being what it is, some first-time homebuyers bragged about the high price they had agreed to pay, thinking that it elevated their standing among friends and relatives. Everyone knew him; he sponsored the first regular black programs on local television, WMAR-TV's *Tomorrow's Stars* and *Goldseker Open House.*

Although the situation would change after the 1968 riots, Goldseker's prices were not an issue for a long time. Blacks had grown to expect gouging. For as long as anyone could remember, Baltimore's blacks had paid more for scarce housing than whites did. As early as 1924, *The Sun* published an article headlined, "THE CONFESSION OF A BALTIMORE LANDLORD." Its verdict: "For a black man renting is an expensive business. His black skin marks him as a source of profit." The unnamed author wrote that a landlord who was content with a

10 percent annual return on his property when tenants were white, expected to get 17 percent when he converted it to black tenancy. Greed speeded up deterioration.

> Take any block in which there has been a recent shift of the two races. Under white occupation, one family doubtless occupied an entire house. This created a feeling of pride in maintenance. Go through the street a few months later and you will not recognize it as the same block.
>
> Under the new tenancy there are two or more families in each house. Individual pride in the appearance of the house and the street has become submerged in divided responsibility. Nobody feels inclined to do all the work of keeping up appearances. A few months bring a change that is reflected along the entire stretch.

Later studies reaffirmed that blacks paid more for housing. A 1936 federal government survey marked "confidential" reported that rents in Baltimore's best white neighborhoods were generally *lower* than in black areas. The pattern of blacks paying more was documented in many other cities, including Chicago and New York.

As blacks began to buy homes in growing numbers after World War II, a new term was coined: "black tax." It could not be found in dictionaries, and even urban affairs literature seldom mentioned it. Yet the term was easy to define and readily understood. "Black tax" connoted the considerable difference between a house's fair market value and the inflated price blacks agreed to pay to speculators. Calling it a tax was justified; blacks had no choice but to pay that surcharge if they wanted a house, because banks and other regular financial institutions would not lend them money. No one talked about a "white tax." Yet whites too paid a heavy penalty. In their eagerness to outrun blacks, they typically sold houses for less than the assessment value and well below the fair market value. That made little economic sense, of course, but many whites wanted out at any cost. In addition to losing money, they suffered an immeasurable emotional price in mounting anger and resentment toward blacks, whom they blamed for their predicament.

12

ЛЛЛЛЛЛЛ

Uneasy Allies

INTEGRATION in Baltimore as elsewhere was a one-way street, a short-lived transitory phase between desegregation and predictable resegregation. Whenever blacks appeared, whites were preconditioned to run. A tipping point was quickly reached, a measure of how many blacks white residents would tolerate before a wholesale abandonment began. The tipping point varied from one neighborhood to another, but it was quite low. Once the cycle began, racial changeover was typically completed in a decade. The lightning pace was not new. The turnover had been equally as fast in the 1910s when blacks moved to McCulloh Street.

In the 1950s and 1960s the rate of racial turnover was about the same in Edmondson Village, a largely Catholic rowhouse area, as it was in the majority Jewish Ashburton, where single-family homes predominated. Blockbusters targeted both neighborhoods. By contrast, there was no overt blockbusting or panic selling in Howard Park, a mostly non-Jewish neighborhood of single-family homes farther up along Liberty Heights Avenue. Yet the pace was the same there too. In each case the first black homeowners were roughly at the same income levels as departing whites, but that made no difference. School desegregation played a key role. The size of initial black enrollment was irrelevant. As soon as even a handful of black students appeared, whites began complaining. Their anxiety increased, regardless of whether or not they had school-age children.

Blockbusting—the name ordinary people applied to any racial change, whether panic peddling was involved or not—became a hot-button issue. In 1956 the city's Commission on Human Relations urged the Real Estate Board to discipline unscrupulous agents through bad publicity, whether or not they were board members. In order to prevent overcrowding and decay, the commission called for the city zoning board to "hold the line against zoning changes" and exhorted the City Council to tighten hygienic enforcement. The commission urged the various authorities to "see that existing regulations are strictly enforced." There is no evidence that any of those calls was heeded.

The Baltimore Jewish Council took a firm position against blockbusting in 1957. It issued a strong statement condemning the "ruthless and deceiving 'block-busting'" as organized crime:

> What is and what is not a racketeering operation may, at times, be a matter of opinion, but there are obvious cases. For example a white home owner who desires to move and sell his house to the highest bidder has a perfect right to sell his house to a Negro. Some may call this "blockbusting," but to deny this seller his right to sell would be denying both to him and to his prospective purchaser their civil rights. However the realtor who, motivated by quick profits, utilizes one artifice or another to stir up panic and thus induce white homeowners to sell is engaged in an obviously unethical and anti-social business practice. The Baltimore Jewish Council will make every effort to curb such practices where they are designed to dislocate established and peaceful Jewish neighborhoods. . . .
>
> We emphasize again that the answer to the problem of changing neighborhoods is *not to panic, but to stay put*. It is sheer folly to abandon costly and treasured homes and synagogues merely because fellow human beings of another color have moved close by.
>
> This is the course of conduct dictated by self-interest. This is the course of conduct demanded of those who believe in the American

and democratic way of life. This is the course of conduct which is the finest exemplification of the highest ideals of Judaism.

Soon afterward Councilman Solomon Liss, a leader in the Jewish community, introduced a City Council ordinance to outlaw blockbusting. He later withdrew it for lack of support, but not before calls were sparked to ban real estate signs that were used to sow panic. Racial change was on everyone's mind. It was happening so fast that a newly formed regional booster group, the Greater Baltimore Committee (GBC), predicted dire economic consequences. "Flight of the medium and upper income families from the city limits and the replacement by persons of both races of the lowest income levels is a threat not only to our municipal solvency but to the economic stability of the entire metropolitan area," warned the developer James W. Rouse, a GBC leader. The following year GBC spun off a separate organization, Baltimore Neighborhoods, Inc., to deal with residential desegregation issues.

As public clamor increased, the previously unresponsive City Council enacted an anti-blockbusting law in 1960. Liss secured an unlikely co-sponsor, Councilman William Donald Schaefer, who was Mayor J. Harold Grady's floor leader. He agreed to muster the votes for the measure, even though he did not see eye-to-eye with Liss. Schaefer's role was curious. He and his mother were among the last white holdouts in Edmondson Village. Yet he had shown no activism on this issue. In fact he exhibited little interest in racial equality during his fifty-year career in public service, which included four terms as mayor as well as two each as governor and state comptroller. But his friend Irv Kovens, who dispensed advice from his west Baltimore furniture store, knew politics. He may have suggested to Schaefer that it did not hurt to be seen on the side of the angels. In 1966 Schaefer also voted for a controversial fair housing bill that the City Council's majority defeated, and he even briefly served as a board member of the integrationist Baltimore Neighborhoods Inc. The anti-blockbusting law itself had no impact because blockbusting was so difficult to prove in court.

The truth was that no one knew what to do, how to counter the tensions generated by racial change. The city was divided: there was no common language, no agreement about terminology. What whites condemned as destructive blockbusting, blacks hailed as liberating desegregation, a long-awaited opportunity to move into better housing. Prominent African-American leaders participated in activities that whites saw as blockbusting. Marse Calloway, a Republican leader, and Willard A. Allen, a Democratic worthy, bought real estate listings from white agencies and sold the properties to blacks. Allen owned an insurance company, which enabled him to finance the houses he sold in neighborhoods that were opening up.

He also was the grandmaster of Prince Hall Masons, a fraternal order that included thousands of the most accomplished African-American men as members. All craved a house.

Most whites believed that racially mixed neighborhoods could not be sustained. The city had become so accustomed to segregation that no other way seemed possible. Even liberals feared that living among blacks would ruin them economically and mark them socially. The walls of separation remained astonishingly high. This was demonstrated in 1962 when the Greater Baltimore Committee's movers and shakers created a new downtown dining club. It was the first one in the city to admit Jews to membership, but when the new Center Club opened, blacks were excluded from membership and would be for several years.

Among the most cynical instigators of racial panic were owners of apartment complexes. Whenever a stable neighborhood began to desegregate, they bestowed a kiss of death on integration by simply evicting all white tenants, who were on monthly rents and leases. Landlords then jacked up rents, changed them to weekly payments, advertised their complexes only in the *Afro-American*, and rented only to blacks. This happened time and time again. A young architect, M. J. Brodie, was among those evicted; he later played an important role as the housing commissioner and development administrator. Apartments, with their concentrated population of renters walking on the streets and waiting at bus stops, influenced the public's perception of a neighborhood. Segregation and resegregation of apartment complexes was so absolute that in 1962 not a single multi-racial complex existed in the metropolitan area.

Baltimore Neighborhoods Inc. hoped to change the situation. Its executive director pleaded with a leading management company: "If the city is to continue as a desirable place to live we must find means whereby whites and Negroes may satisfy their housing needs without planning in terms of housing solely for one group or the other."

A communal emergency also forced the Baltimore Jewish Council to get involved. Several newly built Jewish-owned garden apartment complexes along Greenspring Avenue, near Cold Spring Lane, evicted their mostly Jewish renters, instituting an all-black rental policy. Located nearby were several important Jewish institutions, which had followed their memberships' exodus from east Baltimore to the northwestern edge of the city. How viable could they be if the area now became black?

Sinai Hospital was a poignant example. In 1959 it had relocated from its original home in east Baltimore, near Johns Hopkins Hospital, to a state-of-the-art campus near the Pimlico Race Course. When construction began, the neighborhood was Jewish. By the time the hospital opened, blacks were moving to surrounding blocks. The Baltimore Jewish Council told the garden-apartment-complex owners that they owed it to the Jewish community to rescind their all-black rental policies.

"Although no one should object to a properly integrated neighborhood, Jewish and Negro leaders alike are concerned lest the whole area some day become another Negro ghetto," Leon Sachs told the apartment house owners. The communal stakes were high. "This is a matter of concern not only to Sinai Hospital and Levindale [a geriatric home] but also the Jewish Community Center, the Baltimore Hebrew College and many synagogues—all involving an investment of many millions of dollars." Sachs's efforts failed. Greenspring Avenue garden-apartment-complex owners stuck to their guns and continued to evict whites. The Sinai Hospital neighborhood became African American.

Another force that weakened efforts to create stable integrated neighborhoods was Maryland's largest newspaper company, *The Sunpapers,* owned by families who were part of the city's establishment. *The Sun, The Evening Sun,* and *The Sunday Sun* classified real estate ads according to race. *All Sections of the City, Move Right In,* and *White* were among real estate advertising classifications. So were *Houses for Rent—City–Colored, Colored Rentals,* and *Colored Homes.* These ads became a tool in the blockbusters' bag of tricks. As soon as even a single block was broken, an area could be advertised as *Colored.* Such a description, though patently inaccurate, told skittish white house hunters to stay away and signaled to the existing white owners that it was time to sell. "Use of the designations 'Colored' and 'Negro' have been instrumental in forcing the conversion of many neighborhoods from all-white to all-Negro in the past. If permitted to continue, designations which have never, in the initial stages of change, truly reflected the racial makeup of an area, will force community after community to become all Negro," Baltimore Neighborhoods Inc. noted in 1962.

During more than two decades from the 1940s onward, numerous delegations visited *The Sunpapers* to protest racial designations in real estate ads, particularly the identification of certain properties as "Restricted" or being available only to "Gentiles." The pressure achieved nothing. *The Sunpapers* refused to drop such labels. In 1955 its advertising director expressed surprise at suggestions that such advertising was offensive. So did other executives. It was a newspaper's duty to "inform its readers and serve the city to its best advantage," said *The Sunpapers* president William F. Schmick, Jr. A neighborhood's racial composition was news, he contended, and knowing about it was in readers' best interests.

Equal-housing advocates were at a disadvantage in such encounters. Their numbers were small, and they were divided on many issues, particularly on blockbusting. While the Baltimore Jewish Council had formulated its position, its membership was split on how racial change should proceed and to what extent. Also divided were members of the NAACP and the Baltimore Urban League, who included numerous whites. Some members advocated gradualism; others rejected it. The rift was not only black and white, it was also black and Jewish. Many blacks did not trust Jews, charging that they were growing rich and powerful at the expense of African Americans. Jews, for their part, suspected that blacks harbored anti-Semitism. The rift between the city's leading black and white civil rights families illustrated this tension.

Lillie May Carroll Jackson, the matriarch of the African-American civil rights movement, headed the local NAACP. Her daughter, Juanita, also did civil rights work. They saw blockbusting as a perfectly acceptable real estate tactic because it forced recalcitrant whites to desegregate. Was it the blacks' fault if whites chose to run? By contrast, Sidney Hollander, Sr., the leading white civil rights influence, condemned blockbusters as evil men who cynically and greedily destroyed stable neighborhoods by preventing gradual integration. He dominated the Baltimore Urban League and did not trust the two Jackson women.

Hollander had been born in 1881. At six feet two inches he was an imposing man whose avocation was mountain climbing. His cough syrup company ran itself and made plenty of money, allowing him to champion various equal-opportunity causes. He was a major force in the American Jewish community and from 1939 to 1946 served as national president of the Jewish Federations and Welfare Funds. He also fought tirelessly for black causes. "Sidney Hollander will fight for the black man to the last Jew," it was jested.

In 1947 Hollander sent a letter to Walter White, the national NAACP's executive director. He and White were close friends who occasionally vacationed together, but on this occasion Hollander resorted to a formal letter. He questioned Lillie May Jackson's "veracity and integrity." He said that he was not the only one who had come to doubt her. "Important individuals and organizations here, interested in the same issues as the NAACP, just won't work with that organization as long as Mrs. Jackson is its fuehrer," Hollander wrote. When

It was said of Sidney Hollander that he "will fight for the black man to the last Jew." Nevertheless his relations with the leading black civil rights family were tense. *(Courtesy of Sidney Hollander, Jr.)*

Jackson quickly learned of the letter, the relationship deteriorated further.

Even though their memberships overlapped to some degree, organizational tensions and rivalry existed in many cities between the NAACP, the most important agency for blacks in the struggle against discrimination, and the Urban League, which sought to win the support of white businesses and corporations for equal job opportunities. The issue was control. Whites had been instrumental in setting up both national organizations. But while blacks had gradually gained control of the NAACP, white individuals, foundations, and corporations continued to steer the Urban League by holding its purse strings. This reality underlay the tension between Hollander and Jackson. But her behavior also annoyed him, including her swearing and hollering. Always wearing gloves and a big hat—as respectable ladies did—she was some sight shouting at the top of her lungs, later apologizing,

"God opened my mouth and no man can shut it!" James Rouse thought that "she did not employ physical violence, she used *verbal violence*." That often did the trick. "I'd rather have the devil after me than Mrs. Jackson. Give her what she wants," Governor McKeldin famously said.

Lillie May Jackson had been born in 1889 into a family of teachers, landowners, and small proprietors who claimed descent from Charles Carroll of Carrollton, the Marylander who, as noted earlier, was the only Catholic signer of the Declaration of Independence. She graduated from the Colored High and Training School for teachers and married a traveling projectionist of educational and religious films. Crisscrossing the country with him, she became comfortable speaking to gatherings large and small. Her rise to civil rights prominence began in 1933, after a lynching on the Eastern Shore aroused Maryland's blacks. Out of the blue in west Baltimore arrived the self-styled Prophet Kiowa Costonie, a turban-headed faith healer. While other ministers preached, the twenty-eight-year-old "New Messiah" organized direct action against stores in Baltimore's black neighborhoods that did not employ African Americans. The tactic had been tried earlier in Chicago. Costonie's boycotts and picket lines marked the first time that Baltimore had seen mass organizing in the black community. The *Afro-American* enthusiastically backed the "Buy Where You Can Work" campaign. After Costonie disappeared as mysteriously as he had arrived—some insisted that he was run out of town for seducing young girls—the newspaper's publisher, Carl J. Murphy, handpicked Jackson, his grade-school classmate, to take over the "Buy Where You Can Work" campaign. She emerged as the de facto civil rights leader in Baltimore.

Murphy next assigned Jackson to take over the NAACP's dormant local chapter. In a short time she built it into a powerhouse, the second-largest chapter in the nation. Her daughter, Juanita, headed a separate City-Wide Young People's Forum, whose debates featured the most provocative speakers of the day. When W. E. B. DuBois or the folklorist Zora Neale Hurston appeared, the overflow crowds numbered more than two thousand. Juanita's co-leader at the forum

Wearing her trademark hat, Lillie May Jackson is surrounded by civil rights honors and memorabilia in her Eutaw Place home. *(Special Collections, University of Maryland Libraries)*

was Clarence Mitchell, Jr., an *Afro-American* reporter who was soon to become the national NAACP's lobbyist in Washington. They married in 1938.

In 1934, when Juanita was twenty-two, she was involved in an incident that made the Jewish community cringe. Her City-Wide Young People's Forum sponsored a debate on the situation in Germany, where Hitler had recently risen to power. Leslie Pinckney Hill, president of a teachers' college in Cheyney, Pennsylvania, was one of the panelists. He declared that while Adolf Hitler's Nazi regime was brutal, "in many respects its principle of establishing a pride of race and group salvation would be a great help to colored Americans." He won strong applause. The *Afro-American*'s headline read: "HITLER PROGRAM OK, CHEYNEY HEAD AVERS."

The Jewish community was aghast. People began saying that the daughter and her mother turned all black-white problems into black-Jewish problems. That sentiment deepened in 1936 after Edward L. Israel, rabbi of Baltimore's Har Sinai Congregation, addressed the City-Wide Young People's Forum on "Germany's Treatment of Jews: Is It Justified?" During the question-and-answer period he became so perturbed that he later wrote an article headlined "JEW HATRED AMONG NEGROES" for the NAACP's *Crisis* magazine. "Negroes today are becoming antisemitic because they make generalizations about the Jew on the basis of their distasteful experiences with or their dislike of certain inferior people who happen to be Jews," Israel wrote. Such anti-Semitism was not limited to black intellectuals. He cited *Situations Wanted* ads in *The Sun*, in which applicants for domestic service stipulated that they would work for "Gentiles only."

Rabbi Israel was careful in the wording of his article, but Lillie May Carroll Jackson exploded. In a letter to *The Crisis* she claimed that "when the Gentiles controlled the large stores downtown (having been born and reared in Baltimore) there was no such thing as Negroes not being able to buy in any of the stores." Indeed, for decades until 1960, the discrimination practiced by downtown department stores had soured relations among blacks and Jews. Enforcing restrictions that were harsher than those in the erstwhile Confederate capital of Richmond, Virginia, all major downtown Baltimore department stores barred African Americans from trying on dresses, suits, hats, gloves, and shoes, and insisted that any black sales were "final." Four main stores were Jewish owned; two were not. Ownership made no difference; they all discriminated.

Jackson went on to accuse Jews of rent gouging and of not paying fair wages to domestics. She wrote that Jews had tricked blacks into a political alliance, which resulted in Jews being elected and blacks losing their only representation on the City Council, which had no African-American member for three decades until 1955. "Because both Jews and Negroes represent minority groups, who are being persecuted, the Negroes naturally expect better treatment from the Jewish group," Jackson wrote.

Leon Sachs, executive director of the Baltimore Jewish Council, noted that in discussions with Jackson and Mitchell, "I made it very clear that if you want to fight discrimination in department stores, we are with you 100 percent. If you are going to fight only the Jewish department stores, I am opposed to you 100 percent. I couldn't make it any clearer than that." Jackson and her daughter repeatedly promised not to single out Jewish department stores. But repeatedly the two women broke their word, said Sachs, who accused them of "something bordering on dishonesty." He described Juanita Mitchell as "very erratic." As for the matriarch, Sachs said "she wasn't too bright. . . . I think Mrs. Jackson's strength lay in the fact that she was there early and at the right time, and particularly because the *Afro* was always behind her."

Murphy, the *Afro-American*'s editor and publisher, indeed supported the two women. Improbably, he was a German-language scholar by training and had studied a year at the famed University of Jena, where the philosopher George Wilhelm Friedrich Hegel and the poet and philosopher Friedrich Schiller had once taught. But instead of pursuing an academic career he took over the family newspaper. Everyone called him Mr. Carl, even his children. His Druid Hill Avenue office was a clearinghouse where black communal priorities were identified and strategies plotted. The office was on the third floor of the *Afro-American* building, where Mr. Carl, a short man, sat behind an elevated desk. Thus a visitor still gasping for air from the steep climb had to look up to Mr. Carl from the very beginning. Mr. Carl's Ph.D. degree was in German philology, but he knew his psychology well.

The *Afro-American* missed few opportunities to point out that Jews were a "foreign" minority, lucky to live in America and not in Nazi Germany. "Assuming the right of every individual to conduct his business as he sees fit, the picture of a member of a persecuted race defending other people's exclusion from public institutions isn't particularly pretty," the *Afro-American* editorialized in 1944, when the department store owner Albert Hutzler defended in court the Enoch Pratt Free Library's policy of not hiring blacks. Hutzler was the public library's board chairman, and he told the court that he himself did not hire blacks in his store. Curiously, Hutzler was a close friend of Hollander's, who was among the city's few true and committed integrationists, white or black.

Jackson counted blockbusters among her friends. Manny Bernstein remembered how she and her daughter repeatedly visited his real estate office. When it came time for Clarence's and Juanita's eldest son, Clarence Mitchell III, to get his first full-time job, he became a salesman for the Manning-Shaw blockbusting company. Jackson herself owned and operated several apartment buildings to produce the family's badly needed income.

In 1961 a public clash erupted between Juanita Mitchell and Sidney Hollander, Jr., his father's namesake, who was a market researcher by profession. They were among the speakers in an NAACP meeting devoted to equal housing. Representing the integrationist Baltimore Neighborhoods, Inc., Hollander Jr. advocated a gradual approach. He urged blacks to ask whites to stay in changing neighborhoods; ask white families to buy into black areas; and ask black families to serve as pilot residents by moving to unbroken white neighborhoods. Blacks should also disperse to the counties and try to desegregate white developments there. "This is the only way we can see to keep the city from [becoming] 'a black city' with 'white' counties," the *Afro-American* reported Hollander Jr. as saying.

Juanita Mitchell took exception. She declared that open occupancy, regardless of race or ethnic background, was the only solution. "We don't go for half-compromises. We go for open occupancy straight down the line," she declared. Warren Shaw then stood up. Why would an all-black city be a bad thing? he asked. Regardless of race, color, or creed, people should be able to move wherever they wanted, the blockbuster remarked.

Despite long odds against success, some neighborhoods devised strategies to prevent resegregation. One was Windsor Hills, where several generations of Hollanders lived. An early streetcar suburb built where a grain mill and large estates had existed in the 1750s, it

Juanita Mitchell, looking feisty, was vocal in her belief that blockbusters were good because they opened up housing opportunities for blacks. *(Special Collections, University of Maryland Libraries)*

was a pleasant community whose architectural styles ran the gamut from Victorian to rancher. The grandest house was a mini-estate fashioned after Thomas Jefferson's Monticello; the oddest was an eye-catching modern home constructed entirely of exposed logs; the most futuristic was a Buckminster Fuller geodesic dome that looked like a stranded spaceship.

Windsor Hills' residential development had begun in 1895. After Jewish families moved in about ten years later, original homeowners began to depart. There was little neighborly interaction among homeowners of different faiths. In the 1930s, while the improvement association met and men conducted business—and it was always only men in those days—separate socials were held for Jewish and non-Jewish wives. Beginning in 1955 the cycle repeated itself when Nellie Buchanan became the first African American to settle in Windsor Hills. She was an English teacher at Frederick Douglass High School. Others soon trickled in.

Four years later John and Ernestine Pumphrey, their young sons, and a daughter became the first blacks to move to a tree-shadowed block of Gwynns Falls Parkway on the bluffs of a stream valley in Windsor Hills. Buying directly from the white owner, the thirty-year-old electroplater of printed circuits got a good deal on a green hulk of a house. "I worked at Westinghouse during the week and I would cut people's lawns on weekends, and I just took the bus and walked until I found this house," he recalled.

No Welcome Wagon called on the Pumphreys. A fellow Westinghouse worker evacuated his house next door as quickly as he could. Whites across the street also fled. Some time afterward the Pumphrey family noticed that the city no longer swept the streets or collected the garbage as punctually as when the neighborhood was white. The pattern of declining public services was duplicated in other racially changing neighborhoods.

As all sales now tended to be to blacks, a group of Windsor Hills integrationists launched a self-financed campaign to recruit white homeowners and renters to maintain racial diversity. Two real estate companies were designated as agents and for the recruitment. That was the only way to retain multi-racialism, it was argued. After initial promise, the effort flagged. Another multi-racial group of residents tried to raise money so that Windsor Hills could be marketed to whites. That attempt also flopped. African-American homeowners saw little reason why they should spend their money to attract whites if whites didn't want to move to the neighborhood on their own. Windsor Hills soon became predominantly black.

The lending industry generally denied mortgages to the few whites who wished to move to changing neighborhoods. Getting mortgages was such a problem that in 1961 Baltimore Neighborhoods, Inc. tried to set up a $1 million loan pool to provide financing to white buyers. Nothing came of the plan. When John Michener moved to Windsor Hills in 1966, "twenty mortgage companies" turned down this white Ph.D. who worked for the Social Security Administration. Financing was such a problem nationwide that in 1975 a big Philadelphia builder, Morris Milgram, teamed with James Farmer, one of the founders of CORE (the Congress of Racial Equality), to set up the Fund for an OPEN Society. Still operating in 2009, it made below-market-rate mortgages available to people moving to neighborhoods where their race was underrepresented.

Across town, Bolton Hill grappled with similar problems with different results. Bolton Hill was the name that boosters adopted in the 1950s to counter the community's popular nickname, Gin Belt, presumably earned during Prohibition. In the acute World War II housing shortage, many huge Bolton Hill rowhouses, originally built as single-family homes for the wealthy, had been cut up into units for defense workers. Since the city placed no limit on the number of rental units, the result was that just one group of eight adjoining rowhouses was split into 93 "apartments," housing nearly 250 renters. By the mid-1950s such rooming houses had become death traps where fatal fires were frequent.

Since World War II, longtime homeowners had blamed "hillbillies" for Bolton Hill's worsening conditions. But when Appalachians began returning home after World War II, other whites were not interested in renting or buying substandard housing. It seemed just a matter of time before African Americans would take over, since an overcrowded black slum already existed just south of Bolton Hill. Residents were relieved when a decision was made in the 1950s to demolish the slum so that a colossal state office complex could be built there, next to the Fifth Regiment Armory. But there was also talk about urban renewal, a fearful prospect to whites convinced that federal funding meant the area would turn black.

Bolton Hill's Mount Royal Protective Association had successfully worked to stop blacks ever since the segregationist William L. Marbury created it in the 1910s. Refusing speculators' offers, it did not buy properties in a preemptive move. Instead it kept blacks away through lawsuits, going so far as to argue its case before the U.S. Supreme Court. "No person has the essential liberty to occupy anothers [sic] land," the association's brief argued. "Prejudices cannot be eradicated by law. This is specially true of certain so-called prejudices, which many people feel are not prejudices at all but a mere recognition of the facts of life and nature."

In the late 1950s the association's direction changed. Membership ranks were opened to blacks, and the name was changed to the more neutral Mount Royal Improvement Association. The association even gave its qualified support to urban renewal, as long as certain safeguards were in place. To that end it struck a deal with the Baltimore Urban League. The two set "an informal percentage quota, plus a screening process to keep out undesirables of either race," Gurney Breckenfeld, an editor at *Time* and *Fortune* magazines, wrote in *The Human Side of Urban Renewal.*

The Urban League pledged to keep the number of blacks, estimated at 12 to 15 percent in 1956, below 25 percent. No records survive to show how that was to be accomplished. But executive director Furman Templeton explained: "The Urban League is ready to take what would appear to be drastic action, in order to achieve a stabilized, integrated neighborhood, which is, after all, the democratic goal in housing." At about the same time 211 white Bolton Hill homeowners banded together. They attracted nationwide attention by investing a hefty amount of their own money in a stock corporation, Bolton Hill, Inc. It was charged with renovating problem properties and finding "desirable tenants and purchasers." Bolton Hill remained overwhelmingly white.

13

꘎꘎꘎꘎꘎

From Dream to Nightmare

FLICKERING IMAGES on black-and-white television sets brought the
civil rights struggle to America's living rooms in 1963. In Birmingham,
Alabama, a Ku Klux Klan bomb killed four black girls in a church,
and a public safety commissioner named Bull Connor unleashed police dogs on black demonstrators. In neighboring Mississippi a sniper's
bullet ended the life of civil rights leader Medgar Evers. In Maryland
boycotts and sit-ins erupted into rioting in the Eastern Shore town of
Cambridge. Governor J. Millard Tawes declared martial law and sent
425 National Guardsmen to quell the violence with the help of state
troopers.

Then there was William Devereaux Zantzinger. Draped in white
tie and tails, with a carnation accenting his lapel, at six-foot-one and
200 pounds the partygoer was hard to miss at Baltimore's annual
Spinsters Ball in February 1963. For one thing, he was drunk. The
24-year-old heir to a 630-acre southern Maryland tobacco farm was
a mean drunk, and that night he was on a tear. At a dinner before the
ball he whacked two black restaurant waiters with a white wooden
toy cane, the type that used to be sold at carnivals. After feasting
on prime rib—and, it was noted, departing without leaving a tip—
his party moved to the Emerson, where he assaulted a hotel bellhop
with the cane. He struck a waitress, then stumbled to a crowded bar.

"Nigger, I asked you for a drink," he slurred to the barmaid, Hattie Carroll. When she ignored him, Zantzinger, calling her "a black bitch," prodded her on the head and face with his cane. She fell to the floor, lost consciousness, and died next day of a brain hemorrhage. She was 51, the mother of 11.

Zantzinger's father was a Washington real estate developer, a member of the Maryland state planning commission, and a former state delegate. Now his son, the product of one of the finest private schools in the nation's capital, Sidwell Friends, was about to become the first white man in Maryland history to be charged with murdering an African-American woman. But because Carroll had suffered from dangerously elevated blood pressure, the charge was reduced to manslaughter. Convicted, Zantzinger was given a six-month prison sentence, to be served among white inmates at a distant county prison. The judge delayed the start of the sentence so that Zantzinger could harvest his tobacco crop. This coddling so outraged songwriter Bob Dylan that he wrote "The Lonesome Death of Hattie Carroll" as a protest. "For now is the time for your tears" went the refrain.

Two weeks after Hattie Carroll's death in 1963, Archbishop Lawrence J. Shehan issued a pastoral letter instructing that every Catholic's obligation was to promote racial equality. His Lenten pastoral called "particularly lamentable" the "unreasonable and automatic panic, too often fanned by unscrupulous and disreputable real estate brokers and speculators, which accompanies the arrival of a Negro family in an area previously occupied by white families only. The fight that occurs not only unfairly pre-judges the new neighbors, but it also works an economic hardship on departing property owners, destroys the community, undermines church life, and hits hard on the substantial investments made in schools, rectories, convents, and recreational facilities, as well as in the actual places of worship."

He continued: "The duty of justice and charity applies not only to our churches, our schools, our charitable organizations and institutions, and our hospitals, but also to all of us as individuals. It must guide us in our personal relationships—within our block, our neighborhood, our community; in our social and fraternal organizations; in the business we may conduct; in the labor unions to which we may belong; at work and play; in all the circumstances of everyday life." Shehan's words divided Maryland's 450,000 Catholics. Dismayed by the turmoil at the Ecumenical Council in Rome now known as Vatican II, their faith was again being tested by the church. More tests were to come.

Four months later, on the Fourth of July, 283 protesters were arrested at Gwynn Oak Amusement Park, just across the city line in Baltimore County. The arrests culminated a ten-year campaign to desegregate Gwynn Oak, its Dixie ballroom, rickety Big Dipper wooden roller coaster, Ferris wheel, Rocket to the Moon, and Pretzel rides and bumper cars. Among those handcuffed were 36 clergymen of various faiths, including nationally known religious leaders and several Baltimore priests who had Shehan's permission to participate. The arrests made front pages across America and led television newscasts. They signaled pastors' and rabbis' heightened role in the civil rights movement. Gwynn Oak finally opened its doors to all races eight weeks later, on August 28, the same day that Martin Luther King, Jr., electrified multitudes of civil rights marchers in Washington with his "I Have a Dream" speech.

The struggle continued. Three years later, in January 1966, an Episcopal bishop, a Methodist bishop, and leading rabbis appeared before the Baltimore City Council with Shehan to support a bill outlawing racial discrimination in real estate sales and rental housing. Shehan, elevated to a cardinal by then, spoke first, ignoring death threats. Many in the overflow crowd of two thousand booed. Some spat on him. Several Catholic councilmen deplored the rowdiness but said that the cardinal had asked for it. "It was a bad thing to bring the cardinal down here. This is not the kind of an issue a clergyman should get involved in," one councilman admonished. He accused the cardinal of "moral blackmail." The Real Estate Board led the opposition. Its representative called the bill "a gross and flagrant flouting of the human right of property disposition." Others said that the bill

smacked of "communism." When the vote came, the Catholic majority of councilmen saw to it that the bill was defeated by a vote of
thirteen to eight.

To the national media, Martin Luther King, Jr., had become the
symbol of black America's aspirations for equality. But within the
civil rights movement his nonviolent leadership was under fierce challenge. To firebrands it didn't matter that Congress had passed the
Civil Rights Act of 1964, or that a sweeping voting rights act had
been enacted in 1965. The pace was too slow, they contended. The
rebellion grew so strident that a Mississippi sharecropper-turned-
activist, Fannie Lou Hamer, fired up a Baltimore rally by ridiculing
Dr. King: "While he is having a dream, I'm having a nightmare." Her
alternative to nonviolence was Black Power. Against this backdrop,
a letter that Dr. King received from Baltimore in early May 1967
was remarkable. Its signers were six direct-action activists of varying
militancy who had walked out of CORE. They urged him to come to
Baltimore to lead a march against segregated housing on Memorial
Day, fewer than three weeks away.

Over the years Dr. King had repeatedly visited Baltimore, preach-
ing and raising money. But he had refrained from direct action—protests and demonstrations. The reasons were not entirely clear. Perhaps
he conceded Baltimore to the NAACP, which preferred litigation to
demonstrations, or did not wish to become embroiled in the faction-
alism of CORE and of students at Morgan State College. These two
groups were the cutting edge of direct action. The students sponsored
sit-ins at the Northwood Shopping Center, a Roland Park Company
property not far from the campus. CORE, for its part, designated Baltimore as a "target" city for major organizing. It garnered national
headlines by trying to desegregate about fifty restaurants on the main
road between New York and Washington. Those restaurants refused
to serve not only American blacks but dark-skinned foreigners as well,
making it necessary for the State Department constantly to apologize
to African and Asian diplomats.

Now, writing on the stationery of their organization, complete
with the emblem—a hangman's noose—these six Activists for Fair

Housing told Dr. King that the city was overdue for mass organizing and needed him to spearhead it. "Baltimore has a potential to achieve real and meaningful change as great or greater than any large city in the U.S., if only its large Negro population (43%) could be roused to speak out boldly for its rights," the letter argued. In truth the activists' letter was a cry of desperation. Years of sustained small-scale protests against residential segregation had produced incremental results, but lately progress had stalled. The defeat of various housing bills in the City Council was just one indicator. Baltimore's civil rights movement needed a shot in the arm.

The six activists did their best to entice Dr. King to come to Baltimore. Aware of his outspoken opposition to the war in Vietnam, they pointed out "that one of the leaders in the Peace Movement, Fr. Philip Berrigan," was among their advisers. They underscored that Fort Meade, an important army post, was nearby. Off-base housing barred blacks. That housing belonged to Joseph Meyerhoff, Maryland's largest home builder. Activists for Fair Housing had picketed the apartments repeatedly. They had sought meetings with the developer; they had tried to persuade the Department of Defense that desegregating off-base housing was a federal issue. They had failed miserably. In their letter the Baltimoreans pleaded with Dr. King to take on Meyerhoff.

Since the late 1940s, when the Baltimore Jewish Council had condemned Meyerhoff's discrimination against other Jews, the developer had greatly increased his influence. His real estate empire now spanned 11 states. He championed suburban sprawl as a founding member of the National Homebuilders Association and as chairman of Maryland's state planning commission. He continued to be a rainmaker in American Jewish fund-raising, and he had become an important donor to Republican causes. Meyerhoff's holdings were no longer limited to home building or to some 5,500 apartments. He built shrines to suburban consumerism—shopping malls with gigantic parking structures. He owned a life insurance company, and interlocking directorships gave him a voice on the board of a big old-line Baltimore bank. His generous philanthropy kept the Baltimore

Symphony Orchestra afloat. He was on the board of the city's black hospital. Whenever money was needed for a good cause, the advice was always the same: "See Joe."

Activists for Fair Housing had been working on Meyerhoff for months. They calculated that as pressure mounted, the developer would at least hear them out and perhaps, as a member of a minority group, see their point. But he did not budge or even receive representatives of the organization. Instead he issued a statement arguing that he alone could not change the bigoted housing market. "It is a plain and proven fact that it is not within my power, or that of the Joseph Meyerhoff Corporation (which owns less than 2 percent of the rental housing in the area), or that of any private builder, to alter what has always been a deep rooted pattern of housing in the Baltimore area," he declared. In any case, builders were at the mercy of the buying public, which in turn did not want blacks. "No builder or developer could possibly continue in business if he attempted to ignore the desires of the purchasing or renting public. Open housing is not a problem of builders, or of the building industry alone, but one that the total community must decide through their elected representatives."

Activists for Fair Housing picketed symphony concerts. They held overnight vigils at Meyerhoff's home at 6724 Westbrook Road in Fallstaff, a Homeland-like upper-crust Jewish neighborhood that he built in northwest Baltimore and that barred blacks. Nothing worked. In desperation they decided to shame Meyerhoff before his peers. Newspapers announced the Activists' plans to picket a testimonial dinner honoring the multi-millionaire, who had been awarded the Israeli Prime Minister's Medal. Maryland's political establishment was expected to attend the black-tie gala, along with important business, religious, and civic leaders. The tribute to Meyerhoff hoped to raise two million dollars for Israel, more than twelve million in 2009 dollars. A protest at such an occasion surely would get newspaper and television coverage, perhaps even nationally. But on the eve of the testimonial, the Activists abruptly canceled their picketing. They had "no desire to injure the cause of Israel in any way," the organization sheepishly apologized in a statement. Clearly Joe had very persuasive friends.

That had happened six months earlier. Now the same Activists for Fair Housing exhorted Dr. King to come to Baltimore to spearhead a nationwide drive against Meyerhoff. Their appeal to Dr. King put the matter succinctly: "We hope that later in the summer, if Mr. Meyerhoff is still unmoved, that a number of 'coordinated' demonstrations may be arranged, with your cooperation, to take place simultaneously at his developments in Atlanta (where he just last week signed a contract to start a third large apartment project), Chicago and Baltimore."

The Baltimoreans' letter brought back to Dr. King nothing but bad memories. In 1965 he had been talked into launching a campaign to end slums in Chicago. It was his first organizing foray to the North, and the Windy City nearly knocked him over. After a year and a half of various difficulties, accentuated by escalating white violence, the campaign ended shamefully. Dr. King concluded a high-publicity settlement with Mayor Richard J. Daley, who had no intention to fulfill his part—and Dr. King knew it. He slunk out of Chicago, his credibility in tatters. He never acknowledged the Baltimoreans' letter. He was busy elsewhere; he had too many other commitments. The Poor People's Campaign was under way. Time was running out.

An assassin's bullet felled Dr. King in Memphis on April 4, 1968. Cities throughout the nation erupted in an orgy of burning and looting. Baltimore simmered for two days. On the third day, William L. Hankins was preparing to take in a play with his wife. He had been among the signers of the letter to Dr. King. Late in the afternoon, his telephone rang.

"Hank, can you get some medical people to come to east Baltimore?" a breathless CORE activist asked Hankins, a former Peace Corps volunteer in India who had become the first black administrator at Sinai Hospital.

"Are you people blowing up the city?" was all Hankins could think of saying.

"Baby, it has blown up," he heard on the line.

Guns were everywhere. At the height of rioting, firefighters braved sniper fire from a nearby public housing high-rise, trying to keep a blaze set by the mob from devouring East Lombard Street's shops.

A few yards away, an Israeli immigrant, Jack Goldensohn, stood on the roof of his corned beef sandwich emporium, his steel-grey machine gun aimed at the surging mob. (After the riots, Goldensohn displayed chutzpah by placing the machine gun on his deli counter.) Fear infected otherwise levelheaded people. One radio station owner stood guard at his living room window, armed with a rifle. He was convinced that blacks were about to attack his home in exclusive Guilford, a good distance from the rioting. In the bucolic village of Ruxton, outside the city, a prominent lawyer handed his petrified wife a loaded gun, instructed her to shoot any invader, kissed her goodbye, and headed downtown.

Baltimore emerged from three nights of mayhem during that Palm Sunday weekend with six persons dead, seven hundred injured, more than a thousand businesses ransacked and destroyed, countless houses torched, and more than five thousand people arrested. The National Guard and regular army troops patrolled downtown. Looters wiped out commercial corridors in nine neighborhoods. Pillaging was indiscriminate. Stores were looted without regard to whether their owners were white or black. A substantial number belonged to Jews, including several who had blue numbers inked on their arms, irremovable reminders of their narrow escape from the Final Solution.

Anguish gripped America's devastated cities. To prevent a race war, Congress enacted the Civil Rights Act of 1968, including provisions for fair housing. Few thought that such a measure had a chance when President Johnson had proposed it two years earlier. But with big cities in flames, the House passed the act by a vote of 250 to 172, and the Senate by 71 to 20. Eight days after Dr. King's assassination, President Johnson signed it into law. He engineered the passage so swiftly that Coretta King and many other civil rights leaders were missing from the crowd of 350 guests who witnessed the bill's signing at the hastily arranged East Room ceremony. The White House could not locate them in time, and the signing could not be delayed. "Fair housing for all—all human beings who live in this country—is now part of the American way of life," President Johnson proclaimed.

A previous law, the Civil Rights Act of 1866, had given blacks "full and equal benefit of all laws and proceedings for the security of persons and property enjoyed by white citizens," but it contained no details or federal enforcement provisions. Such teeth were included in Johnson's act, which outlawed discrimination based on race, religion, national origin, and gender in the sale, rental, and financing of housing. The law triggered widespread opposition among landlords, builders, and real estate brokers. Many, however, chose to comply. Four months after the law went into effect, Joseph Meyerhoff obeyed a Defense Department directive and opened his Fort Meade apartment units to all races. He gradually desegregated his civilian complexes as well, and smaller builders and landlords followed suit.

Baltimore nonetheless remained a tinderbox. Governor Spiro T. Agnew nearly rekindled unrest by summoning black leaders to a public tongue-lashing, where he accused the moderates of complicity in the riots. They marched out in protest. That incident brought Maryland's first-term governor to the attention of Richard Nixon, who would make Agnew his vice president. The extremes hardened, the middle ground shrank. That was a nationwide trend. Around the country black and white splits paralyzed the mainstream civil rights movement, whose commitment to interracialism flagged. Veterans departed. Some joined mobilization against the Vietnam War, others focused on the issues that Dr. King had identified as his necessary future thrust—poverty and economic discrimination. Yet others found new causes. One was called community organizing, and Saul Alinsky was its apostle. Unlike the Black Panthers and the Weathermen who advocated revolution, Alinsky wanted to shake up the system and change it from within by democratic means. Within years after the 1968 riots, a network of community organizations operating along his principles became a factor in many American cities, including Baltimore.

Alinsky began organizing in Chicago in 1938 in the same wretched neighborhood that Upton Sinclair had chronicled in *The Jungle*. He was a Jewish agnostic who taught that Moses and Jesus were the first community organizers; St. Paul also was required reading for all who wished to master the organizer's craft. In the spring of 1958 Alinsky received a peculiar invitation, his first from overseas. The Italian cardinal Giovanni Battista Montini, archbishop of Milan, wanted his advice on a thorny problem. In the 1950s some 300,000 people from other parts of the country had moved to the northern industrial city in search of work, swelling its population to 1.5 million. Living in newly constructed public housing slums and in shantytowns, many migrants became alienated, turning to communism and deserting the church. A trusted friend kept telling the cardinal about Alinsky and the tactics he used to organize difficult neighborhoods in Chicago. The questions that the cardinal wanted answered in the spring of 1958 were these: If applied in Milan, would Alinsky's methods work? Could community organizing stabilize the migrant neighborhoods, give rootless migrants a purpose in life and society, and stop the inroads of anti-clerical secularism?

Alinsky flew to Milan, had "three wonderful meetings" with the cardinal, toured neighborhoods, and inspected local organizing efforts. Then he went to Rome to see more community organizing and flew back to Chicago. He never heard again from the prelate. But after Cardinal Montini became Pope Paul VI in 1963, the Catholic church began a massive community organizing drive in the United States. It hired Alinsky as its conceptualizer, an appealing proposition because the church provided two essentials for successful organizing: people and money.

If Communists had been the challenge in Italy, among the church's problems in the United States were millions of Poles, Ukrainians, Italians, and Hungarians who were becoming religiously apathetic and politically alienated. These "unmeltable" white ethnics—who have since melted—were Richard Nixon's and Spiro Agnew's "silent majority," the salt of the earth, who felt nothing but disconnectedness and confusion in a world of fast-paced change. Technology jeopardized their jobs, Vatican II tested their faith, and racial change threatened their ethnic neighborhoods. They didn't like blacks or forced busing in order to achieve integration. But if they fled, city parishes would face extinction.

In 1970 the church established the National Center of Urban Ethnic Affairs, headed by Monsignor Geno Baroni. It was a pacification program that targeted ethnic whites and was funded by the Ford Foundation and the church's nationwide Campaign for Human

Development. The center consisted of three divisions: the Catholic Conference on Ethnic and Neighborhood Affairs; the National Neighborhood Institute for training organizers; and the Organization for Neighborhood Development, a think tank. With the civil rights movement in turmoil, community organizing appealed to Catholic activists around the country. The concept was familiar. In 1933 Dorothy Day and Peter Maurin had begun the Catholic Worker Movement to organize Christian communities to fight social injustices. Now, in the aftermath of the 1968 riots, many activists saw organizing as a domestic application of the new liberation theology sweeping Latin America. Most of the budget of Alinsky's Industrial Areas Foundation soon came from organizing contracts with the church.

Alinsky built a solid organizing base by creating (or aggravating) conflicts as a way to alter dynamics between those who had power and those who wanted it. Critics suspected he was a Communist. But his work did not rest on Marxist principles. Marxism was too rigid and anti-democratic, Alinsky said. Liberalism was too timid and passive. His ego was big, which was one reason why he did not work with Martin Luther King, Jr. Another reason was that Alinsky thought Dr. King lacked the skills to organize in the North, as evidenced by the disastrous campaign to end slums in Chicago, a city where machine politicians understood and respected only the use of "stiletto" tactics, according to Alinsky.

Successful organizing required clearly stated goals, pragmatic flexibility, and a willingness to resort to whatever tactics worked, Alinsky taught. Each situation required different tactics, which should be constantly monitored, refined, and adjusted. People acted out of their self-interests. Blacks and whites, Christians and Jews, Hispanics and Anglos did not have to love one another to work together. Surprising coalitions could be built when people were made to see that their self-interests coincided despite their different color, religion, or social standing.

Alinsky's *Rules for Radicals: A Pragmatic Primer for Realistic Radicals* and *Reveille for Radicals* became the handbooks of community organizing. Among those poring over them was a Wellesley student named Hillary Rodham. In 1969 she wrote a somewhat starry-eyed ninety-two-page senior thesis, "There Is Only the Fight—An Analysis of the Alinsky Model." Alinsky twice offered her a job; instead she decided to go to law school at Yale, where she met a guy named Bill Clinton. Even after Alinsky died in 1972, new acolytes continued to follow and refine his teachings. In 1985 a skinny young man from Hawaii attended the Industrial Areas Foundation's nine-day training session before taking an organizer's job in Chicago. His name: Barack Obama.

Alinsky's tactics were employed in Baltimore so soon after the 1968 riots that the church had not had time to set up the Northeast Community Organization (NECO) and South East Community Organization (SECO), which will be described in Chapter 16. Instead the predominantly black Activists for Fair Housing—the CORE splinter group which by then had shortened its name to Activists, Inc.—took the lead, assisted by a small but energetic group of Catholic social activists, including Jesuit priests and seminarians led by Father John Martinez.

They went after Morris Goldseker, who was notorious for his high prices and strict terms. Activists, Inc. began organizing land-installment contract buyers in Edmondson Village, where Goldseker had sold 712 rowhouses to blacks, and in Montebello, where he had sold 348 houses to blacks. Noisy picket lines were set up at Goldseker offices every day. But Activists did far more. They embarked on a huge data-gathering hunt. Taking full advantage of the primitive computers of the day, they studied acquisition and resale patterns and issued sophisticated research reports. In 1969 the organization filed a land-installment contract buyers' class-action lawsuit against Goldseker, accusing him of anti-trust conspiracy and violations of federal civil rights and Maryland's usury laws. The organization also filed for a "stay of exploitation," asking the court to order Goldseker to renegotiate all contracts, reduce all rents and home installment-contract payments by 37.5 percent, and earmark 10 percent of the company's gross income "to supply mortgage money at no interest to the poor."

Although Goldseker was the only named defendant, the suit challenged the whole decades-old system that forced blacks to use exploitative middlemen if they wished to live in better housing. "We reached the decision that the exploitation in housing was spinning off, a large part, if not most, of the segregation in housing, and therefore we shifted our direction from segregation to housing exploitation," Activists, Inc. chairman Sampson Green told the University of Maryland Baltimore County professor W. Edward Orser in 1981.

Goldseker made a splendid scapegoat. He was a byproduct of redlining, a class symbol and stereotype so crude and instantly recognizable that scarcely any Jews joined the protests. His name was an organizer's dream: Goldseker, Goldseeker, Goldsucker. "You can't mobilize people against the banking system; you can mobilize them only when they have a personal enemy that clarifies the issues. Goldsucker was the personification of the system," Activists member Walter Dean, Jr., explained. Frank Fischer, another member, said: "Goldseker was one of the main participants in an evil system that exploited blacks. This system was the issue, not slum housing."

During his long career, Goldseker dealt with more than a hundred financial institutions, including numerous savings and loan associations, small and large. At Jefferson Federal Savings and Loan his right-hand man had sat on the board. Another board member was Marvin Mandel, speaker of the Maryland House of Delegates, who had been president of Oldtown Savings and Loan before it merged with Jefferson. Both institutions' mortgage money went mostly to finance Goldseker. Mandel resigned his board membership only after becoming governor in 1969.

In the mid-1960s, Maryland's big establishment banks began financing Goldseker. They knew that he would buy whole blocks of rowhouses and sell them to blacks, but leading banks had reached the conclusion that racial change was good for the economy: it kept banks profitable, suburban builders humming, and the real estate industry busy. Between 1965 and 1968, Goldseker was able to borrow $10.5 million—more than $58 million in 2009 dollars—from establishment banks. He received $1.6 million from Maryland National Bank, $1.1 million from Equitable Trust Company, $1 million from Uptown Federal Savings and Loan Association, $700,150 from the First National

Bank of Maryland, and $253,450 from National City Bank of Baltimore, which later became Suburban Trust. During the same period those banks issued hardly any mortgages to blacks trying to buy in Goldseker's price range without using him or any other middleman.

Goldseker won access to bank financing because of a stamp of approval from John Luetkemeyer, president of Equitable Trust Company, the same ultimate power broker who struck a lifelong friendship with Little Willie Adams. In measuring people, Luetkemeyer divided them into the "good" and the "bad." Goldseker qualified as "good" because he had credibility. This opened doors to Goldseker, a difficult customer because he didn't do things the way bankers did. "Certain loans we agreed to make him took some imagination," Luetkemeyer marveled later. "When loans were negotiated, Goldseker would assure: 'Don't worry, they'll always be paid back as agreed.' And they were. His handshake was better than many a contract I signed."

Such loans enabled Goldseker to conduct a phenomenally profitable business. According to an Activists, Inc. study of sixty thousand properties, shown on the facing page, this was the success of Goldseker and his main rivals between 1960 and 1968, with partners identified in parentheses.

Goldseker challenged the Activists, Inc. data. The company opened its books and had an audit of 65 properties. After deducting repairs, wages, various financing charges, and other costs of business, the audit showed a net profit of 18.17 percent per house, a stark contrast to the 85 percent profit margin that the Activists, Inc. survey of 1,678 properties suggested.

A pattern emerged: blacks who had the means and smarts to buy directly from fleeing whites paid prices that were very close to FHA appraisers' valuations. But blacks who placed themselves at the mercy of middlemen paid far more than the appraised value and up to 85 percent more than what those speculators themselves paid when they acquired the houses from panicky whites. A widowed mother of six told the court that when she realized her house contract was with Goldseker, "I stood there and cried like a baby, and God knows I'm still crying. I knew I didn't have a fair chance."

Activists, Inc.: Baltimore Under Siege

Speculators	Houses Bought[1]	Purchase Price	Houses Sold	Sale Price	Average Purchase Price of Resold Houses[2]	Average Sale Price of Resold Houses[3]	Average Markup
Morris Goldseker	1,678	$10,853,767	742	$9,427,723	$6,868	$12,706	85%
Louis Singer	446	2,930,897	250	2,975,578	6,458	11,903	84%
Walter and Al Becker	264	1,826,606	106	1,308,008	7,248	12,340	70%
Stanley E. Sugarman (J. Seaman, C. Caplan)	388	2,824,790	148	1,302,273	5,371	8,799	63%
Morris Wolf (J. Friedman)	416	2,824,890	300	3,351,865	6,974	12,290	60%
Walter Kirson (A. Applefeld, H. J. Gerber)	440	3,243,767	247	2,998,646	7,683	12,140	58%
Anthony Piccinini	313	2,498,160	152	1,823,972	7,775	12,000	54%

Note: The computer database on which this chart is based contains sixty thousand property transfers. For January 1960 to the end of 1964 it contains the seventeen Census tracts where there was most racial change. For January 1965 to December 31, 1968, it contains the entire city.

1. Houses bought by these men in the 1950s or earlier and sold in the 1960s are not included.
2. Increased ground rent is capitalized and figured in. If previously existing ground rent is capitalized and figured in, the average purchase prices and average sale prices should be raised about $800.
3. Activists, Inc.'s previous studies show that these sales prices are $3,000 to $4,000 above fair market value.

In a deposition, Goldseker insisted that his prices were fair. His was a unique service because he provided 100 percent financing without any collateral or guarantees. "The FHA price is different than my price because theirs is a cash market and mine is an installment market. There's more than one fair-market value, depending on which market you're in—cash or installment." If he didn't exist, he added, blacks would be shut out of the marketplace altogether. When Sheldon Goldseker's turn came, he made his uncle's business sound outright humanitarian. "We were the first liberals," he asserted. "We were the first pioneers."

In 1972, after two years of litigation, Activists, Inc. withdrew its suit. Their key witness got cold feet and declined to testify. He was a black real estate broker who had conducted systematic appraisals as a volunteer. "Just about two months before the trial began, the real estate industry opened up an assault on him and his real estate operation, and really threatened him with putting him out of business if he testified," Sampson Green said. With the trial going on, Activists, Inc. had neither the time nor the money to redo systematic appraisals that would prove Goldseker's exploitation.

The Goldseker Company celebrated by buying full-page newspaper ads in the *Afro-American* but also in the dailies. The ads proclaimed that Activists, Inc.'s suit had been without merit from the very start. But long litigation and public bludgeoning took their toll; the company lost its prior prominence. After Goldseker died in 1973, disbelieving Baltimoreans learned that he had bequeathed his wealth to a foundation dedicated to nonsectarian good deeds. In his will, he made sure that blacks were amply represented in the foundation.

The 1968 riots ushered Baltimore into a new political age. To be sure, whites retained the decisive majority on the City Council, thanks to a long tradition of racial gerrymandering. All citywide elected offices—from mayor to state's attorney, the top prosecutor—were in white hands. But Baltimore's population was now 46 percent black, restless and aching for power. No sooner had the riots been quelled than a tall, charismatic lawyer named Joseph C. Howard challenged the city's judicial establishment. He produced studies of the strikingly disparate treatment of black and white defendants in the criminal courts. Howard's specific target was Edwin J. Wolf, for no other reason than that the judge had been appointed so recently that he had to win voters' approval to stay on the bench. Wolf was a Jewish Republican of impeccable credentials. He had practiced law with distinction in Baltimore for forty years, interrupted by gallant service in World War II. Badly wounded while commanding troops at Omaha Beach on D-day, he was wounded again during the Battle of the Bulge.

In normal circumstances Wolf would have been a shoo-in. An election challenge to a sitting judge was unheard-of. But the circumstances were anything but normal. In the aftermath of the riots, Joe Howard's candidacy galvanized blacks to an unprecedented mobilization drive. It was Judge Wolf's historical fate to become the first white officeholder in Baltimore to lose citywide to a black challenger.

In 1970, Parren J. Mitchell challenged a nine-term incumbent congressman from northwest Baltimore, Samuel Friedel, for the Seventh District congressional seat. Mitchell was a brother of Clarence Mitchell, Jr.'s, the NAACP's legendary lobbyist in Washington who had been a factor in all civil rights legislation of the preceding decade. A war hero who was wounded in Italy, "P.J." taught sociology at Morgan State and had headed Baltimore's federally funded anti-poverty agency during President Lyndon B. Johnson's Great Society drive. Small of stature and meek looking, he was not popular among whites. Many considered him devious and divisive—racist was one word that was often used, anti-Semitic was another. The predominantly white district's liberals, a mostly Jewish heavy voting bloc, split. Many stayed with Friedel, who enjoyed a nearly perfect ranking by the then influential Americans for Democratic Action (ADA). But enough voted for Mitchell to enable him to squeak in by thirty-eight votes, thanks to a spoiler, another Jewish candidate, State Senator Carl Friedler. Mitchell became the first African-American congressman from Maryland.

Conspiracy theorists refused to believe that Mitchell had won fair and square. The initial returns favored Friedel. When the official count declared Mitchell the winner, his supporters, including several young Jewish lawyers, guarded the ballot boxes overnight. An urban

legend came out of this. It held that white political kingmakers gave
the election to Mitchell out of fear that blacks would otherwise burn
down the city. Governor Mandel, no stranger to backroom politics,
categorically denied that such a deal was made.

In the same election Milton Allen won the state's attorney's office.
He became the first black since Reconstruction to be elected the local prosecutor in any American big city. The shock had not worn off
when in 1971 the lawyer George Russell mounted a vigorous mayoral
campaign to succeed Thomas J. D'Alesandro III, Old Tommy's son
and a brother of future House Speaker Nancy Pelosi. D'Alesandro
walked away from politics disillusioned by what had happened to
his hometown in the wake of the 1968 riots. After a tough campaign,
where this time the spoiler was none other than Clarence Mitchell III,
a state senator and nephew of Parren Mitchell's, Russell lost to William Donald Schaefer, the white politician from Edmondson Village.
Even so, the future had revealed itself: it would be only a question of
time before blacks would be a majority and hold the reins of municipal power.

For many whites, enough was enough. They voted with their
feet.

*

On April 13, 1976, a visibly disturbed carryout owner, Charles Hopkins, entered City Hall. He had been there the day before, complaining to the mayor and other top elected officials about his landlord
and how city health inspectors had ordered his carryout closed after
only a few days in operation. His problems had multiplied when he
received a $200 gas and electricity bill, quite a bit of bread in those
days. He also needed money to pay a like amount in fines for having
burned an American flag in a personal protest near City Hall. He was
going out of his mind.

Now returning, he demanded to speak with Mayor William Donald Schaefer. When the mayor was said not to be in the building, he
killed City Councilman Dominic M. Leone with a .38-caliber hand-
gun, wounded Councilman Carroll J. Fitzgerald and Kathleen No-

lan, the mayor's appointment secretary, and police officer Thomas Gaither. Witnessing the carnage, the veteran Councilman J. Joseph Curran, Sr., died of a heart attack.

One detail about Hopkins never made the newspapers. One week earlier he had resigned as the founding president of a newly created Activists, Inc. affiliate in east Baltimore. Hopkins was angry and frustrated because members refused to do what he wanted, Sampson Green remembered in 1981. "When he shot up City Hall, you know what that can do to a working-class community, because as far as they knew he was still the president of the association, so they became afraid of the organization . . . "

That was the end of Activists, Inc.

Part Three: 1968–2000

THE NOOSE

"There are no walls around Baltimore County."
—County executive Dale Anderson, 1969

14

ЛЛЛЛЛЛЛЛ

Exiting the City

ESCAPING the city's racial cauldron could not have been easier; an invisible jurisdictional fence ran just a few miles from City Hall. On the other side was Baltimore County, an independent entity with its own government, laws, rules, traditions—and a tax rate half of the city's. So many whites fled there between 1950 and 1970 that the county's population more than doubled, from 270,273 to 621,077. Consequently the share of African Americans in the county fell from 6.6 to 3.2 percent.

Generations of elected county officials used various means to marginalize African Americans, thus contributing to their declining numbers. Housing was made scarce. Schools for blacks were second rate. Until 1939 Baltimore County did not even operate a high school for blacks, a distinction shared by only one other of Maryland's twenty-three counties. It was true that a few high-achievers were given the opportunity to attend the city's Frederick Douglass High School at county expense. But in the name of fiscal frugality, their numbers were limited and they had to pass a county-administered admission test.

White families fleeing the city quickly discovered that desegregation and integration were not pressing issues in the growing county, which was fine by them. Eventually they became aware of a different set of problems.

Petty corruption was a county tradition. Gifts of cash or liquor—by the caseload—had rained on helpful county decision-makers each Christmastime for as long as anyone could remember. Such largesse from favor seekers was expected, as was sponsorship of bull roasts, where the entrenched Democratic machine's foot soldiers—called b'hoys to honor their filial loyalty to the boss—whooped it up amid mountains of steamed crabs, pit beef, and fried chicken, all washed down with pitchers of beer and whiskey chasers while polka bands blared. At election times, Democratic bosses shook down builders and regulated businesses so that cash could be showered on the machine's army of poll workers and another Democratic victory secured.

Tavern owners pitched in, rewarding voters in Democratic strongholds with a free drink. State law prohibited serving alcohol on election days. So? Liquor inspectors and police were part of the Democratic machine's political patronage. They turned a blind eye to pinball machines and other forms of illegal gambling that went on lustily in back rooms. Such gaming increased tavern owners' profits—and strengthened the umbilical cord linking them to the ruling machine.

The construction of the Baltimore Beltway, which opened in 1962, raised graft to new levels. Zoning approvals acquired a price tag, with shopping-center zoning requiring big bribes. Water and sewer connections became marketable commodities. Contractors, engineering firms, and architects openly bought favors. So did ordinary citizens if they built homes without permits, or on floodplains.

Many politicians and bureaucrats accepted cash, and the greediest demanded it. Among the voracious was Spiro T. Agnew, a Republican, who rocketed—in just seven years—from chairman of the county zoning appeals board to Richard M. Nixon's vice president. Even in Washington Agnew continued to receive plain white envelopes of cash. Inside the White House he accepted a kickback from a civil engineer who was still paying for favors that Agnew had bestowed in his previous offices, first as Baltimore County executive, the highest elected office in the county, and then as Maryland's governor. That particular firm kicked back to Agnew 5 percent of its contract awards.

Evidence of systemic kickbacks forced Agnew to resign as vice president on October 10, 1973. Ironically, he was not the federal

Having resigned from the vice presidency, Spiro T. Agnew departs
Baltimore's courthouse. Years earlier, county residents had rebelled against
his urban renewal plan, seeing it as a Trojan horse to bring blacks into the
county. *(Special Collections, University of Maryland Libraries)*

crimebusters' intended target; prosecutors were after his Democratic
successor as county executive, Dale Anderson. Tried in 1974, Anderson went to prison for extorting bribes and failing to report them as
income. Another trial took place simultaneously in another courthouse. That accused was Samuel A. Green, Jr., a former Democratic
County Council chairman who was serving his second term as state's
attorney, the elected top prosecutor. He too went to prison. Among
his crimes was his propensity to make criminal cases disappear. He

usually did it for money. But when one twenty-five-year-old shop-lifting suspect didn't have the requisite amount of cash, Green hap-pily accepted a "carnal bribe" from her, according to the indictment. Green was some man: court testimony showed that he hired nine fe-male office staffers on the mutually understood condition that they serve his sexual needs.

Green had come from patrician roots. One forebear was Harriet Chew, a daughter of Benjamin Chew's, chief justice of Pennsylvania's Supreme Court at the time the United States broke away from Britain. She married Charles Carroll, Jr., of Maryland, son of the only Catho-lic signer of the Declaration of Independence. At Green's heirloom-filled home in Ruxton, a quaint village favored by the fox-hunting set, an antique etching showed Chew talking with George Washington. Genealogy was not among Green's interests, but his wife, identified in the *Blue Book* as the former Camilla de Chantal Corcoran, treasured that picture.

More typical of Baltimore County were the hundreds of thou-sands of newcomers who moved there after World War II as part of a suburban migration that transformed the nation. Like Agnew and Anderson, many were returning veterans eager to make up for lost time. Grown up amid the Great Depression, their generation had glimpsed the future during the 1939 New York World's Fair. Forty-four million visitors—fully one-third of the nation's population at the time—saw with their own eyes a consumerist fairyland. General Mo-tors showed a futuristic city ruled by cars and highways. Chrysler assembled Plymouths right before visitors' eyes in a theater equipped with a new technology called "air-conditioning." The AT&T pavilion introduced a robotized, synthetic voice. Next door, IBM showcased electric typewriters and a machine called the electric calculator that used punch cards. It was a primitive forerunner of programmable computers. NBC awed fairgoers by transmitting live pictures to small boxes with tiny screens in rooms seating twenty-five people. The first transmission was devoted to the arrival of one million tulips from Holland, part of that country's exhibit. The picture was in black and white, but viewers saw the colors in their minds.

The defeat of Germany, Italy, and Japan in World War II ushered America into a sustained period of growth and affluence. Gross domestic product more than doubled between 1945 and 1960, as did car ownership. Retooled war industries flooded stores with television sets, refrigerators, lawn mowers, washing machines, and toasters. Advertising, now driven by opinion researchers trained in psychology, created a nation of mass consumers who wanted more of everything—more TV dinners, more breakfast flakes, more frozen orange juice. Above all they wanted more and better housing. And new taxpayer-paid roads, including the huge interstate system that revolutionized motor travel after the Eisenhower administration built it for defense purposes at the height of the Cold War.

Builders were happy to oblige. One of them was William Levitt, a demobilized lieutenant from the navy's construction battalions. His Levittown in Long Island, New York, became the prototype for post-war suburban tract housing. He built inexpensive, mass-produced houses on slabs, using prefabricated elements just as in the military. Copying Levittown's methods in Baltimore County was Victor Posner, the onetime blockbuster and future Wall Street corporate raider. He constructed so many rowhouses that in 1954 he was ranked as Maryland's largest residential developer. The next year proved that it had been a fluke, when Meyerhoff regained the No. 1 ranking.

In later years the Agnews and Andersons of America would rail against federal meddling and governmental subsidies, but they themselves benefited from taxpayer handouts like no previous generation. Thanks to the GI Bill, returning veterans were entitled to stipends for education in addition to a monthly payment to help with living expenses. This was a godsend for Agnew, a Greek immigrant restaurant owner's son who had married his high school sweetheart in 1942 and soon had children. Before the war he had studied chemistry at Johns Hopkins, but he had lost interest and dropped out.

Agnew served five years in the army, including frontline duty in France. He must not have been much of an officer because he was never promoted beyond the rank of lieutenant. Back home the GI Bill enabled him to go to law school at night at the University of

Baltimore, where standards were not rigorous. A veteran's mortgage allowed him to acquire a home. Like millions of other veterans around the nation, he became a suburbanite. Agnew moved to Baltimore County in 1946, two years before the Supreme Court voided racially restrictive covenants and eight years before school desegregation. Race played no part in his decision.

His rancher in Lutherville—a onetime religious campground—was modest; a typical home in those days contained fewer than one thousand square feet of space. But the name of his subdivision, Country Club Park, had a nice ring to it. The idyll did not last long. When war broke out in Korea, Agnew was recalled to military duty. He was forced to sell the home. On his return, all he could afford was Loch Raven Village, a community of two-story rowhouses near Towson built with taxpayer-subsidized FHA loans. On his street the struggling lawyer was sandwiched between the families of a transit bus driver and a postal worker.

Agnew's years in Loch Raven Village marked a turning point. He became involved in community issues. Like his father, he was a registered Democrat, but he soon changed his party registration to Republican. He was rewarded with a patronage job that he badly needed, because he wasn't much of a lawyer. He became a member of the board hearing zoning appeals. He was so little known that *The Sun*, in reporting his appointment, referred to him as Spiro T. Anger.

Dale Anderson had been born in the southern Illinois town of Metropolis, across the Ohio River from Paducah, Kentucky. Metropolis was Huckleberry Finn country, part of a region called Little Egypt because the Mississippi and Ohio rivers were prone to periodic floods like the Nile, and because towns carried names like Cairo, Thebes, Palestine, and Lebanon. Anderson's parents, Baptists, were so inspired that they christened him Naaman, "Pleasantness" in Hebrew. He hated his given first name and never used it.

In 1937 Anderson joined an uncle who owned an auto supply shop in Baltimore. When the war came he volunteered for the army air corps, rising from private to captain but never shipping overseas. On his return he settled in Fullerton, Baltimore County. His work as a Democratic precinct leader won him a patronage job as a night clerk in a magistrate's court. That's how one advanced in politics in those days.

Neither Agnew nor Anderson realized it at first, but they appeared on the Baltimore County scene at a time when regional power dynamics were changing radically. In 1950 the City of Baltimore's population peaked at 949,708. The next Censuses would record only a modest initial decline, but that was due to a substantial black migration from the Carolinas that statistically replaced white families departing to the county. When that migration stopped in the 1970s, the city's population began shrinking. The city grew more black; the county remained nearly all white. An astonishing 83 percent of the white growth occurred outside the city while 83 percent of the black growth occurred within the city.

In early recorded times, the land area of Baltimore County was huge. It was still considerable after the City of Baltimore and Carroll, Anne Arundel, Howard, and Kent counties were carved out as independent jurisdictions. But although the county had eight times more land than the city, its population was small until World War II, and concentrated near the city line. That left the rest of the county empty. The City of Baltimore, by contrast, was running out of land. It had everything else: people, wealth, political clout, daily newspapers, and radio and television stations. And the city dominated the whole state of Maryland economically, culturally, and politically. Not only did the city reign as the region's unchallenged center of manufacturing until the 1960s, it was also home to nearly all the banks, hospitals, offices, theaters, concert halls, and colleges. The city had the Colts, the professional football team that had moved to Baltimore in 1953, and the baseball Orioles, which had relocated from St. Louis the following year. The city even boasted America's biggest bowling alley—its five floors contained more than one hundred lanes.

Baltimore's fortunes turned after World War II ended and armament manufacturers scaled back, retooled, and terminated tens of thousands. Meanwhile the federal government disbanded big war-procurement bureaucracies in Baltimore, and several floors in downtown office buildings were left vacant. There was more bad news. The day after Christmas 1954 brought the startling announcement that O'Neill's department store was going out of business. O'Neill's, at Charles and Lexington streets, was a mercantile icon like no other. It offered an unsurpassed selection of bridal gowns, First Communion dresses, and good linens. Many Catholic families patronized O'Neill's for an additional reason: a miracle was said to have happened there during the Great Fire of 1904. As a firestorm of flames and cinders spread through the downtown business district, the department store's distraught owner, an Irish immigrant named Thomas O'Neill, raced in his carriage to the nearby convent where his sister led a religious life. He begged the Sisters of Charity to pray for him. They did so, fervently, and the fire stopped at the walls of his emporium. The grateful O'Neill willed his wealth to the Catholic archdiocese. Eventually Thomas O'Neill's fortune paid for a new hospital, several high schools, and the new Cathedral of Mary Our Queen, dedicated in 1959. There, in a chapel near the altar for everyone to see, O'Neill's was immortalized. A triptych showed flames shooting up around the store while a nun—his sister—prayed. A group of boys standing next to her included George Herman "Babe" Ruth, holding a baseball bat and ball, and a studious-looking Asa Yoelson, a rabbi's son better known as Al Jolson, the future singer and vaudevillian. Both had been wards at a reformatory school where O'Neill served as a trustee.

The closing of the celebrated O'Neill emporium overwhelmed the entire downtown retail district with gloom. "It affected us all," remembered Walter Sondheim, an executive of a rival department store. Flagship stores on Howard Street saw sales drop. Equally important, the carriage trade shrank on nearby Charles Street, condemning fancy food stores, fashionable jewelry dealers, and fine furniture merchants to an irreversible spiral of doom.

After O'Neill's closed, the other shoe fell soon enough. The federal government's steadily expanding Social Security Administration decided to centralize its national headquarters operations, which were scattered among ten commercial office buildings in downtown Baltimore. A site in the city was investigated but rejected. Instead a headquarters campus was constructed in Woodlawn, a farming community along the soon-to-be built Beltway in Baltimore County. In 1967 the agency began moving 8,200 employees to Woodlawn. The exodus devastated downtown service retail businesses, from diners to dry cleaners. Office vacancies skyrocketed.

Downtown Baltimore had been under a massive assault since 1944. That year the city hired Robert Moses to plan a new crosstown expressway. No one could argue against better roads; during the war, the few existing arteries in the city had created one of the nation's worst transportation nightmares. Moses, New York's indefatigable parks and roads czar, chose a sunken expressway path. He proposed bulldozing through Howard and Charles streets, piercing the heart of the downtown retail district. His plan would have saved, barely, the Roman Catholic basilica, the Walters Art Museum, and the Enoch Pratt Free Library, but dozens of churches and public buildings were earmarked for demolition. All told, Moses proposed to raze two hundred city blocks and relocate some nineteen thousand residents, most of them black. "Nothing which we propose to remove will constitute any loss to Baltimore," he assured.

The Moses plan cast a pall over the whole center city. Residential property owners, victimized by banks' redlining since the 1930s and fearing that their areas were destined to go black, had another excuse to skimp on improvements and upkeep. Retailers too refrained from investing, using the capital to construct suburban stores instead. America's other cities thrived and expanded during the postwar consumer boom. Not Baltimore. The first major downtown office building to rise since the 1927 stock market crash was not built until 1961.

As it turned out, the east-west expressway was never constructed. But over three decades highway builders acquired and demolished thousands of rowhouses along the road alignment that Moses had identified and others revised. Other renewal projects abounded, with the result that roughly 94,000 people, mostly black, were relocated between 1965 and 1980. The uprooting of more than a tenth of the city's population increased neighborhood instability, magnified by the steady abandonment of neighborhoods by whites.

The collapse of the public transit system contributed to the city's decline. A dense network of streetcars and trolley lines ran through downtown to the suburbs, bonding the whole region together. Indeed, O'Neill's had been at the terminus of two streetcar lines. Reliance on public transport had only increased during the war, when gasoline and tire rationing forced residents of all social backgrounds to ride streetcars and trolleys. Once the privations of war were over, they could choose. And choose they did, aided by National City Lines, which took over the transit company in 1945.

National City Lines was a holding company owned by General Motors, Firestone Tire, Standard Oil of California, and Phillips Petroleum, which acquired streetcar operators in more than a hundred U.S. cities. As it did everywhere else, NCL began systematically replacing the Baltimore Transit Company's streetcars with GM buses, equipped with Firestone tires. Those buses consumed plenty of fuel, which the two oil company partners were only too happy to provide. Meanwhile the remaining streetcar lines experienced unexplained operational difficulties. The Public Service Commission cited the No. 8 streetcar line as the most egregious example. The No. 8, the longest line in the system, connected Baltimore County's county seat, Towson, with downtown Baltimore and the western suburb of Catonsville. So busy was the No. 8 streetcar line that it alone carried 10 percent of the entire transit system's passenger load. Mysteriously, the No. 8 line's vaunted reliability went to ruin. Instead of arriving at predictable intervals, streetcars came late and in twos or threes, leading to charges that they blocked traffic and caused congestion. Critics howled that streetcars should be banned. Traffic planners concurred.

But operational problems persisted even after buses replaced streetcars and trolleys. Service became more infrequent and erratic. Baltimore Transit buses were like bananas, residents joked, "because they are yellow and come in bunches." Baltimoreans, accustomed to transit vehicles that on some lines had run at two-minute intervals during the rush hour and every seven minutes at other times, made other arrangements. In 1948 the Baltimore Transit Company's ridership declined by 9.9 percent. The very next year it fell by 20.4 percent, by 28.3 percent in 1950, and by a further 34.2 percent in 1951. The transit company responded by cutting routes and hiking fares, and then cutting some more. Riders got the point and bought cars.

With cars, people could live farther out. Instead of having to depend on the public Lexington Market downtown or on smaller municipal meat and produce markets scattered elsewhere, families could buy their provisions at new supermarkets, which were opening in the county at breakneck speed. Almost all families shopping there were white, whereas increasing numbers of shoppers in the city were black. A final blow to downtown shopping occurred after the riots in the early 1970s, when department stores abandoned a traditional courtesy that had been much appreciated by customers using public transit. Free deliveries of purchases large and small—even handkerchiefs and neckties—were discontinued, and so was the free collection of returns.

Between 1955 and 1965 the city lost eighty-two industries, sixty-five to Baltimore County. Only six new firms moved to the city, where jobs became difficult to get, particularly in manufacturing and menial labor. Additional jobs were lost when hospitals, colleges, corporations, and prestigious churches relocated to the county. Over their histories, the oldest of those institutions had moved several times, but all the previous moves had been within the city.

Baltimore County became a latter-day Klondike. Residents included corporate executives and other powerful people whose civic commitment to city institutions wavered. By this time such earlier arrivals as Agnew and Anderson had put down roots in the county. Agnew was a late bloomer who had tried all kinds of jobs before finding his niche. Anderson was a go-getter who started a construction business in 1950, quickly establishing himself and thriving.

These were the men who would guide Baltimore County when it began challenging the city as the metropolitan area's most important jurisdiction.

15

⊓⊔⊓⊔⊓⊔⊓

Metropolis

SPIRO T. AGNEW'S early political career intertwined with Dale Anderson's. But as the Republican moved on to bigger and better things, the Democrat stayed in Baltimore County, becoming county executive. Anderson's administration kept blacks and poor whites out. It was like a "white noose" that strangled the increasingly black city socially and economically, the U.S. Commission on Civil Rights charged in 1974.

Anderson's tenure as a county official ran from 1958, when he was first elected to the County Council, until his conviction and resignation from the county executive's office in 1974. These were years of all-encompassing social change, from civil rights to Women's Lib to the counterculture's rebellion against traditional values. Amid such tumult, Anderson set policy as a member of the planning board, the recreation and parks board, the social services board, and the Regional Planning Council, a conclave of the metropolitan area's highest elected leaders. His clout was immense. In addition to being the undisputed political boss of Baltimore County—the last in a long line of bosses, as it turned out—he also was one of the 303 members of the Democratic National Committee at a time when that still mattered. He was a conservative voice, an "at-all-deliberate-speed" man—in the phrase used by the U.S. Supreme Court to urge along school desegregation—and his speed was deliberately slow.

Dale Anderson, seen here cutting a ribbon of fake $10,000 bills at a bank opening, was convicted of accepting bribes and of tax fraud. He struck a deal with voters—he kept blacks and poor whites out of the county and voters kept reelecting him. *(Special Collections, University of Maryland Libraries)*

Anderson's outlook on life was formed while growing up in Little Egypt, where behavior, customs, and speech patterns reflected the influence of early settlers who had trekked from Kentucky, Tennessee, and North Carolina. Add to that the proximity to Missouri—and even Arkansas—and there was no question that southern Illinois was a long way from Chicago and Springfield, both in distance and attitudes. In the Civil War many residents had sided with the Confederacy. Soon thereafter the area experienced a period of protracted violence over issues that echoed the war. First, dozens were killed in family vendettas bigger and bloodier than the later but more famous feuds among the Hatfields and McCoys. In 1922, when Anderson was just five years old, nineteen scabs and two union members were massacred

during a coalmine strike in neighboring Williamson County. Most
were mowed down in gunfire, but some had their throats cut.

As lawlessness continued, the Ku Klux Klan took over. It had been
a factor in the region since the 1880s, boasting a membership of several thousand in Williamson County alone. Federal authorities saw
the Klan as a stabilizing force. They deputized more than five hundred
Klan members to conduct liquor raids, including leading citizens and
many ministers, as Paul M. Angle detailed in his book *Bloody Williamson: A Chapter in American Lawlessness.* Under the leadership of
a former revenue agent who kept a submachine gun and a six-shooter
at his bedside, hooded Klansmen hounded blacks, Catholics, and immigrants. The Klan's main target was Jewish. Charlie Birger, born
Shachna Itzik Birger in Russia, had lived an adventurous life since
coming to America. He had ridden up San Juan Hill as one of Theodore Roosevelt's Rough Riders and spent some time as a cowboy in
the West. In southern Illinois he lorded over bootlegging, prostitution,
and gambling in the sooty coalfield camps.

By the time he was finally captured, Birger had become a folk
hero of sorts. He was the last man to be hanged in Illinois, which then
changed to electrocution. Five hundred ticketed spectators fought for
the privilege of witnessing the hanging in 1928; five thousand others
gawked from outside the jail compound as vendors peddled cotton
candy, soda pop, and popcorn. Birger rejected the hangman's offer of
a white hood. "I've never liked Klux colors," he said, insisting on a
black one. Then he looked at the sky, laughed, and said, "A beautiful
world."

This was the lawless environment in which Anderson grew up.
The Klan was not quite as powerful in Metropolis, Massac County,
where his father worked in a plant that made auto parts. The Andersons were "a good family," Dale's brother Don said, but outlaw
violence shaped their fates too. The boys' mother, a half-Cherokee
named Belle, lost her first husband to a revenge killer. The way the
story was told, he caught a fellow poker player cheating and called his
hand. That night the cheat shot him dead in his sleep.

Residential segregation in southern Illinois was even stricter than
in the nearby South. That was because of numerous "sundown towns"

that surrounded Metropolis. Those towns had expelled all black residents beginning in 1863, the year of the Emancipation Proclamation and the Battle of Gettysburg. Since then, no African Americans had been tolerated after dusk. One such nearby town was Anna, whose residents said the name stood for "Ain't No Niggers Allowed." (Until the 1970s, highway signs warned, *Nigger, Don't Let the Sun Go Down on You in Anna-Jonesboro.*)

When Anderson graduated from high school, Metropolis offered no prospects. In 1937, shortly after floods of biblical proportions devastated Little Egypt, he escaped to Baltimore. The twenty-one-year-old encountered a metropolis nearly as segregated as the town he left. He fit right in. That was a thing people noticed about Anderson: despite his Southern drawl, he thought like locals. When he ran for the Baltimore County Council in 1958, the weekly *Union News* described him, a builder of cottages and a member of the American Legion, as "an unknown in County affairs." The machine put him on its ticket, and he won handily. He was a likable fellow but prone to dark moods. Occasionally his taste for stingers—brandy and white crème de menthe—revealed a terrible temper, and he would do something for which he would have to apologize. "That's the Indian in me," he would say.

In 1958, when Anderson joined the County Council, nearly ten thousand new houses were constructed, most sold to families from the city. Land-hungry developers continued to buy farms, particularly near the soon-to-be-opened Beltway. Shopping centers would rise on some of them, new residential communities on others. But which plats to rezone and which not? Anderson and his six fellow councilmen decided that. You-scratch-my-back-and-I-scratch-yours was their watchword. During rezoning, each councilman single-handedly decided what requests should be approved or rejected in his district, and the rest of the councilmen automatically supported one another's decisions. One politician claimed that rezoning was done on napkins in the back room of a popular tavern.

The council conducted a comprehensive rezoning only every four years. In the interim a zoning commissioner appointed by the county executive and confirmed by the council handled zoning requests.

Grand amounts of money rode on his rulings. A favorable decision could produce a windfall for a developer; a rejection could spell ruin. Not surprisingly, money talked. And money often changed hands several times because the commissioner's decision could be appealed to the three-member Board of Zoning Appeals. If the board decided that the commissioner had made an error or that the use of surrounding land had changed, it could nullify his decision.

Because of a political fluke, Agnew sat on the appeals board. As far as Anderson was concerned, the Republican was a showboat and a troublemaker. For instance, in 1958 Agnew demanded that the county's top prosecutor go after an illegal junkyard, whose well-connected owner had ignored the board's order to close. A grand jury refused to indict the junkyard owner, but Agnew's bluster garnered plenty of headlines, including this from *The Sun*: "AGNEW CALLS FOES AFRAID — 'THEY CAN'T CONTROL ME.'" Readers got the idea that Agnew was a shining knight, unlike the bunch he worked with. And what a bunch that was! In a single month in 1959, a Democratic member of Agnew's board was indicted for malfeasance, and the zoning commissioner's wife was found to have profited from a land deal whose zoning her husband approved. The next year the zoning commissioner himself was fired for accepting "consultant fees" from a supermarket chain seeking favorable zoning. Prosecutors found it hard to get to the bottom of things: the zoning commissioner's files had disappeared.

During all that time Agnew managed to keep his hands clean. But every day he became more tempted.

In January 1961 Anderson decided that Agnew must go. The latter had recently caused trouble in Anderson's district by approving a large rowhouse development. Owners of existing single-family homes were up in arms, and understandably so. Agnew's decision also might have wider implications. It exacerbated development pressures at a time when the new Beltway was about to open. More crucial, it threatened to erode a long-standing county policy. Ever since the first zoning law was enacted in 1949, the county had confined rowhouses and high-density apartments mostly to one geographical area, the east-end communities of Dundalk and Essex–Middle River. During World War ll tens of thousands of war workers—often from Appalachia—had flocked there, transforming vast expanses of farmland near the Bethlehem Steel and Glenn L. Martin plants into a hodgepodge of cheap housing. The area had acquired the county's largest concentrations of poor whites and African Americans, along with intractable social problems aggravated by joblessness when the defense industries cut back. By contrast, practically no rowhouses and low-end apartments were allowed in better-off sections of the county, which were mostly zoned for homes on one-acre lots or larger. Anderson believed that geographically targeted high-density zoning had served the county well, and the courts had sustained the policy. He agreed with Oliver Herman Laine, a local geographer and educator, who called rowhouses "undesirable" in a 1953 Ph.D. dissertation and urged the county to prohibit them "in all areas north of the proposed Beltway."

Anderson engineered Agnew's ouster. The move sparked a heated controversy and eventually backfired when Agnew launched a campaign for county executive. In normal circumstances a Republican would have had no chance. But in 1962 Agnew's Democratic opponent was Michael J. Birmingham, a caricature of an old-style political boss—a bald, potbellied, inarticulate septuagenarian nicknamed "Iron Mike" because of his authoritarian ways. When self-government came in 1956, this building supplies merchant had claimed natural rights and grabbed the new position of county executive. Two years later he allowed Christian H. Kahl, a younger and more flexible politician, to succeed him as the executive, but by 1962 Birmingham was again longing for a piece of the action. Ignoring pleas to stay out, he muscled himself into the primary election race and narrowly defeated Kahl. It was a fratricide, the two men had been that close. Once, they had made a 133 percent profit overnight by flipping seventy-three acres of east-county farmland they bought together. Kahl simply had his council buddies rubber-stamp a zoning change to rowhouses, and Birmingham then signed it. When asked whether that constituted a conflict of interest, Birmingham famously answered that it did not conflict with *his* interest, and that in any case he had been involved in several previous transactions like that without anyone complaining.

Against such a candidate Agnew was an attractive alternative. His ideas sounded enlightened. He advocated legislation to license handguns, rifles, and shotguns. He favored auto-emission controls and tighter curbs against industrial pollution. He was open to talk about cooperation with the city, including revenue sharing. "All in all, Agnew offered a nice mix of liberalism, modernism, and pragmatism," observed Theo Lippman, Jr., who followed Agnew's career as an editorial writer for *The Sun*.

To voters hungry for change, Birmingham's person became the biggest election issue. He embodied everything that was wrong and odious about the entrenched Democratic machine—greed, unresponsiveness, and heavy-handedness. Things got ugly. Huge numbers of unhappy Kahl supporters, including entire east-end Democratic clubs, defected to Agnew's camp in the general election. With their support, "The Man with the Plan," as Agnew touted himself, became county executive.

Agnew's tenure coincided with the county's greatest growth period. But he also had to devote attention to racial issues. Most of the equal-housing activity was still taking place in the city, but television also sometimes featured footage about the decade-old campaign to integrate Gwynn Oak Amusement Park in Woodlawn, or about pickets outside segregated apartment complexes in the county. A spirit of confrontation was in the air. Agnew pledged to steer a middle course between "the hatreds of segregationist dogma on the one hand and the unreasonable ultimatums of some power-crazed integrationist leaders on the other." But the more strident and confrontational the civil rights movement grew, the more its uncompromising demands angered him. When his own Community Relations Commission endorsed open housing, Agnew ousted its chairman, accusing him of having "confused civil equality with social acceptance."

"Open occupancy legislation, the attempted crashing of private membership clubs, unlawful trespassing and unlawful demonstrating, violate the civil rights of others just as clearly as segregation violates the civil rights of the Negro," he declared. "I take a strong position that it is wrong to tell the owner of a private dwelling place, be it single family or multiple unit, that he must offer it for rent or sale to anyone with whom he does not wish to do business. This applies whether or not he is biased and applies regardless of what his bias may embrace. If he dislikes Greeks he should not have to deal with Greeks, and the government that infringes upon his discretion in this respect abrogates his freedom of selection, and disregards the intent of the Constitution of the United States."

Agnew wanted to modernize Baltimore County government. He wanted to abolish patronage in the police and fire departments. He recognized that amid the tremendous population boom, the county faced monumental planning and infrastructure tasks. An example was Towson, the sleepy county seat just eight miles from Baltimore's City Hall. Built like a one-horse town, it was bursting at the seams and needed room to grow. It was obvious where the future growth of Towson should be directed: toward two black settlements that dated back to slavery times. The settlements had deteriorated into slums, their residents living as renters in crumbling dwellings owned by whites. The idea had been kicking around for a while; Laine, the geographer and a later founder of community colleges, had made it the thrust of his 1953 dissertation. "The slum area of [black] East Towsontown should be redeveloped into commercial use, such as warehousing and office building space, thus relieving the [white] residential area west of York Road from further encroachment by expanding business services." Catonsville, on the west side of the county, faced the same predicament and the same solution. But before the project could move forward, the county needed federal funding.

In 1960 voters had approved urban renewal under Kahl. But four years later, when Agnew introduced legislation to implement an urban renewal program, a savage battle broke out. Hundreds of protesters attacked his bill as a Trojan horse that would usher in "undesirables from the city," as a ringleader at unruly public hearings, Joshua Cockey, put it. He condemned Agnew's proposal as part of a worldwide Communist conspiracy.

Cockey operated a for-whites-only swim quarry in a village north of Towson that bore his family's name. The Cockeys had lived in

Maryland since 1667, after having first sweated it out in Barbados for thirty-three years. They came from England, but family tradition held that the first Cockey was an Italian cook in the army of William the Conqueror, who overran England in 1066. The man claiming this colorful genealogy charged that the agent spreading the "malicious, socialistic cancer" in Baltimore County was Agnew's urban renewal chief, Vladimir A. Wahbe, who boasted quite a family history of his own. Born in Palestine of Lebanese parents, he had once worked as the chief city engineer of Damascus, Syria. He spoke English with a noticeable accent; he also spoke French, Arabic, German, Hebrew, and Greek. His Russian was serviceable, of course, because his father had been the superintendent of Russian-language schools in the Middle East, a position for which he was qualified thanks to his education in czarist Russia. When the family prayed, it prayed in Russian in an Orthodox church.

Protesters shrieked that Communists had sent Wahbe, a naturalized American citizen, to turn the county over to blacks by imposing "open occupancy under federal control." The agitation, coordinated by the extreme right-wing John Birch Society, spread like a wildfire. When urban renewal came up for referendum in 1964, voters crushed Agnew's plan. Political repercussions would last a long time: no subsequent county executive dared even to utter the term "urban renewal." Even in 2010 voters would not allow the county to use its condemnation powers for economic development purposes.

The debacle killed Agnew's reelection hopes. In 1966 he instead ran for governor, another seeming kamikaze mission for a Republican. But again he got lucky. Democrats emerged from a bloody primary with George Mahoney as their nominee. The paving contractor had run six times for various offices, losing every time. He had never angled for the segregationist vote; in fact he had been quoted as favoring open housing laws. But Alabama governor George C. Wallace's presidential campaign had proven that bigotry sold well in Maryland. This time segregation became Mahoney's theme. Ingeniously he devised a slogan that took care of both segregation and the gun issue: "Your Home Is Your Castle—Protect It." This allowed Agnew to cast himself as a moderate alternative, though he too opposed open housing. "There is no middle ground in this election," Agnew proclaimed. "The electorate of Maryland must choose between the bright, pure, courageous flame of righteousness or the evil of a fiery cross." Agnew won, but he failed to carry Baltimore County, where petitioners had unsuccessfully tried to get a referendum to ban any local open-housing law.

Anderson got the message. As county executive "he did everything except stand in the school house door to preserve his county as a white-only suburban enclave," *The Sunpapers* editorialized. But that was *The Sunpapers*, his nemesis, which his voters despised, preferring to take Hearst's reactionary *News American*. From World War II the more conservative *Sun* in particular had moderated its racial views. A foundation honoring the civil rights activist Sidney Hollander, Sr., recognized that in 1946 when it gave its first annual award to *The Sunpapers*—part reward, part incentive. The papers had backed aid to Morgan College. They had also dropped racial designations from crime headlines, though news stories continued such identifications until the 1960s. Editorially the papers remained quite conservative, but that did not affect news coverage. A few years later reporters James D. Dilts and Mark Reutter had little trouble getting their thorough and tough articles on housing into the paper, including stories about Goldseker and his links to establishment banks.

Without access to federal funds, Anderson embarked on a rump renewal program for Towson. A tunnel through the heart of the business district was scrapped. Instead a bypass road was constructed, flanked by government and commercial offices. The end result was the same: East Towson's black community shrank. Another pocket of African Americans, Sandy Bottom, disappeared altogether, becoming the site of a high school, police and fire department headquarters, and, eventually, the county jail. In Catonsville, snack shacks and no fewer than ten gasoline stations replaced black homes at Baltimore National Pike and the Beltway.

The removals of blacks in Towson and Catonsville were not isolated incidents but part of a pattern. Using their zoning powers, the

County Council and the zoning commissioner decimated at least twenty old African-American settlements throughout the county. Yale Rabin, a Massachusetts Institute of Technology professor, coined the term "expulsive zoning" to describe the Baltimore County government's actions. His studies identified similar zoning practices in fifty-four other localities around the nation, including Pulaski, Tennessee; Hamtramck and Detroit, Michigan; Charlotte, North Carolina; Nashville and Jackson, Tennessee; Kansas City, Missouri; Selma, Alabama; Mount Laurel, New Jersey; and El Paso, Texas. In Norfolk, Virginia, one of every four black families was displaced to make way for highways and urban renewal that would lessen the need for school desegregation.

A textbook example of expulsive zoning was Turner Station, which had Baltimore County's largest concentration of blacks, nearly nine thousand in the 1950s. By 1980 so much of the community was rezoned for industry that the black population was recorded at only 3,557. A nearby white residential area, also in the shadows of Bethlehem Steel's Sparrows Point mill, was left untouched. The evicted blacks received no relocation compensation, and most were forced to seek housing in the city.

Rabin detected patterns. Black areas were rezoned for business or industry while adjoining white neighborhoods were left intact. At the same time the county prevented existing black communities from expanding by zoning the surrounding land as low-density and therefore too expensive for blacks to acquire. "Zoning and other development control activities in Baltimore County have served to reinforce local discriminatory attitudes and practices, and have played a major role in significantly altering the income distribution of the Black community in the county through systematic displacement of low-income Black households," Rabin wrote.

African Americans lived in segregated pockets. Some were "isolated from their surroundings and particularly from adjacent white residential areas by discontinuous street patterns," wrote Rabin, whose conclusions county officials did not contradict. Other black hamlets were "characterized by unpaved streets and a generally low level of public improvements, while adjacent white residential areas often have paved streets and are better served by public improvements."

Opposition to open housing had been one of Anderson's election planks. After Dr. Martin Luther King, Jr.'s death triggered widespread rioting and Congress passed the Fair Housing Act of 1968, residential construction activity in the county ground to a halt—as it did throughout the metropolitan area—while builders waited to see whether the federal government would use FHA loans as a hammer to force white suburbs to desegregate. That did not happen. Anderson rebuffed suggestions that he should help implement open housing. "There are no walls around Baltimore County," he contended. "I've said before and I'll say again, I didn't pass the law and I don't intend to enforce federal laws. That's for the federal government to do."

In 1970 the U.S. Commission on Civil Rights probed Baltimore County's racial practices during three days of public hearings. In his testimony, Anderson stood his ground. He rejected calls for thousands of low-income units. "We cannot go about . . . making the same mistake that we made in major cities by just moving our problems across the [city] line into the county. That is not the answer to these problems." He added: "There are many people in Baltimore County that need help, and I think they should be helped first with local tax money."

The catch, according to other testimony at the hearings, was that the county steadfastly refused to take care of its needy who ended up becoming wards of the city, relying on its overburdened social services. Each week, half a dozen county families applied for public housing in the city, which had no residency requirements, because there was no public housing in the county. Four such projects had existed in the county during World War II—operated by the city housing authority—but the county made sure that they were razed by 1954. In the 1970s the city housing commissioner, Robert C. Embry, Jr., tried to kindle cooperation in the matter, but Anderson ignored his letters. Because of noncompliance, the county lost millions of dollars in federal housing grants each year, but Anderson was willing to pay that price.

The Civil Rights Commission's hearings were held at the sprawling headquarters of the Social Security Administration in Woodlawn,
west of the city. With four thousand African Americans among sixteen
thousand employees, the expanding federal agency was the county's
largest employer of blacks. The whole situation irked Anderson. No
entity in the county promoted open housing more vigorously than the
Social Security Administration, an agency of the U.S. government. It
had not escaped Anderson's attention that Robert M. Ball, the SSA
commissioner from 1962 to 1973, was a dues-paying member of Baltimore Neighborhoods, Inc., and that his deputy, Louis Zawatzky,
sat on the integrationist organization's board with his name listed
on the letterhead. The two men believed in integration. When the
Board of Realtors refused to provide listings of homes for sale so that
employees would see a full range of offerings before agents screened
them, a leading Realtor, Grempler, was persuaded to put a multiple
list machine in the SSA housing office. Anderson could not believe
what he heard next: SSA employees were allowed to participate in
open housing activities on government's time. House hunters could
even meet Realtors and realtists in a designated office at the Social
Security Administration headquarters before going to see properties
during work time.

In 1972 the Social Security Administration announced an expansion that would move 2,800 additional low- and middle-income
workers, most of them black, to Woodlawn. Anderson fiercely opposed the plan. There was no housing for them, he said, and none
should be constructed because "not one house in that bracket will
pay enough taxes to educate one child, and how many of those people
coming in here are going to have one child or more?"

Anderson's uncompromising positions inevitably led to clashes
with the county planning department, headed by innovative men like
George Gavrelis and Leslie Graef, graduates of Harvard and MIT, respectively. The county executive accused them of keeping information
from him and charged that planners conspired with citizens to defeat
controversial zoning proposals. Anderson grew so upset that in 1972
he abolished four key positions in the planning department, which

was in the middle of completing a forward-looking plan to guide the county's long-term growth. Gavrelis resigned in protest. Graef was fired.

A few months later that same year, Anderson ordered real estate agents to report all sales to blacks to the police. He said he was acting at the request of the Real Estate Board. That board, indeed, after adopting a new "code of equal opportunity," had asked all its members to notify the county police intelligence division whenever they signed a lease or contract involving a black moving into "predominantly or totally white county areas." Anderson was merely enforcing that practice, wanting to make sure that blacks were protected, the county executive said. A representative of the Civil Rights Commission did not buy Anderson's explanation. He charged that the county executive's intention was to "clearly intimidate rather than help the potential black buyer in the county." None of this hurt Anderson politically. He forged an unspoken pact with the electorate: he kept his end of the bargain by excluding blacks and poor whites from the county. Voters, in return, kept reelecting him. It worked like a charm. In 1983, seven years after he was released from serving thirteen months of a five-year prison sentence for corruption, voters elected him to the Maryland House of Delegates.

16

꒐꒐꒐꒐꒐꒐꒐

Persistent Patterns

DALE ANDERSON died in 1996. Ten years later a researcher called the
Baltimore County Historical Society, trying to locate his papers. "Who
is Dale Anderson?" he was asked. The county truly had marched on.
Its population was larger than the declining city's. The number of African Americans had grown so greatly that blacks accounted for close
to 25 percent of the county's 787,384 residents. One of seven County
Council members was black, as were four legislators. The school superintendent was an African American.

The evolution was not easy. Theodore G. Venetoulis learned that
early on. No sooner had the Goucher College political science lec-
turer been elected county executive in 1974 than he found himself
embroiled in a tug-of-war with the County Council. In his election
campaign, Venetoulis had promised a clean break from the corruption of the Anderson years. But the County Council rejected his
choice to implement open government, a chief aide to Jim Wright,
the powerful Democratic speaker of the House of Representatives
in Washington. Councilmen did not want an outsider as the head
administrator, and there was the matter of the nominee's wife, an
African American. "There was this resistance to outsiders in general,
women and blacks," Venetoulis remembered. He pushed on. After
the County Council passed his breakthrough growth-management

legislation, he appointed a woman to coordinate the program and deal with developers—a brusque and burly chain-smoker with close-cropped reddish hair and a predilection for green polyester pantsuits. The old-b'hoys' network was abolished, expulsive zoning ended, and blacks appointed to substantive posts in the county government.

Still, a high degree of residential segregation persisted. Racial change was mostly limited to one section in the northwest—Liberty Road, an old turnpike that was an extension of the city's Liberty Heights Avenue, where Forest Park and Ashburton already had transitioned from non-Jewish to Jewish and then from Jewish to African American. Beginning in 1950, this succession sequence was repeated in the county.

The cycle began that year when Howard Rowe tried to buy a home in Lochearn, a leafy Liberty Road community of cottages, brick colonials, ranchers, and Protestant churches just across the city line. A decorated veteran of the New Guinea and South Philippines campaigns, he was drawn to Lochearn by a newspaper ad that promised: "Live like a king for less than rent at Lochearn." But even though the ad featured a Veterans Administration logo, the sales office rejected Rowe because he was Jewish. Homes in Lochearn could be sold only to "Gentiles," he was told—two years after the Supreme Court struck down discriminatory covenants. The Baltimore Jewish Council took up his cause. The first Jewish residents arrived in Lochearn in 1951. Friction soon grew so serious that the Baltimore Jewish Council convened meetings of synagogues to discuss "the problems of Jewish-Christian relations" in the community. By the early 1960s so many non-Jewish homeowners had departed that the real estate industry perceived the whole corridor from Lochearn to Randallstown pretty much as a Jewish market. Other whites were steered elsewhere.

Randallstown was the end point of Liberty Road's suburbanized stretch, a onetime farming and chrome-mining community dating back to 1719. Its most famous son was James Ryder Randall, a newspaperman and offspring of the village's founding family. Upon learning in 1861 that a classmate had been wounded in a Baltimore street skirmish with Union soldiers, he described his torment in a poem that became a Confederate battle hymn and, in 1939, the Maryland state anthem, words and all:

> The despot's heel is on thy shore, Maryland!
> His torch is at thy temple door, Maryland!
> Avenge the patriotic gore
> That flecked the streets of Baltimore,
> And be the battle queen of yore,
> Maryland! My Maryland!

> I hear the distant thunder-hum, Maryland!
> The Old Line's bugle, fife, and drum, Maryland!
> She is not dead, nor deaf, nor dumb—
> Huzza! she spurns the Northern scum!
> She breathes! she burns! she'll come! she'll come!
> Maryland! My Maryland!

After the Civil War Randallstown thrived. In the 1880s it supported two physicians, three blacksmiths, three storekeepers, a Methodist church, and a Catholic parish. Black servants and laborers had their own churches in segregated pockets. In 1922 trackless trolley service linked Randallstown with City Hall, twelve miles distant. With newcomers came colonials and cottages. Many of those early houses were built of fieldstone by Italian immigrant masons. The ambience remained semi-rural. In the early 1960s the custodian at the historic Mount Olive Methodist Church still took care of three cows, a horse, two goats, and some seventy-five chickens on the church property in the heart of Randallstown. But as cookie-cutter subdivisions rose in open fields to obscure the stone houses, the town lost its charm. Liberty Road became a congested strip of sprawl. Every carpet installer, car dealer, mattress shop, gas station, and fast-food restaurant seemed to be in business there, contributing to a nightly freak show of brake lights and blinking neon.

The first black family moved to Lochearn in 1968, a few weeks before Dr. Martin Luther King, Jr.'s assassination. Its arrival triggered fear and trepidation. Baltimore Neighborhoods, Inc. spent countless hours trying to calm residents. After nine meetings the integrationist

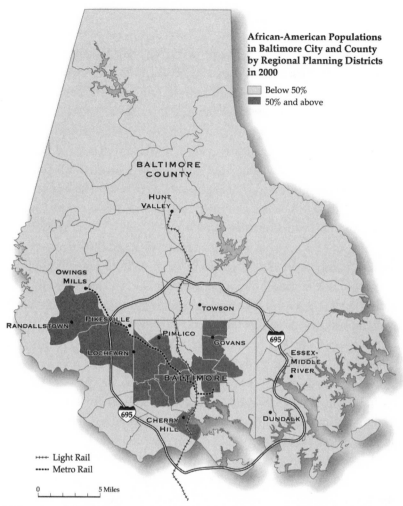

This map of black concentration in Baltimore County shows the established pattern of neighborhoods first transitioning from non-Jewish to Jewish and then to African American.

organization reported that ninety-five families on Forest Garden Drive "seem willing to accept and welcome their new Negro neighbors"; two were selling, and twenty-three were undecided. Half a mile up the road, a homeowner was threatened and his children intimidated when it was learned that he was selling to a black family. Leading the harassment was a member of the Real Estate Board, who lived in the neighborhood.

A man wearing an undertaker suit appeared, distributing "THIS HOUSE IS NOT FOR SALE" signs. Was he the same man who had brought such signs to Goose Hill two decades earlier? No one knew. But as soon as his sign appeared, so did "FOR SALE" signs. Most buyers were black, usually families with children. They quickly altered the complexion of public elementary schools and produced jitters in the neighborhoods in which those schools were located. Community organizations complained that real estate agents showed houses only to blacks. They lobbied for a sign ban, which the County Council passed, and anti-blockbusting legislation, which it did not. By 2000, Lochearn had become 77 percent black, and Randallstown 65.5 percent. Big-name retailers and restaurants moved out, even though the incoming black families' buying power usually was no different from that of departing whites. "Resegregation today is just as much a reality in the suburbs as it was fifty years ago in the city, but the pace is much slower," the Barnard College professor Gregory Smithsimon observed in 2008 after studying Liberty Road.

The departing Jewish families did not move far. They headed in the direction of Owings Mills and Reisterstown. In those two old farming communities they met an earlier phalanx of migration that had been moving out of the city along Reisterstown Road and its parallel, Park Heights Avenue. That Jewish vanguard reached Pikesville in the early 1960s. With an interchange on the new Baltimore Beltway, Pikesville was transformed from a sleepy farming village of churches, state police headquarters, and an old Confederate veterans home to the capital of Jewish Baltimore County. Ranchers and split-levels mushroomed on generous lots; synagogues were built, as were shopping centers catering to Jewish tastes. A backlash developed. In 1964 ethnic brawls broke out at Pikesville's bowling alley, pizzeria, and movie theater. One prominent Jewish family's home was burned down. The root cause was envy, a Philadelphia researcher wrote in a report to the Baltimore Jewish Council. He cited a Pikesville resident who complained about "Jews trying to 'show off' with their new and more beautiful homes, flashy cars and expensive clothes."

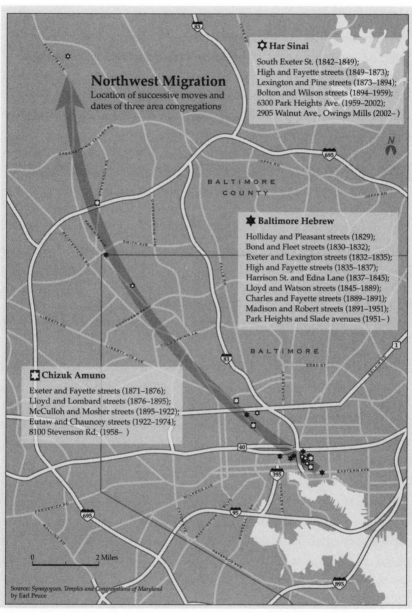

Northwest Migration
Location of successive moves and
dates of three area congregations

✡ **Har Sinai**

South Exeter St. (1842–1849);
High and Fayette streets (1849–1873);
Lexington and Pine streets (1873–1894);
Bolton and Wilson streets (1894–1959);
6300 Park Heights Ave. (1959–2002);
2905 Walnut Ave., Owings Mills (2002–)

✡ **Baltimore Hebrew**

Holliday and Pleasant streets (1829);
Bond and Fleet streets (1830–1832);
Exeter and Lexington streets (1832–1835);
High and Fayette streets (1835–1837);
Harrison St. and Edna Lane (1837–1845);
Lloyd and Watson streets (1845–1889);
Charles and Fayette streets (1889–1891);
Madison and Robert streets (1891–1951);
Park Heights and Slade avenues (1951–)

✡ **Chizuk Amuno**

Exeter and Fayette streets (1871–1876);
Lloyd and Lombard streets (1876–1895);
McCulloh and Mosher streets (1895–1922);
Eutaw and Chauncey streets (1922–1974);
8100 Stevenson Rd. (1958–)

0   2 Miles

Source: *Synagogues, Temples and Congregations of Maryland*
by Earl Pruce

The moves of three leading synagogues from east Baltimore deeper and
deeper to the northwest.

A decade later no hostility greeted Jews when Owings Mills became the farthest outpost on the community's migration. Since the
1880s the Jewish community had made three major moves: out of
east Baltimore's slums to the Eutaw Place–North Avenue areas, then
onward to Garrison Boulevard, Liberty Heights Avenue, Reisterstown
Road, and Park Heights Avenue, and finally deeper and deeper into
Baltimore County. Despite the changing geography, the community
maintained its cohesion. Seventy percent of Jews lived in a handful
of contiguous zip codes, mostly in Pikesville and Owings Mills. One
cause of cohesion surely was real estate discrimination, but that was
increasingly part of a painful past. The contemporary Jewish community stuck together by choice.

The 1968 riots unleashed an African-American tidal wave that
swept over Liberty Road. Whether Social Security Administration employees or not, many moved from the Pimlico area in the city, which
Johns Hopkins geographers Lata Chatterjee, David Harvey, and Lawrence Klugman identified in 1974 as having the highest home turnover rate in the city. Thirteen miles south of Owings Mills, Pimlico
straddled Park Heights Avenue and Reisterstown Road. Coming from
the north, the neighborhood began at Northern Parkway in the city,
which more or less demarcated the races from the 1970s onward. To
the north were the Jewish Community Center, the Baltimore Hebrew
College, prestigious synagogues, and choice residential areas stretching all the way up to Owings Mills. To the south was Pimlico.

Pimlico was another neighborhood that over the years had transitioned from non-Jewish to Jewish to African American. In 1907,
when the area was still quite rural and sparsely populated, a Catholic
missionary priest had founded St. Ambrose's parish on Park Heights
Avenue. Later a school was added. The church kept growing. In
1929, just seven months before the stock market crash, a new eight-
hundred-seat sanctuary was dedicated. St. Ambrose's continued to
build through the 1950s even as parts of the neighborhood became
heavily Jewish. Families of Eastern European origin brought zest to
streets around the famous racetrack. Jewish organizations followed,
including the Talmudical Academy, B'nai B'rith offices, and Sinai

Hospital; shopping centers and private entrepreneurs thrived. Pimlico was a neighborhood of amazing stories and tall tales, some of which the filmmaker Barry Levinson spun in *Tin Men* and *Diner,* cinematic scrapbooks of his growing-up years.

Park Heights Avenue and Reisterstown Road were extensions of Pennsylvania Avenue. Since the late 1890s blacks had been slowly but steadily moving north along the artery, whose southern portion contained the community's segregation-era retail and entertainment hub. By the late 1950s blacks had reached Park Circle, near Pimlico, where the whites-only Carlin's Park had closed a few years earlier. Carlin's was one of the few public venues that had allowed Jews to use an Olympic-size swimming pool.

Pimlico was in the midst of racial changeover when the 1968 riots came. Remaining Jewish and white Catholic homeowners fled within a few years. Black homeowners also packed up, many heading for Liberty Road because African Americans from lower socioeconomic strata were settling in as homeowners and renters in Pimlico. The low-income influx was among the consequences of a policy change that the FHA implemented nationwide. After decades of catering to middle-class families, the agency devised programs to help low-income buyers, who did not need to put any money down if they acquired an existing home in any city. In Baltimore, so many low-income families took advantage of the so-called 221(d)(2) program that nothing-down FHA loans replaced the controversial land-installment contracts and rent-to-buy deals, which for decades had been the predominant financing vehicle of sales to blacks.

Pimlico became the epicenter of the new nothing-down mortgages. "Superficially it looks as if the FHA is involved (or is being used) in an aggressive block-busting operation," the Johns Hopkins geographers told the FHA in a 1974 consultants' report. "The area has become substantially black in the last ten years and there is a continuing process of relocation and change both from white to black and from one group of blacks to another." When the ground was broken on one apartment building, the neighborhood was Jewish. Six months later, when the roof was topped, the area was going black.

Racial and socioeconomic change continued to drag Pimlico down-hill. The decline accelerated after city officials, with the approval of the federal Department of Housing and Urban Development (HUD), resettled in Pimlico hundreds of poor blacks whose homes in other parts of the city had been bulldozed to make way for road construc-tion and various urban renewal projects. Scattered public housing projects followed, including one project developed by Allen T. Quille, the parking lot operator. These actions were in keeping with a prac-tice that city and federal authorities had followed since World War II: public and subsidized housing was placed in areas of least resistance. Pimlico was such a place. The results were disastrous. The area re-segregated, becoming a dysfunctional pocket of concentrated poverty where human life was cheap and drugs and sex plentiful.

Not many scholars had studied class succession within African-American neighborhoods, the phenomenon that the Johns Hopkins geographers encountered in Pimlico. By contrast, other types of eth-nic and economic neighborhood succession had long intrigued social scientists who developed theories to explain why certain population groups quickly abandoned racially changing areas while others did not. In 1999 Gerald Gamm published a provocative study, *Urban Ex-odus: Why the Jews Left Boston and the Catholics Stayed.* Contrast-ing the two different outcomes, he argued that the strict geographical borders of parishes set by a central church authority gave the Irish Catholic neighborhood in Boston a solidity that the adjoining Jewish neighborhood lacked. Synagogues had no geographical borders; they made decisions autonomously of any central authority and were free to move when circumstances warranted. Once Orthodox synagogues relocated, members had to move too in order to be within walking distance on the Sabbath. A high number of Jewish renters added po-tential for mobility.

That was Boston. In Baltimore the parishes' institutional role as a natural stabilizer was questionable. Catholic churches and parochial schools did stay open and operational even after racial change oc-curred and flocks dispersed. The black upper and middle classes of the time were significantly Catholic, but they seldom encountered a welcoming priest or parish. Fulton Avenue's St. Martin's and its pastor, Monsignor Louis O'Donovan, actively fought to stop blacks in the 1940s and failed. A few years later Monsignor Louis Vaeth had no better success in containing blacks at St. Bernardine's in Edmondson Village. Their ultimate failure as pastors was that they left both parishes so weak that they survived on life support. So it was significant that a few years after those debacles, the church began using totally different tactics. It set up Alinsky-inspired community organizations to deal with racial issues. A high-turnover area (in home sales) between York and Harford roads in northeast Baltimore's Govans area showed how that was done.

That area consisted of a geographically limited but expanding black concentration amid enclaves of middle-class Irish and German Catholics, who objected to desegregation. Nevertheless they tried to cope with the probability that they might soon have black neighbors, if they didn't already, because more than one-third of the area's ninety thousand people were black. When the specter emerged of an influx of FHA-financed low-income African-American homeowners, all kinds of fears erupted. Surely a deluge of ghetto renters would be next. Why not move now?

Many fled, but many others fought back. They coalesced around the Northeast Community Organization (NECO), which was launched in 1970 after three years of meticulous planning and preparations, spearheaded by Alinsky's successor at the Industrial Areas Foundation, Edward T. Chambers, and the Baltimore archdiocese's controversial Urban Commission. NECO's launch was impressive: 692 delegates staged the multi-racial organization's inaugural congress, a spirited event that resembled a political convention. The delegates represented 158 constituencies ranging from block clubs to churches of several denominations to improvement associations. The executive director and the lead organizer were both veterans of Alinsky's Chicago operations. Another organizer came from the Southern Christian Leadership Conference in Memphis, Tennessee. In addition to yet another full-time organizer, two part-timers were employed. One was a student from the University of Maryland School of Social Work who specialized in community organizing; the other was a former reporter for the *Chronicle of Higher Education.*

A serious white Catholic backlash soon developed. Critics, including real estate brokers and other businesses, attacked NECO as a sinister outside power grab. Several parish councils resigned from NECO and withdrew their funding, but that mattered little because most of the money came from the church's nationwide Campaign for Human Development. A big ad in the *Catholic Review* accused NECO of "creating elaborate plans to conduct a 'block-busting' program." "Help free us from the arrogant use of the economic power of the Archdiocese of Baltimore," it said, urging Catholics to use the "ballot box in this battle"—the collection basket: "Don't contribute."

Alinsky's teachings called for tactics that produced results. In the early 1970s NECO accused a Towson Realtor, Joseph L. Mann, of blockbusting. It picketed the man's home on a street of pricey split-levels near Goucher College, but without success. Other tactics also failed. In desperation, NECO bused in noisy black protesters to the Immaculate Conception Catholic Church, a cathedral-like edifice on a hill overlooking Towson. Their chanting and shouts interrupted the Sunday calm and upset thousands of middle-class whites who attended the mass there along with the Realtor and his family. That evening the spectacle was replayed on television for all to see. The parish pastor acted quickly. He confronted the Realtor. Whether it is true, as some alleged, that the builder was threatened with excommunication, he promised to sin no more. The pastor was Monsignor Joseph M. Nelligan. He was the cardinal's finance chief, placed in charge of the Towson parish because it was the archdiocese's cash register at collection times.

NECO scored other victories. Its complaints persuaded the U.S. Department of Justice to investigate steering by real estate agents. Two blue-ribbon real estate firms, Russell T. Baker and Temple Peirce, signed agreements pledging to show houses to whites as well as blacks. Panic-peddling speculators were confronted and driven out. Then a disaster struck. In 1973 the NECO president, Walter Brooks, resigned. He was a public television producer, an intense man who sported a

Malcom X goatee. Announcing his resignation at a press conference, he charged that infighting had hampered his leadership at NECO and that racism stymied progress. An internal rift developed, damaging the NECO brand.

In 1977 the Catholic church supplanted NECO with a larger umbrella, the citywide Baltimoreans United in Leadership Development (BUILD). The new organization redefined community issues. It concentrated on economic demands, from fighting against mortgage and insurance redlining to campaigning for a living wage. It was still operating more than three decades later, defying Alinsky's view that community organizations should not become permanent fixtures.

Racial change came, but thanks to NECO and BUILD it proceeded gradually. An example was St. Matthews Catholic parish on Loch Raven Boulevard, near Good Samaritan Hospital, whose pastor, Monsignor Clare O'Dwyer, had been among NECO's founders. Over the next four decades St. Matthew's evolved into a polyglot parish, one of the most diverse in the archdiocese, with congregants coming from forty-two countries. Members included so many Kenyans that a later pastor, BUILD activist Joseph L. Muth, Jr., studied Swahili. *Habari nyumbani*, he would ask, how are things at home? He was quite an apparition: a white Santa Claus look-alike wearing African liturgical robes and speaking in tongues.

*

The 1974 study by Chatterjee, Harvey, and Klugman identified eight housing submarkets in Baltimore, each with different characteristics. They ranged from the inner city, which the federal government had redlined in 1937 and where mortgages could not be obtained, to the white-ethnic southeast Baltimore, which was largely unaffected by racial change. Sellers there spurned FHA sales. They did not like federal involvement or inspections that might result in costly orders for mandatory repairs. FHA loans had another drawback: the seller agreed to pay possibly thousands of dollars in points as a precondition for a good interest rate. Who needed that? East Baltimoreans financed their loans through Polish, Czech, Slovak, and Italian savings and loan associations, which offered decent terms. These were neighborhood institutions, and it was in their best interest to keep the tightly knit rowhouse enclaves in ethnic Catholic parishes intact. As a result, racial and class change bypassed certain neighborhoods altogether for a long time.

In 1971 the Catholic church created the South East Community Organization (SECO) to prop up the neighborhoods and ease the transition to multi-racialism that eventually came, largely in the form of a Hispanic influx. SECO's godmother was a social worker named Barbara Mikulski, who launched a political career that culminated in her election as the first woman U.S. Senator from Maryland.

In west Baltimore's Edmondson Village, the Hopkins geographers encountered a surprisingly low turnover rate. It seemed inexplicable in view of the frantic pace in Pimlico. They searched for an explanation and came up with a theory that the early black Edmondson Village home buyers were still shell-shocked from their buying experience in the 1950s and 1960s. They had bought at the peak of aggressive blockbusting. With little money or advice, they had entered into exploitative rent-to-buy contracts with speculators. Whether they got burned or not, the experience so taxed them emotionally that they did not care to relive it. "All I know is that I drove a cab for the next 365 days without a day off, trying to juggle two payments," Adolph Simmons recalled 50 years later. Then he clammed up. This was probably what the Johns Hopkins researchers had in mind when they said that the Edmondson Village market was characterized by "stickiness."

Simmons lived on Mount Olivet Lane, a pleasant street overlooking a grassy open field leading to the Gwynns Falls stream valley. The stability on his block was astonishing. Until the early 2000s, many houses were still in the name of the African Americans who had purchased them in the 1950s and 1960s, or their heirs. Homes typically transferred within the family, preventing normal ownership rotation and the improvements that went along with it. Many streets acquired a tatty look. The offspring didn't care. They likely lived along Liberty Road and had little interest in the old neighborhood. They chopped their inheritance into rental apartments, and when those failed to make money they sold to speculators. For a second time in fifty years, Edmondson Village faced an unsettled future.

Younger African-American families did not gravitate to the Liberty Road corridor solely because of real estate steering. Mass transit also steered them there. Baltimore's original 1966 transit plan envisioned six rapid-transit lines radiating out from the city center. By 1983 only a single line had been built, a Metro subway that ran midway between the Liberty Road and Reisterstown Road corridors. That alignment was chosen after fierce battles. The public's fear of crime and undesirables carried along the rails was strong. So were the racial overtones of their arguments. To placate anxious residents and businesses, politicians and transit officials made intriguing decisions. Even though Owings Mills was the line's northwestern terminus, the Metro stopped well short of the shopping mall, the centerpiece of the planned town center. A subsequent light-rail line stirred even more opposition. Completed in 1992, it ran through mostly white neighborhoods from the airport to downtown, then followed the Jones Falls stream bed to Hunt Valley, an important employment center in the county. Although Ruxton was on the line, trains skipped the wealthy county village because its influential residents vetoed a stop. They did not want outsiders. In Linthicum, Anne Arundel County, homeowners accepted a light rail station but only on the condition that no parking was provided.

In time blacks concentrated along Liberty Road because it was the place to be. They included people like James Dean, a retired management consultant who had lived in the Netherlands and Germany. He bought a 1950s fieldstone rancher. A Rolls Royce in his driveway suggested that he could have lived anywhere. Others constructed brand-new homes, including McMansions. Churches followed black upwardly mobile professionals, or "buppies," out of the city. As blacks spread, the question was sometimes asked whether Owings Mills too would eventually face a transition from Jewish to African American, following the established Baltimore pattern. As in 1910, blacks and Jews in 2010 were uneasy neighbors.

One important city institution that announced a move to Liberty
Road was Bethel African Methodist Episcopal Church, a 14,000-
member congregation. It acquired 256 acres of farmland for a new
worship center that included a 3,000-seat sanctuary, school, and
athletic complex. The site was a onetime plantation in the middle
of an undeveloped farming area, chosen because of its convenience
to both Baltimore and Howard counties, where more than half the
church membership had moved. Old Court Road at that point was
a mere winding, two-lane country road, so a church—and a black
mega-church at that—unsettled white neighbors. They entangled the
project in endless litigation, claiming that any construction would dis-
turb the remains of slaves who had toiled and died on the plantation.
Bethel argued that all graves were likely to be in a clearly marked
cemetery that would not be touched. But white protesters insisted
that corpses of slaves might be anywhere and that bulldozing could
pose health hazards. It was bizarre. "I don't know what the devil this
case is about," a frustrated judge exclaimed after hearing hours of
testimony.

Bethel's plans to move underscored how important, city-rooted
African-American institutions had arrived at a crossroads. Their best
bet, if they wished to grow and prosper, was to follow their middle-
class membership out of the city. Just two minutes away from Bethel's
proposed site, occupying both sides of Old Court Road, was New
Antioch Baptist Church, a four-thousand-member African-American
congregation. It too saw its future in the county.

Bethel's plan to leave the city carried strong symbolism. The
church dated to 1785 when a group of African Americans, upset
about discrimination, split from the Lovely Lane Meeting House,
the birthplace of American Methodism. Bethel eventually acquired
a former German Lutheran church downtown, where it stayed until
Mayor Preston razed the racially mixed neighborhood just north of
City Hall. The church then relocated to Druid Hill Avenue, buying a
Gothic stone church from a departing white Protestant congregation.
That move happened in 1910, the year when W. Ashbie Hawkins's

acquisition of 1834 McCulloh Street around the corner prompted the City Council to enact the nation's first residential segregation law.

Bethel was a fighting church, so important in the African Methodist Episcopal movement that 14 of its pastors were elected bishops. Its reach was wide. The church sponsored vitally needed community outreach programs in the increasingly impoverished neighborhoods surrounding Druid Hill Avenue. Its telecasts were seen in 123 countries. Baltimore mayor Sheila Dixon was a member, as were the city comptroller, several state senators and delegates, and members of the City Council. The pastor, Frank M. Reid III, was the stepbrother of Kurt L. Schmoke, Baltimore's first elected African-American mayor, who after three terms in office became Howard University's law dean. So even though Reid insisted that he would not close the landmark sanctuary on Druid Hill Avenue, his intention to move Bethel to the county caused quite a stir.

The African-American community was scattering, but there was little soul-searching about the wider implications of such geographical dispersal. Howard, Anne Arundel, Carroll, and Harford counties had growing black populations, often quite segregated. The City of Baltimore remained the center, but the black community's onetime heart, Pennsylvania Avenue, had stopped beating. Its storied nightspots and shops had long ago been reduced to rubble. Remaining retail was of the get-by variety. Even a much-ballyhooed food market, modernized with millions of dollars in taxpayer money, was not making it.

Just two blocks east of Pennsylvania ran Druid Hill Avenue. From the early 1900s until the 1950s it had been an address coveted by the black elite. But once racial barriers came down, the middle class deserted to the suburbs. Houses were abandoned and boarded up because of simple economics: they were contaminated with layers and layers of poisonous lead paint. The liabilities frustrated landlords and scared away new investors. The same calamity also befell McCulloh Street, one block farther east. Just a few hundred yards away, on the other side of Eutaw Place, stately Bolton Hill houses fetched record prices. But Bolton Hill was upscale, white, and picturesque, resembling Washington's Georgetown, while Druid Hill Avenue and Mc-Culloh Street were underclass, black, and run-down.

Not everyone gave up hope. A community development corporation built modern rowhouses, with garages, on vacant land. Black middle-class professionals snapped them up; they were good deals, close to downtown and public transit links. Other ambitious plans were in the works. A private landlord rehabbed W. Ashbie Hawkins's onetime acquisition at 1834 McCulloh Street. The rowhouse had been vacant and vandalized for several years. It became a rental property again, just as it had been in 1910. It was among a handful of houses on the block that were not boarded up.

The significance of 1834 McCulloh Street was forgotten; Hawkins's name produced blank stares. No one, black or white, wished to remember Baltimore's pioneering role in residential segregation or subsequent real estate bigotry. It was as if those things had never happened, such was the communal amnesia that hit the population. The numerical majority of Baltimoreans had moved after World War II at least once because of racial reasons, but few dwelled on those experiences. African Americans suppressed memories of racial segregation. Jews avoided talk of past anti-Semitism. The traumatic turnover of neighborhoods had been completed within ten or fifteen years. There had been resistance and tense moments, but deadly violence somehow was avoided. Whites seldom fought back, unlike families in Chicago and Detroit who resorted to brute force to repel blacks. Baltimore seemed to agree that these unpleasant matters were best forgotten. Things had changed for the better in the end, had they not? Many neighborhoods had opened up, even Roland Park. More fashionable and wealthier than it had perhaps ever been, it had a smattering of black residents and so many Jews that two synagogues opened nearby.

Having cut grass in his youth for Roland Park swells, James Crockett watched all this with fascination. Born in Jim Crow Baltimore, he was a jack-of-all-trades, a pioneering African-American firefighter who had operated a corner grocery and held a patronage job at the election board. In the mid-1950s he began working for

Manning-Shaw, the city's leading blockbuster, as a sideline, selling houses to fellow blacks in white neighborhoods. Eventually Crockett became the first black appointed to the Maryland Real Estate Commission, and early in the millennium he became president of the city Board of Fire Commissioners.

One day in May 1985 Crockett went to a real estate auction on Park Heights Avenue. The property being sold was the old clubhouse of Jack Pollack, the political boss, who was long gone, as was his Democratic machine. Crockett was about to walk away when the auctioneer whispered, "Stick around." He did. In the absence of bids, Crockett ended up acquiring the former Trenton Democratic Club building for $11,000, a steal at less than the suggested minimum bid. He sold the building to a black church. "How about that!" Crockett chuckled. There was a sparkle in his eye. He was an old-style black Republican at heart, delighted to have squeezed a profit out of Jack Pollack.

Crockett was a wry man, full of observations about life and the human condition. He had seen so many fundamental changes in his lifetime that he no longer kept count. He thought that one of the most important transformative events had occurred after World War II, when hot water on demand became widely available. A quick wash after work enabled regular people to participate in civic life, and the 1950s and 1960s bore many fruits of that activism. The racial condition was more complicated. Despite much progress, prejudices prevailed.

In the 1990s Crockett spotted a novel phenomenon: some white families began considering houses in predominantly black neighborhoods, if the architecture was outstanding, the price compelling, and future prospects promising for regentrification. White families buying homes from African Americans as part of a normal real estate rotation startled Crockett. He had never seen that happen in Baltimore before. Something new was going on.

Crockett did not make the connection at the time, but he had witnessed one of the consequences of the subprime mortgage craze.

Epilogue: An American Dilemma

IN 1944, when the Swedish social scientist Gunnar Myrdal published a seminal survey of race relations, *An American Dilemma,* Jim Crow still ruled courtrooms, public accommodations, education, and workplaces in many sections of the country. But Myrdal saw a new day dawning: "The Negro problem is not only America's greatest failure but also America's incomparably great opportunity for the future," he wrote four years before the Supreme Court struck down racially restrictive covenants and ten years before the school desegregation order. "Not since Reconstruction has there been more reason to anticipate fundamental changes in American race relations, changes which will involve a development toward the American ideals."

Part of Myrdal's prediction came true more than two decades after his death. In 2008 an emerging new America—a highly diverse, suburbanized, cell-phone-connected internet nation—elected a self-described "mutt" to the White House. Widely celebrated as a milestone in race relations, the moment was rife with contradictions. For one thing, many of those voting for Barack Hussein Obama lived in a segregated neighborhood, worshiped in a segregated house of God, and sent children to an effectively one-race school. A survey of sixty-nine urban centers revealed that more than half of blacks resided in areas that were more than 50 percent African American, while more than two-thirds of whites lived in places where blacks accounted for less than 5 percent of the population.

Other uncomfortable reminders of racial realities surfaced frequently, including racial profiling. Police stops of African-American motorists were so common that DWB was said to mean "driving while black." Blacks also often had difficulties in hailing a cab after dark—even if the driver was African American. In 2009 police arrested Professor Henry Louis Gates, Jr., Harvard University's prized head of African-American studies. Returning from a two-week trip to China, he had broken into his own home because the front door was stuck. Cambridge police, alerted to the scene, suspected he was a burglar. Just a few months earlier, Eric Holder, Obama's attorney general, had offended some by castigating Americans as "a nation of cowards" for their failure to confront racial issues. After Gates's arrest, everyone had an opinion, but no concensus was reached. Different peceptions based on race were a fact of life.

This was the America that Obama inherited, along with the worst economic mess since the Great Depression. Triggered by the collapse of the subprime mortgage sector, a series of destructive tsunamis hit the financial world. The causes of the subprime crisis were complicated and contradictory. The Carter administration's 1977 Community Reinvestment Act (CRA), which forced banks to help previously disqualified borrowers realize their dream of homeownership. For a long time CRA enforcement was perfunctory. A 1979 survey of the thirteen biggest lenders in Baltimore showed that only 1.6 percent of their mortgage loans went to majority black census tracts. Low figures were the rule in other parts of the country as well. In 1995 the Clinton administration demanded that banks do more. Seeing a huge potential for profits, the financial sector responded. In the next seven years the number of mortgage firms doubled, from twenty thousand to forty thousand. A spree of risky lending followed.

A two-tiered system of financial services had existed for a long time. In the 1940s, 1950s, and 1960s, lenders gave mortgages and consumer loans to whites fleeing to the suburbs while blacks had to rely on financing from predatory speculators. That two-tier market now exploded. Banks closed branches in the inner city and minority areas, leaving financial services to check-cashing outfits, payday loan offices, and other assorted loan sharks. When whites applied for money to buy homes, they were offered conventional mortgages, particularly if they were middle-class suburbanites. But when blacks and Hispanics applied, even big-name lenders offered only higher-priced or predatory loan products.

Race was such an overriding consideration that *high-income* African Americans in predominantly black neighborhoods were three times more likely to receive a subprime home loan than *low-income* white borrowers, according to a 2004 study. At the time more than 20 percent of all residential mortgages consisted of risky "nontraditional" loans, compared to just 2 percent in 2000. The business was lucrative, generating hefty commissions and origination fees. Subprime mortgages were eight times more likely to default than conventional loans, but issuers did not care. Real estate firms sold houses to "Ninjas," buyers with no income, job, or assets, whom lenders approved nonetheless.

Baltimore became a hotbed for subprime mortgage abuses. But that was the second act. The first act opened in the mid-1990s. Called flipping, it was the bastard son of redlining and blockbusting. Among the earliest to call attention to the systematic flipping of bottom-rung properties was *The Sun*'s John B. O'Donnell, a meticulous and battle-hardened former City Hall reporter. In a front-page article on August 1, 1999, he told the story of how Ingrid met Chuck. Ingrid Simon, thirty-seven, was a lifelong renter from the Mondawmin area, a seven-dollar-an-hour security guard who wanted a home for herself and her teenaged daughter. So it was like an answered prayer when Chuck Famous in 1998 offered to sell her a Forest Park fixer-upper for $65,000, with just $500 down. If she had done her homework, she would have found out that the silver-haired onetime Florida mortgage broker had bought the same house for $15,000 five weeks earlier and had done next to nothing to improve it. Not knowing any better, she took a mortgage from Chuck Famous with an 11.5 percent interest rate that could rise to 18 percent but never go lower; similar mortgages for buyers with best credit carried a 5.63 percent rate at the time.

Flipping was little different from systematic speculation on substandard rowhouses after World War II. Except that as a criminal enterprise it was more corrosive because quick-buck artists not only gypped buyers but also gave kickbacks to greedy appraisers whose fraudulent paperwork was accepted by corrupt mortgage brokers and sleazy title company officials. "In both scenarios, black families were paying more for houses than they were worth," observed Kenneth Strong, who fought flipping at the nonprofit Community Law Center. "In both cases, the risk of foreclosure was greater because of inflated prices. [Lingering] redlining aggravated those risks by higher mortgage rates or barriers to buying a home in a stable mixed neighborhood."

Over several years O'Donnell documented dozens of similar flipping cases. Flipping created a culture of fraud. By 2005, when the 100th prosecuted offender was sentenced—one of the worst defendants receiving a five-year jail term—hundreds of Baltimoreans had lost their homes while thousands of others tried to avoid foreclosure. The racket was a chief reason—along with lead-paint contamination—why boarded-up rowhouses pockmarked so many city neighborhoods. The curse was not over yet when subprime lending came in vogue. Again black neighborhoods were hit hard. More than 33,000 homes were foreclosed on between 2000 and 2008, when Baltimore became the first city to sue a lender under the 1968 Fair Housing Act. The city accused Wells Fargo of reverse redlining, which was forbidden by the courts. The suit alleged that two-thirds of Wells Fargo's foreclosures in Baltimore were in city census tracts that were more than 60 percent African American while only 15.6 percent were in census tracts that were less than 20 percent black.

As subprime mortgages spread throughout the country, they intensified segregation. But they also allowed a counter trend to occur: in some locales, old segregation patterns began to break down. One such community was Harlem, a huge chunk of undervalued prime real estate just a quick subway ride from the heart of Manhattan. Whites had not bought or rented in Harlem since the transition to an

African-American community was completed in the 1950s, but four decades later they rediscovered Harlem. Low prices trumped racial fears. When Manhattan's real estate prices inflated, some real estate brokers recommended Harlem as a lower-cost option. Whites moved to certain sections north of Central Park. Banks, increasingly comfortable with taking risks, saw no problem in financing loans that had been hard to obtain.

Some blacks saw the white infiltration as a threat. "HARLEM UNDER SIEGE," declared a headline in the local *New Amsterdam News*.

"In the past few years the 'Village of Harlem,' as older residents still call it, has become a 21st century laboratory for integration," the *New York Times* observed in 2008. "Class and money and race are at the center of the changes in the neighborhood. Lured by stately century-old brownstones and relatively modest rents, new faces are moving in and making older residents feel that they are being pushed out. There have been protests, and anger directed as much at the idea of the newcomers as at them personally."

Elsewhere throughout the country, subprime mortgages allowed black urban dwellers to move to suburbia. "Keep it real, the romance of the ghetto is gone for many," the *Sun Reporter* in San Francisco wrote about Oakland, California. So many blacks left that the once majority-black city across the bay became two-thirds white, Asian, Hispanic, or Pacific Islander. Blacks moved out because "they want a yard, a school with better teachers and facilities, and a chance to move up the economic ladder. As soon as we can, the black middle class moves to suburbia or exurbia, and integrates and assimilates into white communities," the newspaper wrote.

So many Oakland blacks headed for nearby Antioch that their share there shot up from less than 3 percent to 20 percent, while this Contra Coast County bedroom community's population, estimated at 73,386 in 1995, rose to 101,000 eight years later. Among the black transplants were more than 1,500 public-housing renters. With federal Section 8 vouchers covering two-thirds of the rent, one 42-year-old mother of five from Oakland found that she could rent a large new home, with a pool, for $2,200 a month, and that

Section 8 covered the rent. Tensions increased. Whites complained about cultural and lifestyle conflicts; blacks filed a class-action suit against the local police department, accusing it of "a deliberate policy of coercion, intimidation and threats." Antioch's foreclosure rate—23 of every 1,000 homeowners—was among the highest in California.

The old pattern of resegregation following desegregation characterized many changing suburbs. But much of the resegregation was what Myrdal called "voluntary withdrawal" by blacks. "It is impossible to draw the line between voluntary withdrawal and forced segregation, and the latter is practically always contributory to the former, indirectly if not directly. The effects—in terms of cultural isolation and lack of equality of opportunity—are the same," Myrdal wrote in 1944. Voluntary withdrawal occurred widely in social settings, school cafeterias, playgrounds, and churches. It was not limited to blacks; many other ethnic groups, including whites, also practiced voluntary withdrawal but without similar negative consequences.

By the time Obama took office, vacant homes defaced cities and suburbs. "FOR SALE" signs typically advertised properties that were bought at the height of the real estate bubble at prices that bore little relevance to their underlying value, and then were heavily mortgaged at a predatory rate. What made the situation unparalleled was a huge surplus of houses that existed in many areas of the country. During the Great Depression, Baltimore and many other cities had experienced practically no housing vacancies, meaning that foreclosed homes found ready renters and were not left vacant and boarded up. Now, as families continued to lose homes and future foreclosures loomed, thorny sociological questions emerged: What would happen to the human fabric of communities with high foreclosure rates, including assumptions about their racial makeup? Would the economic disaster intensify segregation or break it down?

Past financial crises had worsened prejudices. The serious economic troubles of the 1880s and 1890s produced populism and hostility toward blacks, Catholics, and Jews. Soon thereafter eugenics gave bigotry a respected academic gown and the endorsement of the federal government. Against that background, it was significant that while prejudices continued to exist, ideological racism was limited to a few on the lunatic fringe, unlike during the heyday of eugenics when it permeated all aspects of life.

The United States in the beginning of the Obama administration is a different country. It is at a momentous turning point. The GI generation is almost gone; the baby boomers are aging. The Millennial Generation will soon wield power. Born in the years from 1982 to 2003, the Millennials are the biggest and most racially diverse generation ever: 40 percent are of African American, mixed race, Latin American, or Asian origin, compared with 25 percent of the preceding two generations. They think and do things differently. Surveys show that they are big on volunteerism, but community has a different meaning for them. Living in a global village brought about by an instant-communications revolution, theirs is a generation united by shared concerns and ideas, not necessarily by race or where they live. They are the vanguard of a new America where, by 2040, whites will no longer be the majority population, a proposition that the Founding Fathers would have rejected as insane.

These epochal demographic changes will spawn unpredictable consequences for all aspects of human interaction. Neighborhood succession will continue, but new patterns will emerge. Over time, the country will morph beyond recognition. Obama truly is the face of the future.

Acknowledgments

WHEN ACTIVE RESEARCH for this book began in 2000, a crucial generation of post–World War II real estate brokers was passing away without anyone having recorded their stories. Theirs was the generation that transformed the racial character of American cities and included Baltimoreans James Crockett and Stanley Sugarman. They had been longtime sources for my work at the Baltimore *Sun*, and became good friends. In countless interviews and tours of neighborhoods, they shared their recollections and dug up old contracts, restrictive covenants, rent-control decisions, and other detritus from decades of selling American dreams and, sometimes, nightmares. They led me to real estate buddies. That's how this book began; it could not have been written without their help.

As the scope widened, I established a rule: although I was always looking for information, I never conducted a planned interview without first sending a letter that summarized the intended book. It asked a set of specific, individualized questions. That enabled me to gauge the person's involvement and memory of events during a follow-up telephone conversation. Some people begged out, others I screened out. Manuel Bernstein, the leading blockbuster of upscale white neighborhoods, received such a letter. When he failed to respond to it, I sent him another letter. His business associates assured me that he would never talk. One day my telephone rang at *The Sun*. It was Bernstein.

He lived mainly in Florida, but we met twice in an office that he kept in Pikesville. Both times he deflected questions by claiming they had nothing to do with real estate. He apologized for his hearing, which offered another excuse to avoid sensitive questions. Still, he talked. He had never granted an interview before. Two conditions: no recording devices, and "A book is fine but I don't want to read about this in the newspapers."

Melvin S. Sykes fought Bernstein during the Ashburton blockbusting days. A small, quiet man, he was pretty much unknown in the wider community. Among Jews he was honored as a *macher* to whom others deferred because of his intellectual brilliance, legal knowledge, and good judgment, and because he led an Orthodox life. He handled only appeals cases. We met in his kitchen on Martin Luther King, Jr.'s birthday in 2003. With my letter in front of him, underlined and full of scribbled notes, he wanted me to tell him specifically what I wanted. He returned from his basement with big files under his arms. "My father was a judge, and he told me never to throw away anything," he explained.

Sykes had trial transcripts and complaints about Manning-Shaw, critical material. Like Bernstein, he was selective. He scrutinized each document. He made two piles. One I could copy, but the other I could not even read because principals were still alive. One document that I sorely wanted was a seven-hundred-page Real Estate Commission hearing transcript. It was not there. But he did find a receipt for having photocopied it. Maybe there was more in Sykes's catacombs?

Literally hundreds of people helped me in the preparation of this book, which germinated during my thirty-five-year career at *The Sun*. If I must pinpoint a starting point, it may have been in 1979 when I wrote a series on Baltimore's African-American power brokers. William L. Adams refused requests for an interview, even though we had met and chatted at political meetings at his Club Casino on Pennsylvania Avenue. So I began interviewing old associates from his numbers days, assuming he would become so curious that he would have to see me. I knew I had gotten to Adams when Henry G. Parks, one of his partners, remarked: "I don't know why Willie wants me to talk to you because nothing good will come of this." Adams finally invited me to his home. In his living room he talked freely but often vaguely. The trick was to know so much about him that we could have a conversation instead of an interrogation.

Parks was right: four months after my series was published, Adams was indicted on ridiculously flimsy charges that linked him to a numbers operation through a nonsensical analysis of wiretaps. He was acquitted.

By the time I began working on the book, Adams was living in a long-term care facility for rich people in Roland Park. I last met him at City Hall around 2000. I introduced myself, but there was no recognition. Except that a few moments into our chat—he was organizing a parade of vintage cars on Pennsylvania Avenue—he fixed his steel-grey eyes on me and said: "So you are the fellow who likes to walk around the reservoir." There was nothing wrong with his memory that day.

The incident he referred to had occurred seventeen years earlier. In the summer of 1983 I was in Baltimore, headed for Moscow after completing an assignment in South Africa. One morning before leaving for another week of Russian studies in Washington, I was walking my future wife's black poodle around Lake Ashburton. When I spotted Adams ahead of me, I started walking faster. He was deep in his thoughts. Eventually he heard my footsteps, and turned, with nothing but fright in his eyes. No white guy appeared in his neighborhood at 6 A.M. without a mission. Had the grim reaper finally arrived in the guise of a dog walker? "Good morning, Mr. Adams," I said, explaining who I was. "Have a nice day." Then I almost ran away, sensing that I had intruded.

Countless others helped me. Ed Kane, dying of cancer, recorded hours of recollections about Baltimore before and after World War II. He had been the Baltimore Gas and Electric Company's troubleshooter in neighborhood relations. Wearing that hat, he was involved in the business community's campaign against NECO, the Alinsky-type umbrella group.

Milton Bates, an erstwhile organizer for Henry A. Wallace's Progressive party, shared his memories about politics and growing up in Easterwood Park. We met every Saturday for several years. His was an American story from the early 1950s that was revealed only to close friends: having finished law school, he passed the bar examination but flunked the character review board because of his political views. With the law career blocked, he became a home-improvement contractor. One day in 2005 he suggested that I meet a friend of his. The friend was Sidney Weinberg, who for decades had been the accountant for burlesque and gambling figures on The Block, Baltimore's red-light district. He helped me with connections among people and told me amusing tales, including how the comedian Lenny Bruce was bought out because his language was too raunchy for Baltimore. In the meantime, love was in the air: Bruce fell in love with a girl from a whorehouse across the street from the gambling joint where Weinberg did the books. Another story involved a lawyer representing nightclubs who prepared income tax returns for strippers in exchange for sex. He was later elected city comptroller, the No. 3 job in the municipal government. I knew the man. He was an oddball.

Stanley Sugarman, for his part, brought me together with William Grigsby, emeritus professor of economics at the University of Pennsylvania, who took a deep interest in what I was doing. Sugarman thought the world of Grigsby, who had studied Baltimore in the 1970s for his important scholarly work on housing markets and on the dynamics of change in neighborhoods, and had actually sought out landlords to talk to. We finally met in 2007 at the funeral of Sugarman's wife and talked about the book at lunch. Grigsby read every word in various versions, critiquing chapters and challenging assumptions. I cherish his long letters, some written in longhand.

I would like to thank James (whose last name I have forgotten). We were at an Inner Harbor health club chatting about this and that. When he heard about my book project, he gave me the telephone number of Thomas Cripps, a retired Morgan State University history professor and a leading expert on African-American films. Cripps helped with the structure of the book and historical accuracy—and, of course, took me on tours of Goose Hill, where he grew up.

Hal Riedl I met while he was working as a case evaluator at Baltimore's central lockup and I was writing editorials about the collapsing criminal justice system. He read several versions, raising the right questions about facts and their interpretation. He is still with the prison system; in another life he deserves to be an editor.

Howell Baum, James H. Bready, Stephens Broening, Joan Jacobson, Mark Reutter, Robert Ruby, Scott Shane, and C. Fraser Smith read the manuscript at various stages. Each made suggestions that led to many improvements in the evolving concept and execution of the book. My thanks to Joe Mathews. I benefited greatly from several 6 A.M. meetings with Judge Kenneth L. Johnson, a onetime lawyer for Activists, Inc. Summer, spring, or fall we sat for a couple of hours on his outside porch in Roland Park. He shared his knowledge about Morris Goldseker and secured rare documents, including court transcripts from the National Archives in Philadelphia.

My debt to generations of librarians is immense. Those assisting me at *The Sun* early on in my career included Dee Lyon and Esther Blake, who regaled me with stories about black Baltimore. Of later librarians, Paul McCardell and Jean Packard were particularly eager to help. I owe them big time.

At the Jewish Museum of Maryland, archivist Erin Titter was resourceful. I had come looking for the minutes of the Baltimore Jewish Council. Instead she found the largely unsorted archives that Leon Sachs had kept. Without them this book might have never become compelling enough to write. The importance of that collection is heightened by the fact that I never was able to locate the meeting minutes.

At the University of Baltimore a big *dziekuje* (thank-you) goes to the head of special collections, Thomas Hollowak, who in free time safeguards Baltimore's Polish heritage. The National Archives, Sheridan libraries at Johns Hopkins, the University of Maryland, Towson University, and Howard University also treated me right.

Decades ago the Maryland Historical Society conducted a wide-ranging oral documentation project that focused on civil rights, particularly on the contributions of Theodore R. McKeldin and Lillie May Jackson. Unfortunately much of that important material has been lost because the tapes are so fragile that scholars are not allowed to hear them, and their contents have not been transferred. Only relatively few written transcripts exist; most tapes are only summarized.

A word about local governmental archives. Incredibly, Baltimore County has not saved the records of any of its county executives. Some of Spiro T. Agnew's papers from his county tenure, including all press releases, are in a vice-presidential collection at the University of Maryland. By comparison, Baltimore City Archives keeps separate files for each mayor in a vast collection that covers all municipal agencies and multitudes of subjects from the early days of the city. The scandal is that when that official depository of records, including films, recently moved, its new home again lacked climate control.

The Enoch Pratt Free Library, where Jeff Korman was invaluable, faces a related problem. Among the library's holdings are vertical files, alphabetized by many subjects, including housing, race, commerce, religion, and education. Oversized envelopes contain not only newspaper clippings but also reports, plans, press releases, and evaluations, and have provided grist for many books and dissertations. Those files, dangerously brittle, are Baltimore's collective scrapbook. They are an invaluable resource, sometimes containing material from the late 1890s onward. Their scanning must be priority No. 1.

The Enoch Pratt director Carla Hayden has returned the badly neglected public library system to respectability. Despite constant budget woes, new books have been acquired, gaps in old collections plugged. The library has even opened new branches for the first time in more than three decades. The library offers patrons free access to ProQuest, a commercial company that sells searchable newspaper archives that in the cases of the *New York Times*, the *Washington Post*, and the *Wall Street Journal* go back to their first issues. After the manuscript was nearly completed, the *Afro-American* became available on ProQuest. *The Sun*, by contrast, is only partially available, and Mencken's paper, *The Evening Sun*, not at all. There is even a fifteen-year gap in the paper's own morgue. During that time before the computerization of the library in the 1980s, stories were clipped but never filed. It was justified as a cost-cutting measure.

The internet was vital. Such was its head-spinning evolution that I ended up repeating key searches several times because so much new material was being added. During one such repeat search I found the obituary of Warren S. Shaw on the website of his Oberlin high school. This led to Laura Smith, his sister, who knew little about him but had the scrapbook that her mother had kept. She even had the guest book used at his funeral.

Over decades, many people helped me understand Baltimore or otherwise contributed to the book. They included Cornelius Behan, Troy Brailey, Walter Carr, Sr., George Collins, Herbert Davis, James Dilts, Jo and Gil Fisher, Larry Gibson, Hirsh Goldberg, Neil Grauer, Sampson Green, Homer Favor, Daniel P. Henson III, Eric Holcomb, P. David Hutchinson, and Tom Horton. Also Steven Israel, Ron Kreitner, A. Robert Kaufman, Gregory L. Lewis, John McGrain, Joe Mathews, John Michener, Martin Millspaugh, Dr. Keiffer Mitchell, Michael Bowen Mitchell, Ralph Moore, Kalevi A. Olkio, Walter S. Orlinsky, W. Edward Orser, Dick Parsons, Ron and Pat Pilling, Garrett Power, Vinnie Quayle, Fran and Debby Rahl, Albert Reichelt, Gene Raynor, Dan Rosen, Barbara Samuels, Gilbert Sandler, Eric Siegel, Mark Sissman, Malcolm Sherman, Fred Shoken, Walter Sondheim, Rochelle Rikki Spector, Larry Stappler, Robert Steinberg, Bill Struever, Richard Swirnow, Thomas Toporovich, and Rabbi Samuel Vitsick. Thanks also to H-Urban, a bulletin board for scholars, who were generous with their counsel. A special thank-you to Robert Cronan for his intelligent maps, and to Clayton Elerbe, who kept my computer from crashing.

I thank Ivan Dee, a rare trade publisher who reads unsolicited manuscripts by unknown authors. He is a national treasure. As they say in Finland, *tuhannet kiitokset*, a thousand thanks, because a hundred is not enough.

A. P.

Baltimore
November 2009

Notes

ABBREVIATIONS USED IN THE NOTES:

BCA = Baltimore City Archives
EPFL = Enoch Pratt Free Library
JMM = Jewish Museum of Maryland
MHS = Maryland Historical Society
NA = National Archives
UB/Langsdale = University of Baltimore special collections
UMCP = University of Maryland, College Park
VF = vertical files

Chapter 1. 1910

page
5 Shipwreck: *The Sun*, June 8, 1910.
5 Three days in lifeboats: June 9, 1910.
6 Hawkins's real estate deal: Deed SCL 2587/275, Baltimore City courthouse.
6 Arrests in Baltimore: *Washington Post*, July 5, 1910.
7 Intensifying segregation: William B. Gatewood, Jr., "Black Americans and the Quest for Empire, 1898–1903," *Journal of Southern History*, vol. 38, no. 4 (November 1972), 553.
7 Popular culture spread: Richard Wormser, *The Rise and Fall of Jim Crow* (New York: St. Martin's, 2003), 103.
7 Novelty film: Thomas Cripps, *Slow Fade to Black: The Negro in American Film, 1900–1942* (New York: Oxford University Press, 1993), 9–12.
7 Tillman quotation: Edmund Morris, *Theodore Rex* (New York: Random House, 2001), 55.
7–8 Lynching data: Archives of Tuskegee Institute, www.law.umkc.edu/faculty/projects/ftrials/shipp/lynchingyear.html.

8 Overall position of blacks: Rayford W. Logan, *The Negro in American Life and Thought: The Nadir, 1877–1901* (New York: Dial Press, 1954), 52.

8 The low point of nadir: James W. Loewen, *Sundown Towns: A Hidden Dimension of American Racism* (New York: Touchstone, 2006), 24–116.

8 McMechen's move: A myth insists that nearby McMechen Street was named after him, a claim that is preposterous. Even so, the *Maryland Historical Magazine* (vol. 84, Summer 1989, p. 139) accepted it. The street was so named long before McMechen moved permanently to Baltimore in 1904.

8 McMechen quotation: *New York Times*, Dec. 25, 1910.

8 Juvenile court: *The Sun*, July 6, 1910.

8 Whites threw stones: *The Sun*, Sept. 9, 1910.

8 Early housing: Mary Ellen Hayward, "Baltimore's Alley Houses: Homes for Working People Since the 1780s," in *From Mobtown to Charm City* (Baltimore: Maryland Historical Society, 2002), 38. Also, Ralph Clayton, *Black Baltimore, 1820–1870* (Bowie, Md.: Heritage Books, 1987), 3.

9–10 Borders shifting: Christopher Phillips: *Freedom's Port: The African American Community of Baltimore, 1790–1860* (Urbana: University of Illinois Press, 1997), 104–105.

9 Ethnic churn: This kind of ethnic rotation was typical of American cities. Louis Wirth documented it in *The Ghetto* (Chicago: University of Chicago Press, 1928), 226–228.

9 Population explosion: James B. Crooks, *Politics and Progress: The Rise of Urban Progressivism in Baltimore, 1895 to 1911* (Baton Rouge: Louisiana State University Press, 1968), 8.

9 Sanitation crisis: Alan D. Anderson, *The Origin and Resolution of an Urban Crisis: Baltimore, 1890–1930* (Baltimore: Johns Hopkins University Press, 1977), 69. Charles C. Euchner, "The Politics of Urban Expansion: Baltimore and the Sewerage Question, 1859–1905," *Maryland Historical Magazine*, vol. 86, no. 3 (Fall 1991), 282.

10 The Great Fire: Sherry H. Olson, *Baltimore: The Building of an American City* (Baltimore: Johns Hopkins University Press, 1980), 218.

10 Population redistribution: *The Sun*, July 6, July 13, Sept. 13, and Oct. 8, 1910.

10 Shepherded flock: It was phased out during World War II.

10 Eutaw Place history: http://boltonhill.org/neighborhood/n_history.htm.

11 Jewish migration: Isidor Blum, *The Jews of Baltimore* (Baltimore-Washington: Historical Review Publishing, 1910). See also Earl Pruce, *Synagogues, Temples and Congregations of Maryland, 1830–1990* (Baltimore: Jewish Historical Society of Maryland, 1993), 68.

12 Confederate nostalgics: William L. Marbury (Jr.), *The Story of a Maryland Family* (Baltimore: privately printed, 1967), 36.

12 African-American migration: *New York Times*, Nov. 24, 1903. See also Cynthia Neverdon-Morton, "Black Housing Patterns in Baltimore City, 1885–1954," *Maryland Historian*, Spring/Summer, 1985, and Janet E. Kemp, *Housing Conditions in Baltimore* (Baltimore: Federated Charities, 1907), 16.

12 Racial elasticity: *Afro-American Ledger*, Sept. 4, 1909.

12 Real estate vacuum: The coup de grace came in 1919 when a nine-alarm fire destroyed the main buildings of the old campus.

14 Booker T. Washington: "Law and Order and the Negro," *Outlook*, Nov. 6, 1909; *Afro-American Ledger*, Jan. 14, 1911.

14 The blacks' deteriorating position: William George Paul, "The Shadow of Equality: The Negro in Baltimore, 1864–1911," unpublished Ph.D. dissertation, University of Wisconsin, 1972.

14 Department store discrimination: *Afro-American Ledger*, Apr. 16, 1910.

14 Segregated music: Kenneth S. Clark, *Baltimore: Cradle of Municipal Music* (Baltimore: City of Baltimore, 1941), 33. The colored band existed until 1964 and was forbidden to play jazz or other syncopated music. *Afro-American*, May 16, 1941, listed the program of the symphony orchestra's opening concert as including works by Schubert, Beethoven, and Verdi. A comprehensive overview of segregated municipal music is in the same paper, Apr. 22, 1933. See also F. Corine Anderson Free, "The Baltimore City Colored Orchestra and the City Colored Chorus," unpublished Ph.D. dissertation, University of Alabama, 1994.

15 Synagogue construction: Pruce, *Synagogues,* 54–59.

15 The letterhead: BJC file 1585A, JMM.

15 Jewish residents: The 1909 *Jewish Social Directory* included eight families living in the 1800 block of McCulloh Street and many more on adjoining blocks. See also *Afro-American Ledger*, Oct. 1, 1910.

15 White abandonment: See *The Evening Sun*, Oct. 27, 1909, and July 6, 1910.

15 Dual real estate market: See Karl and Alma Taeuber, *Negroes in Cities* (Chicago: Aldine, 1965), 28–37. See also Harvey Luskin Molotch, *Managed Integration: Dilemmas of Doing Good in the City* (Berkeley: University of California Press, 1972), 15–19.

16 Transportation: *The Evening Sun*, Aug. 24, 1910.

16 Absence of white demand: *The Sun*, Sept. 22, 1910.

16 No ordinary man: He is not to be confused with the unrelated Mason A. Hawkins, who also was active in the Niagara movement. Mason Hawkins was the principal of the Colored (Douglass) High School and a professor at Morgan College.

16 NAACP: See Mary White Ovington, *History of the* NAACP, originally written in 1914. www.si.umich.edu/CHICO/Harlem/timex/history.html.

16 NAACP Legal department: Susan D. Carle, "From *Buchanan* to *Button*: Legal Ethics in the Early History of the NAACP, 1910–1920," *Advocate*, Spring 2001, 12–26. See also Garrett Power, "Apartheid Baltimore Style: The Residential Segregation Ordinances of 1910–13," *Maryland Law Review* 42 (1983), 289, 305.

16 Garvey zealots: Marcus Garvey, *Philosophy and Opinions of Marcus Garvey* (New York: Atheneum, 1992), 293–300.

16 Margaret Franklin Brewer: No person by that name or any combination appears in city directories, telephone books, or the 1900 or 1910 Censuses. It is conceivable, as genealogist Sandra Napier thinks, that she is the "M. R.

Brewer," at the time forty-one, whom the 1900 Census lists, with a seventeen-year-old daughter, as sharing a mansion at 1400 McCulloh Street with her elderly gun manufacturer parents, three unmarried adult sisters, and an adult brother, all born in Virginia. In that case, 1834 McCulloh would have been an investment property, which seems likely in the absence of city directory listings for her at that address. If she indeed was the seller, the plot thickens. M. R. Brewer's brother, B. Howard Richards, was a real estate broker, who in 1914 reorganized the dormant local real estate board.

17 Black home ownership: Cited by Garrett Power in "Apartheid Baltimore Style," 308. Power provides a comprehensive account of Baltimore's residential segregation ordinances. He mistakenly states that it was McMechen who bought 1834 McCulloh Street, when it was in fact Hawkins. The grantor index for 1910 recorded Hawkins as having bought several houses in racially changing areas.

17 Demarcation line: *New York Times*, Dec. 25, 1910.

17 Early renters: *The Sun*, Sept. 9, 1910.

18 Female teachers: *Afro-American Ledger*, Oct. 10, 1910.

18 What Hawkins paid: *The Sun*, Sept. 22, 1910.

18 Mortgage: "W. Ashbie Hawkins Mtg. to Ridgely Bldg. Asso.," Grantor index SCL 2587/276, Baltimore City courthouse.

18 Price slide: *Afro-American Ledger*, Oct. 1, 1910.

18 Sidewalk confrontation: *The Sun*, Sept. 8, 1910.

19 Hammen's campaign: *The Sun*, Sept. 14, 1910.

19 Marbury's ownership of land: Deed JB 1002/151, Baltimore City courthouse.

19 Hawkins on Marbury: W. Ashbie Hawkins, "A Year of Segregation in Baltimore," *Crisis*, Nov. 1911.

19 First segregation draft: *The Sun*, Dec. 20, 1910.

20 Benefits of segregation: *The Sun*, Sept. 27, 1910.

20 Apparent provocations: *The Sun*, Sept. 26, 1910.

20 Bogus letter: *The Sun*, Oct. 11, 1910.

20 Editor's response: *The Sun*, Oct. 13, 1910.

21 Origins of agitation: *The Sun*, Oct. 27, 1909.

21 Locust Point curfew: Interview with Rochelle Rikki Spector, whose parents operated a grocery store in Locust Point, Jan. 23, 2002. Her family moved out of Locust Point one day after they saw her walking back from grade school hand-in-hand with a Catholic boy.

21 Irish longshoremen: *The Sun*, Oct. 8, 1910.

Chapter 2. Good Government

22 The bill's adoption: Edgar Allan Poe to Mayor J. Barry Mahool, Dec. 17, 1910, Mahool file 451, BCA. Poe later became Maryland's attorney general. He and his five brothers are remembered at Princeton University, their alma mater, for their football feats against Yale. See *Princeton Weekly Bulletin*, Oct. 13, 2003.

22 Lincoln and segregation: The fourth Lincoln-Douglas debate, Sept. 18, 1858.

23 Northern cities: Stephen Grant Meyer, *As Long as They Don't Move Next Door: Segregation and Racial Conflict in American Neighborhoods* (Lanham, Md.: Rowman & Littlefield, 2000), 14.

23 Expulsion of blacks: Many such towns remained all white until the 1980s. See Loewen, *Sundown Towns*. See also Elliott Jaspin, *Buried in the Bitter Waters: The Hidden History of Racial Cleansing in America* (New York: Basic Books, 2007).

23 Baltimore's distinction: *New York Times*, Dec. 25, 1910.

23–24 Letter from the Philippines: Mayor Barry Mahool to Charles Woodruff, Mar. 26, 1916, Preston file 21D, BCA.

24 Prevented from moving: *The Sun*, Feb. 5, 1911.

24 Colored Methodist preachers: Daniel P. Shaw to Mahool, Jan. 16, 1911, Mahool file 406, BCA.

24 Councilman's reply: Dashiell to Shaw, Jan. 17, 1911, Mahool file 406, BCA.

24 Hopelessly unclear: *The Evening Sun*, Feb. 4, 1911.

24 A pastor wrote: *Afro-American Ledger*, Dec. 24, 1910.

25 Blacks dominated: Clayton, *Black Baltimore*, 4, 5.

25 Proposed reenslavement: Speech of Colonel Curtis M. [sic] Jacobs, Feb. 17, 1860, 8, Maryland Hall of Records. See also Willa Banks, "Curtis Washington Jacobs: Architect of Absolute Black Enslavement, 1850–1864," *Maryland Historical Magazine*, vol. 104, no. 2 (Summer 2009).

25 Free-Negroism speech: Jacobs speech, 10.

26 Occupied Baltimore: T. Courtenay J. Whedbee, *The Port of Baltimore in the Making; 1828 to 1878* (Baltimore; F. Bowie Smith & Sons, 1953), 71–82.

26 Mobtown: *Baltimore American*, Nov. 5, 1895.

26 Gunshots into alleys: See Crooks, *Politics and Progress*, 41; *American* and *The Sun*, Nov. 6, 1895.

26 Breaking his jaw: Frank R. Kent, *The Great Game of Politics* (Garden City, N.Y.: Doubleday, 1930), 205.

27 Blaming blacks: Margaret Law Callcott, *The Negro in Maryland, 1870–1912* (Baltimore: Johns Hopkins University Press, 1969), 82–91.

27 Campaign slogan: *The Sun*, Apr. 23, 1899.

27 Appeal to voters: Cited in *New York Times*, Oct. 27, 1901.

27 George Wellington Bryant: *Washington Post*, Mar. 11, 1894.

27 Bryant sentenced: Callcott, *Negro in Maryland*, 94–95.

27 Cash box: *Chicago Daily Tribune*, Mar. 9, and *New York Times*, Mar. 10, 1897.

28 Prey to demagogues: Callcott, *Negro in Maryland*, 162. Blacks accounted for a quarter of all registered voters in Maryland and tended to vote as a bloc for the party of Abraham Lincoln. (In 1910, 18,307 illiterate whites also were registered, or 8 percent of all white registrants. They voted mostly for Democrats.)

28 Edwin Warfield: *The Sun*, Oct. 22, 1903.

28 Election platform: Its author was Edgar Allan Poe's father, John Prentiss Poe, who was dean of the University of Maryland law school.

28 White control: *The Sun*, Sept. 17, 1903.

28 Obsession: Callcott, *Negro in Maryland*, 101.

28 Referendum language: Cited in Callcott, *Negro in Maryland*, 127.

29 Republican concerns: Crooks, *Politics and Progress*, 61–83.

29 Printed leaflet: P. S. Henry, "A Poem on Segregation," June 25, 1913, Preston file 21-D, BCA.

30 Population figures: Among other minorities were 306 Chinese and eight Japanese, who were regarded as white.

30 Lafayette Square: *Washington Post*, Sept. 26, 1913.

30 Wholesale murder: C. E. Stonebraker to Preston, May 12, 1913, Preston file 21-D, BCA.

30 Expressed sympathy: Preston to Thomas S. Jenkins, Aug. 21, 1913, Preston file 21-D, BCA.

31 White students: *Chicago Tribune*, Sept. 15, 1890. One of the graduates, Harry Sythe Cummings, won election that year as the City Council's first African-American member ever.

31 Students' threat: *American*, Sept. 16, 1894; *New York Times*, Sept. 15, 1890.

Chapter 3. Race Science

32 Dinner guests' song: *The Sun*, Feb. 4, 1910.

33 Progressives and blacks: Crooks, *Politics and Progress*, 211.

33 Shrinking tolerance: John Higham, *Strangers in the Land: Patterns of American Nativism 1860–1925* (New York: Atheneum, 1963).

33 Kansas City: Roy Lubove, *The Urban Community: Housing and Planning in the Progressive Era* (Englewood Cliffs, N.J.: Prentice-Hall, 1967), 43.

34 Veiller quotation: Lubov, *Urban Community*, 58.

34 Housing types: James F. Waesche, *A History of the Roland Park–Guilford–Homeland District* (Baltimore: Maclay & Associates, 1987), 33–60.

34 Roland Park as a siphon: Ibid., 67.

34 Churches: Elizabeth Fee, Linda Shopes, and Linda Zeidman, eds., *The Baltimore Book* (Philadelphia: Temple University Press, 1991), 33.

35 Kansas City philosophy: Lubove, *Urban Community*, 47.

35 Removal of blacks: Jim Holechek, *Two Cross Keys Villages: One Black, One White . . . and the Leaders Who Created the World Around Them* (New York: iUniverse, 2003), 7. They were evicted to the nearby village of Cross Keys. Many found work as cooks, butlers, domestics, and gardeners in the houses of Roland Park's prosperous whites. See *The Evening Sun*, Mar. 8, 1934. In the early 1960s a planned community of residences and retail stores was built along Falls Road, near where the old Cross Keys had existed. Two high schools, Poly and Western, also were built on portions of the land.

35 Deed restriction: Schmucker & Whitelock opinion to Bouton, Oct. 5, 1893, Roland Park Company papers #2828, Box 2–5, Cornell University.

36 Firmer legal footing: *The Sun*, Sept. 9, Sept. 22, 1910.

36 Charles T. Levine: *The Sun*, Jan. 6, 1911.

36 David Bachrach: *New York Times*, July 26, 1963.

36 Julius Levy: Philip Kahn, Jr., *A Stitch in Time: The Four Seasons of Baltimore's Needle Trades* (Baltimore: Maryland Historical Society, 1989), 149. Sherry Olson, in *Baltimore: The Building of an American City* (Baltimore: Johns Hopkins University Press, 2000), claims that neighbors expressed their un-happiness by making sure that the Levys did not get milk, bread, and news-papers delivered to their home. This claim, repeated by several other authors, likely is a canard. For one thing, Olson places the Levys in Guilford, where they never lived.

36 Bouton and Jews: Cited in Susan L. Klaus, *A Modern Arcadia: Frederick Law Olmsted Jr. and the Plan for Forest Hills* (Amherst: University of Massachu-setts Press, 2002), 116.

36 Sales ban: Garrett Power, "The Residential Segregation of Baltimore Jews: Restrictive Covenants or Gentlemen's Agreement," *Generations*, Fall 1996, 5–7.

36 Rival communities: See Chapter 9.

36 Bouton's position: Robert M. Fogelson, *Bourgeois Nightmares: Suburbia, 1870–1930* (New Haven: Yale University Press, 2005), 137.

37 Ancient kings: http://www.familyofbruce.org/biopage.htm#US.

37 Growing up: William Cabell Bruce, *Recollections* (Baltimore: King Brothers, 1936), 58.

37 Black Republicans: William Cabell Bruce, *The Negro Problem* (Baltimore: John Murphy, 1891), 26.

37–38 View of progressivism: Nelson D. Lankford, *The Last American Aristo-crat: The Biography of David K. E. Bruce, 1898-1977* (Boston: Little, Brown, 1996), 12.

38 Grasty's early years: J.[acques] K[elly], "Grasty Buries Machine Politics," *News American*, Mar. 18, 1973.

38 Grasty and white supremacy: *The Sun*, Sept. 23, 1913.

38 Anti-Semitism: See Chapters 9 and 12. *The Sun*'s relationship with the Cath-olic hierarchy was also sometimes rocky. In 1934, Archbishop Michael J. Curley had a ban read from pulpits forbidding Catholics to read the paper after a story drew parallels between the zealotry of Ignatius Loyola and Adolf Hitler.

39 Democrats' numbers racket: The actual game volume may have been much higher because of the difficulty of establishing accurate dollar equivalents over such a long period of time. John D. Lawson, *American State Trials*, vol. V (St. Louis: F. H. Thomas Law Book, 1916), 216–329, reprints much of the trial transcript.

39 Numbers trial: *News American*, Mar. 18, 1973.

39 Marbury's house: A picture of the elder Marbury in all his glory appears in Marbury, *Story of a Maryland Family*, 98. A minimum of five servants was a standard for a family of Marbury's means living in a big house, "but families of modest means supported at least one servant," according to Francis E. Beirne, *The Amiable Baltimoreans* (New York: E. P. Dutton, 1951), 272.

39 Genealogy: *The Sun*, Oct. 28, 1935.

40 Marbury slaves: Prince George's County Freedom Records, Maryland State Archives.

40 Pray for heroes: *Baltimore News*, Jan. 19, 1923.

40 Town's name changed: It is today known as Clinton.

40 Inferior race: *Baltimore News*, Jan. 6, 1910.

41 Fifteenth Amendment: Maryland finally ratified it in 1973.

41 Pure happiness: William L. Marbury (Jr.), *In the Catbird's Seat* (Baltimore: Maryland Historical Society, 1988), 21.

41 Mayoral run: *Baltimore News*, June 8, 1910.

42 de Gobineau: Marbury, *Catbird's Seat,* 51, 321.

43 Germans: Charles Benedict Davenport, *Heredity in Relation to Eugenics* (New York: Henry Holt, 1911), 212.

43 Irish: Ibid., 214.

43 Italians: Ibid., 218.

43 Jews: Ibid., 216.

44 Movement patrons: H. T. Webber in Lucy James Wilson, ed., *Eugenics: Twelve University Lectures* (New York: Dodd, Mead, 1914), 139.

44 Eugenics Record Office: C. B. Davenport in *Eugenics,* 2–3.

44 Baltimore eagerly: Ibid., 3.

44 Eugenics at Johns Hopkins: Robert A. Steinberg, "Hopkins Men of Science and the American Eugenics Movement," undated and unpublished Master of Liberal Arts thesis, Johns Hopkins University Department of the History of Science, Medicine, and Technology, 1–64.

45 Vivid imagery: Wormser, *Jim Crow,* 121.

45 Roosevelt warning: Cited in David R. Roediger, *How Race Survived U.S. History from Settlement and Slavery to the Obama Phenomenon* (London: Verso, 2008), xviii.

45 Wilson warning: Address in Pueblo, Colo., Sept. 25, 1919.

Chapter 4. Segregation by Collusion

47 Urban black population: Tom C. Clark and Philip B. Perlman, *Prejudice and Property: An Historic Brief Against Racial Covenants* (Washington, D.C.: Public Affairs Press, 1948), 13.

47 Covenant: SCL 47/3750, Baltimore City courthouse.

48 Morgan Park: Roland C. McConnell, *The History of Morgan Park: A Baltimore Neighborhood, 1917–1999* (Baltimore: Morgan Park Improvement Association, 2000), 49. A persistent white buyer broke those covenants in 1967, nineteen years after the Supreme Court had declared them unenforceable.

48 Earliest covenants: *Gandolfo v. Hartman*, 49 Fed. 181 (C.C.S.D., Calif., 1892), LEXIS. See also Tim Wu, "Treaties' Domains," University of Chicago Law School working paper No. 82 (March 2005), 41–48, and Charles Abrams, *Forbidden Neighbors* (New York: Harper & Bros., 1955), 217. The court verdict, ironically, came at the height of anti-Chinese pogroms in California, the same year that Congress passed, and the president signed, a law halting further large-scale immigration from China.

48 Covenants and courts: *Meade v. Dennistone*, 173 Md. 295, 196A. 330. 1938 Md., LEXIS.

49 Chicago: St. Clair Drake and Horace R. Clayton, *Black Metropolis: A Study of Negro Life in a Northern City* (New York: Harcourt, Brace, 1945), 178–179.

49 Real estate boards: Cited in Rose Helper, *Racial Policies and Practices of Real Estate Brokers* (Minneapolis: University of Minnesota Press, 1969), 221.

50 Thirty-two states: Wendy Plotkin, "Deeds of Mistrust: Race, Housing, and Restrictive Covenants in Chicago, 1900–1950," www.wendy.plotkin@asu.edu.

50 Preston was the first: He wrote about the project in the *Baltimore Municipal Journal*, Mar. 16, 1917.

50 Disputed election: *New York Times*, Nov. 11, 1911. A grand jury was convened to investigate the contested Democratic primary, but it could do nothing because Preston's machine had combined the contents of various ballot boxes into huge sacks, rendering a recount impossible. A close general election was equally murky.

50 St. Paul Street: *The Sun*, Sept. 16, 1911, and Nov. 11, 1928.

51 Gallows Hill: It was located on the west side of St. Paul Street, according to *The Sun*, Nov. 11, 1923.

51 St. Francis Xavier: *Afro-American*, Nov. 25, 1911.

51 Hugh Jennings: *The Sun*, Dec. 12, 1930.

51 Demolition: St. Francis Xavier won a reprieve until 1933, when it was razed to become a parking lot. In 2007 the last Italianate rowhouses on St. Paul Street were razed for the expansion of Mercy Hospital. There were faint protests because hardly anyone knew anything about the neighborhood's history.

52 Mark Twain: *The Sun*, July 11, 1937; *Afro-American*, July 17, 1937.

52 Demolition timetable: Mayor Preston, writing in *The Sun*, Jan. 20, 1923.

52 Preston characterization: *Baltimore News Post*, July 15, 1938.

52 Mortality rate: *Baltimore Municipal Journal*, Mar. 16, 1917.

52 Preston ordinance: *The Sun*, July 2, 1918.

52 Chicago plan: Real Estate Board to Preston, July 20, 1918, Preston file 106, BCA.

53 Buckner reply: Real Estate Board to Preston, Aug. 16, 1918, Preston file 106, BCA.

53 Buckner house: C. Philip Pitt to Preston, Aug. 15, 1918, Preston file 106, BCA.

53 Buckner pledge: Power, "Apartheid," 315.

53 Standard contract: A copy of the Real Estate Board's standard sales contract may be found in BJC 333, JMM.

53 Early zoning: David M. P. Freund, *Colored Property: State Policy and White Racial Politics in Suburban America* (Chicago: University of Chicago Press, 2007), 46.

53 Heuisler advice: *The Sun*, Dec. 29, 1923, *Washington Post*, Jan. 14, 1928.

54 Pitt solution: *Afro-American*, Jan. 24, 1924.

54 Pitt comment: *The Sun*, Jan. 6, 1924.

54 Jackson solution: *The Sun*, Jan. 17, 1924.

54 Joint Committee: Plaintiff's exhibit No. 89, MJG 95-309, U.S. District Court for Maryland.

54 Population data: "Study of the Recreational, Social and Cultural Resources of the Jewish Community of Baltimore," mimeographed document issued in New York by the Jewish Welfare Board, 1925, 23–24, JMM.

56 McCulloh Street: Ibid., 23.

57 Sugar Hill: The family of future Supreme Court justice Thurgood Marshall lived there briefly.

57 Five suburban developments: They were Cherry Heights, Kelly Avenue, Bare Hills, Morgan Park, and Wilson Park.

57 Equal to Roland Park: *Afro-American Ledger*, Apr. 22, 1910. The irrepressible W. Ashbie Hawkins and George McMechen were general counsels of the development company.

57 Streets dead-ended: James Crockett interview, Dec. 13, 2002. See also Chapter 15.

57 Carnegie in Scotland: Andrew Carnegie, *The Negro in America: An Address Delivered Before the Philadelphia Institute of Edinburgh, Oct. 10, 1907* (Cheyney, Pa.: Committee of Twelve, undated), 13.

58 Mount Washington opposition: *Baltimore News*, Sept. 25, 1913.

58 Preston opposition: *The Sun*, Sept. 25, 26, 28, 1913.

58 Neighbors' views: *Baltimore News*, Sept. 26, 1913.

59 Northeast Baltimore site: McConnell, *Morgan Park*, 6. See also *The Sun*, May 5, 1917, and *Jeffersonian*, May 12, 1917.

59 Morgan charter: McConnell, *Morgan Park*, 76.

59 Final attempt: Ibid., 1–9.

60 Wilson Park: Karen Lewand, *North Baltimore: From Estate to Development* (Baltimore: City Department of Planning and the University of Baltimore, 1989), 45.

60 *The Evening Sun*, July 30, 1943.

Chapter 5. Mapping Bigotry

61 HOLC mapping: All information about residential security maps is based on documents, questionnaires, and appraisals in the HOLC City Survey Files (Record Group 195) in the National Archives at Adelphi, Md.

62 The list: Homer Hoyt, *One Hundred Years of Land Values in Chicago* (Chicago: University of Chicago Press, 1933), 314–316. Hoyt was among the founders of the Urban Land Institute, an independent organization originally created by the National Association of Real Estate Boards.

63 Eugenics influence: Steven Selden, *Inheriting Shame: The Story of Eugenics and Racism in America* (New York: Teachers College Press, 1999), 69.

64 HOLC instructions: Early British eugenicists had argued that the Church of England represented the highest form of Christianity. This gave a hallowed status to its Episcopal branch in the United States, followed by other Protes-

tant denominations. All other religions were seen as inferior, a value judgment accepted by HOLC mapmakers.

64 Lenders and race: Amy E. Hillier, "Spatial Analysis of Historical Redlining: A Methodological Exploration," *Journal of Housing Research*, vol. 14, no. 1 (2003), 144.

64 Thirty-seven lenders: Amy E. Hillier, "Redlining and the Home Owners' Loan Corporation," *Journal of Urban History*, vol. 29, no. 4 (2003), 400.

64 Philadelphia map: http//cml.upenn.edu/redlining.

65 HOLC office: *The Sun*, July 25, 26, 1933.

65 Verge of insanity: Olson, *Baltimore*, 333–334.

65 Hammond suicide: *Baltimore News*, Dec. 18, 1933.

66 Need for secrecy: *Waverly: A Study in Neighborhood Conservation* (Washington, D.C.: Federal Home Loan Bank Board, 1940), 7.

66 Baltimore foreclosures: Residential foreclosures did increase, from 2,128, in 1926, to as high as 2,845 in 1933.

66 Saved from foreclosure: *The Evening Sun*, Oct. 31, 1935.

67 Housing starts: Record Group 195 (Baltimore), National Archives, Adelphi, Md.

67 HOLC guidelines: "Instructions for Filling Out," Record Group 195.

67 Four categories: These categories—"best," "still desirable," "definitely declining," and "hazardous"—are from the Oct. 17, 1936, "Confidential Report of a Survey in Baltimore Maryland for the Division of Research & Statistics of the HOLC," 9 (Record Group 195), NA.

67 Three communities: The category included separately developed Ednor Gardens and Lakeside.

67 Top ranking: Other A-graded Baltimore neighborhoods included Ten Hills, Hunting Ridge, Pinehurst, Rodgers Forge, Anneslie, Stoneleigh, and Dumbarton.

67 Roland Park and Forest Park: "Explanation," Record Group 195, NA.

70 Importance of newness: All this came together in the Waverly Test Program that HOLC developed for thirty-nine blocks, consisting of more than seventeen hundred lots along Greenmount Avenue in Baltimore. HOLC planners and architects hoped to turn the declining area into a buffer between the Roland Park Company's Guilford and Northwood. They saw no value in the original Victorian architecture of Waverly's old buildings. Instead, if detached houses were of frame construction, as most were, HOLC wanted to strip them of all Victorian influences. A pronounced dormer defining the roofline was to be eliminated so that a bay would not look so dominant. A "more modern" porch would be installed, with a new railing and non-Victorian columns. Similarly, a mansard-roofed Second Empire brick building would be altered to look like a Colonial Revival house. Alternately, slender porch columns could be added and extended to the frieze. With a fancy entrance canopy, the home could be transformed into an ersatz Greek Revival plantation house, not quite a Tara but far more imposing than before. Drawings in *Waverly*, 39, show examples of recommended architectural modifications.

70 Red explained: "Instructions," Record Group 195, NA.
70 Lending criteria: "Baltimore, Maryland," May 29, 1937, Record Group 195, NA.
70 Inevitable deterioration: "Confidential Report of a Survey in Baltimore, Maryland." Oct. 17, 1936, Record Group 195, NA.
70 Block evaluations: A review sheet marked D-4, Record Group 195, NA.
71 Jewish neighborhoods: Kenneth T. Jackson, *Crabgrass Frontier: The Suburbanization of the United States* (New York: Oxford University Press, 1985), 197–198. See also Kenneth T. Jackson, "Race, Ethnicity and Real Estate Appraisal: The Home Owners Loan Corporation and the Federal Housing Administration," *Journal of Urban History*, vol. 6, no. 4 (1980), 423.
71 Dumbarton restrictions: Beryl Frank, *A Pictorial History of Pikesville, Maryland* (Towson: Baltimore County Public Library, 1982), 78.
71–72 Suburban Club: Philip Kahn, Jr., *Uncommon Threads* (Baltimore: PECAN Publications, 1996), 184.
72 Mortgage terms: "Confidential."
73 Consequences of redlining: Ibid.
73 FHA role: Hillier, "Redlining," 407.
73 Salzman offers: E. Lester Muller to Salzman, Sept. 11, 1941, W. Edward Orser's private collection, Baltimore.
73 Salzman complaint: Sidney Salzman to the Director, Federal Housing Administration, Sept. 10, 1941, Orser collection.
74 Salzman's tenacity: John G. Rouse to Salzman, Oct. 14, 1941; FHA sales contract, Nov. 10, 1941, both in Orser collection. The author's telephone interview with Anne Salzman, widow, Nov. 15, 2003.
74 Hawkins's death: Obituary in the *Afro-American*, Apr. 12, 1941.

Chapter 6. The Good War

75 Six months before war: *The Sun*, Aug. 23, 25, 1941; *The Evening Sun*, Aug. 27, 1941.
75 Lifestyle changes: *The Evening Sun*, Aug. 21, 23, 27, 1941.
75 War production: Harold Randall Manekee, *Maryland in World War II: Industry and Agriculture* (Baltimore: Maryland Historical Society, 1951), 9, 15.
76 Flying to Europe: *New York Times*, Nov. 8, 1936.
76 Germans: *Washington Post*, Oct. 17, 1937.
76 *Liberty* ship launch: *The Sun, Washington Post*, Dec. 7, 1941.
77 Shipyard strikes: *New York Times, Wall Street Journal*, July 31, 1943; Chicago *Defender*, Aug. 7, 1943. A solid review of industrial race relations is contained in John R. Breihan, "Wings of Democracy? African Americans in Baltimore's World War II Aviation Industry," in Jessica Elfenbein, John Breihan, and Thomas Hollowak, eds., *From Mobtown to Charm City* (Baltimore: Maryland Historical Society, 2002).
77 Outperforming whites: *The Evening Sun*, Apr. 16, 1942.
77 One-million mark: A Sept. 28, 1942, *Washington Post* editorial estimated Baltimore's population at 1.2 million.

78 "Come North Now" editorial: Cited in Antero Pietila, "Working on a Black Plantation," *Buncombe*, a review of Baltimore journalism, no. 3, 1972.
78 "We Must Have War" editorial: *Afro-American*, July 15, 1939.
78 Bonanza: Thomas J. S. Waxter to McKeldin, Aug. 19, 1943, McKeldin file G1-48, BCA.
79 Housing shortage: *The Sun*, May 19, 1942. Interview with Clinton Dean, a West Virginia war worker, Dec. 1, 2003.
79 Wolman testimony: *The Evening Sun*, June 1, 1941.
79 Spot checks: *The Evening Sun*, Sept. 21, 1942.
80 They need them: Address of H. Streett Baldwin, July 20, 1943, McKeldin file G1-48, BCA.
80 Scum: Cited in Eric Holcomb, "From Herring Run to Cherry Hill: The Politics of Racism and the Location of War Housing for Negro Workers," an unpublished paper for the Commission on Historic and Architectural Preservation, 1995, 2.
80 Trailers: *The Sun*, July 16, 1943.
80 National problem: *The Sun*, July 25, 1943.
80 Competitive capitalism: *Baltimore News Post*, Jan. 8, 1960; *The Sun*, Oct. 10, 1937.
80 Bid to oust Tydings: See Robert J. Brugger, *Maryland: A Middle Temperament, 1934–1980* (Baltimore: Johns Hopkins University Press, 1988), 516–517. Also Philip Grant, Jr., "Maryland Press Reaction to the Roosevelt-Tydings Confrontation," *Maryland Historical Magazine* 68 (Winter 1973), 422–437. Harold A. Williams, *The Baltimore Sun, 1837–1987* (Baltimore: Johns Hopkins University Press, 1987), 241.
81 Beloved Baltimore: *The Evening Sun*, Oct. 3, 1943.
81 Summarizing letters: *The Evening Sun*, Oct. 6, 1943.
82 Poem's author: *The Evening Sun*, June 11, 1947.
82 Baltimore girl: Ibid.
82 Leading insurance man: Harry F. Kleinfelter to McKeldin, Aug. 14, 1943, McKeldin file G1-48, BCA.
82 Bigotry of officials: *The Sun*, July 24, 1943.
83 Ethnic and class tensions: *The Sun*, Aug. 18, 1943.
84 Alarming overcrowding: *Afro-American*, Aug. 2, 1943. "Report of the Governor's Commission on Problems Affecting the Negro Population"(Baltimore, March 1943), VF Housing—Baltimore, EPFL.
84 Dormitories for blacks: Ibid.
84 Evacuation: A Sept. 28, 1942, *Washington Post* editorial mentioned this possibility and noted that the War Relocation Authority was empowered to force such a population shift.
84 Commission urged: "Report of the Governor's Commission," VF Housing–Baltimore, EPFL.
85 Breaking the deadlock: "Public Press Statement of Mayor Theodore R. McKeldin," July 10, 1943, McKeldin file G1-48, BCA.
85 Interracial commission: Francis A. Davis, chairman, to Mayor McKeldin, July 10, 1943, McKeldin file G1-48, BCA.

85 Some basis of fact: McKeldin to J. Harvey Kerns, executive secretary, Baltimore Urban League, June 29, 1943, McKeldin file G1-48, BCA.
85 Palace coup: Arthur to F. Murray Benson, Aug. 4, 1943, McKeldin file G1-48,
BCA.
86 Dodo: Holcomb, "Herring Run," 7, 8.
86 Meningitis cases: *The Evening Sun*, May 20, 1942.
86 At least 26,000: *The Sun*, Oct. 12, 1945.
86 CPHA: "Memorandum on Negro Housing in Metropolitan Baltimore," Aug.
1944, VF Housing–Baltimore, EPFL.

Chapter 7. Crossing Fulton Avenue

89 Landscaped median: The city removed the landscaped median after racial
change occurred. Fulton Avenue was designated as a truck route. A more
modest median was constructed in 2007.
89 The Moon: E-mail from Louis S. Diggs, Dec. 20, 2008.
89 Covenants lapsed: "Report on real estate meeting Feb. 16, 1945," BJC 333,
JMM.
90 Fired off letters: Sachs to Robert Seff, Jan. 2, 1945, BJC 333, JMM. Sachs
also addressed his letter to the following speculators: Samuel Fox, Harry
Merowitz, Robert Leavitt, Leon Crane, Samuel Kalis, Harry Blumberg, William Sinsky, Alex Cooper, Philip Needle, M. Goldseker, Frank Caplan, Victor
Posner, Harry Sachs, Morris Harmatz, Lawrence Lockwood, A. S. Appelstein,
Benjamin Preissman, and Milton F. Kirsner.
90 Before anything: "Real estate meeting, Feb. 16, 1945," BJC 333, JMM.
90 As ugly: "Report on mass meeting Feb. 23, 1945," BJC 333, JMM.
91 Prominent advertisements: *The Sun* and *The Evening Sun*, Feb. 28, 1945.
Also, Mar. 3, 1945.
91 Whites demanded: McKeldin to Mrs. M. E. Weber, McKeldin file G1-48 (Aug.
22, 1945), BCA.
92 Appealed for calm: McKeldin to Frank S. Miller, Sr., McKeldin file G1-48
(July 27, 1945), BCA.
92 This was not: H. O'C. Cross, Sr., to McKeldin, McKeldin file G1-48 (July 27,
1945), BCA.
92 School board member: He was George McMechen, the lawyer who had rented
1834 McCulloh Street from W. Ashbie Hawkins in 1910.
93 At one event: Charles Whiteford in OH 8166, See also OH 8144, MHS.
94 Pebbles: Interview with Stephens Broening, Feb. 12, 2009.
94 Sheer willpower: *Christian Science Monitor*, May 3, 1939; *New York Times*,
July 12, 1942; *New York Times*, May 5, 1943.
94 District of Columbia mayor: E-mail from Hirsh Goldberg, Feb. 5, 2008.
95 Needed the money: Sturm to Sachs, Aug. 27, 1946, BJC 333, JMM.
95 Segregationist agitation: Mass meetings were held in the church hall, with the
monsignor present.
95 Under normal conditions: Clifton R. Jones, "Invasion and Racial Attitudes: A
Study of Housing in a Border City," *Social Forces*, March 1949, 285–290.

95 Better educated: Jones, "Invasion," 285–290.

96 One speculator to another: Handwritten roster of property transfers in BJC 333, JMM. The Banfields became social activists and mainstays of the interracial Baltimore Ethical Society and Baltimore Baha'i Society. One of their granddaughters is Jada Pinkett Smith, the actress, whom they reared.

96 He also bought: E-mail from Karen Banfield Evans, Apr. 15, 2009.

96 Another prominent: *Afro-American*, Mar. 10, 1945.

96 Threats against: *Afro-American*, Mar. 10, 1945.

96 He spoke of: Sachs, BJC 333 (Mar. 2, 1945), JMM.

96 The early blockbusters: *The Evening Sun*, Mar. 20, 1943; *The Sun*, Mar. 24, 1943. Correspondence from the Fulton Avenue Improvement Association (BJC 333, JMM) contains information culled from the *Daily Record* that tracks sales and identifies the blockbusters.

97 Herbert Kaufman: *The Sun*, Nov. 8, 1958; *The Evening Sun*, July 27, 1973.

97 Victor Posner: Mark Reutter, "The Posner Chronicles: The Builder," *Warfields*, May 1990; *Wall Street Journal*, June 23, 1981.

97 Census: *The Evening Sun*, Mar. 5, 1943.

97 Tightening codes: Ordinance 384 (1941).

97 Rats: *The Sun*, Apr. 8, 1943.

98 Statistics from 1950: *An American City in Transition: The Baltimore Community Self-Survey of Inter-Group Relations* (Baltimore: Maryland Commission on Interracial Problems and Relations, and Baltimore Commission on Human Rights, 1955), 233.

98 Leading speculators: BJC 333, JMM.

98 Survey: Baltimore Urban League survey, Mar. 11, 1946, BJC 333, JMM.

99 Sales mechanism: Land-installment contract regulations tightened later; this description applies to the 1940s and early 1950s. In 1951, state law required foreclosure in delinquent land-installment contracts. But many landlords avoided that by offering the contract buyer a onetime cash payment.

99 As early as: *Afro-American*, Feb. 4, 1899.

100 Herbert Kaufman: *The Evening Sun*, May 8, 1943.

100 Double billing: *The Sun*, Dec. 14, 1954. Victor Posner exited bottom-rung real estate around 1950, becoming a builder of inexpensive mass-produced rowhouses in eastern Baltimore County.

100 Fly-by-night operators: William Manchester, *The City of Anger* (New York: Dell, 1984), 244–256.

100 Roughly fifteen: Telephone interview with Aaron Baer, Apr. 20, 2004. Sugarman, Crockett, and Swirnow backed his version.

101 Could ignore the board: *The Sun*, Mar. 28, 1945.

102 A polite stranger: The whole section on Goose Hill is based on Thomas Cripps's recollections in several interviews.

103 First homeowner: Cripps interview, Mar. 17, 2007.

103 Legal murkiness: Sugarman interview, Dec. 28, 2002.

103 Buyers' ignorance: Full name omitted by *The Evening Sun*, Dec. 14, 1954.

104 One elderly couple: *The Evening Sun*, July 21, 1950.

104 Nothing helped: *The Sun*, Dec. 13, 1954.

Chapter 8. Covenants Crumble

105 Three of the nine: *Washington Post*, Jan. 16, 1948.

105 Landmark case: Peter Irons, *The Courage of Their Convictions: Sixteen Americans Who Fought Their Way to the Supreme Court* (New York: Penguin, 1990), 63–80.

106 Truman quotation: Clark and Perlman, *Prejudice and Property*, 22.

106 Cadwalader and Barton: "Motion of the Mount Royal Protective Association, Inc. for leave to file brief as amicus curiae" (October term, 1947). *Baltimore Afro-American*, Nov. 25, 1929, described the enforcement mechanism, naming the block captains and lieutenants.

108 Ghetto system: *Baltimore Jewish Times*, May 14, 1948.

108 Temporary setback: *Afro-American*, May 8, 1948. The newspaper greatly exaggerated the age of Eutaw Place homes and the lot sizes in areas it recommended.

108 Wise choice: Ibid.

108 Without questions: Ibid.

109 Internal census: "Resources of the Jewish Community," 24.

109 Aged Jews: See Anita Kassof, Avi Y. Decter, Deborah R. Weiner, eds., *Lives Lost, Lives Found: Baltimore's German Jewish Refugees, 1933–1945* (Baltimore: Jewish Museum of Maryland, 2004).

109 Not Jewish: "Resources of the Jewish Community," 20.

109 Beginning in 1944: *The Evening Sun*, Oct. 5, 1944; *The Sun*, Sept. 1, 1946. Interview with Matthew Tayback, a city health official who dealt with problems with Appalachians during World War II, Dec. 24, 2003.

109 Ethnic redrawing: Ralph S. Weese, "Report on the Housing Market, Baltimore, Maryland, Standard Metropolitan Area, as of September 1, 1953," Federal Housing Administration, 11-16. VF–Housing, EPFL.

110 Racial transition: *Afro-American*, Aug. 21, 1948.

110 Threatened to kill: Reports dated June 4 and June 11, 1952, BJC 1604, JMM; *Afro-American*, July 15, 1952.

110 Mendel Glaser: Robert A. Steinberg, *1730 Ruxton Avenue: The Story of Mike and Ida Glaser and Their Children* (Baltimore: privately printed, 1997), 1–37.

111 Bootlegger: Steinberg, "Ruxton," 18. Interview with Steinberg, May 8, 2005.

112 Pollack's record: *The Observer*, Jan. 13, 1934. Pollack's rap sheet is on file in *The Sun* library, marked "confidential."

112 Nearly absolute power: Gilbert Sandler, *Jewish Baltimore: A Family Album* (Baltimore: Johns Hopkins University Press, 2000), 160–164. *The Sun*, Apr. 7, 1950, described the extent of Pollack's power; *The Evening Sun*, Apr. 26, 1951, showed how people no longer living in the district used relatives' addresses in order to register to vote. Hundreds of dead people also voted.

112 Liquor inspectors: *The Sun*, Feb. 26, 1959.

112 Political identity: *Washington Post*, Oct. 12, 1958.

112 Stronghold: Harvey Wheeler, "Yesterday's Robin Hood: The Rise and Fall of Baltimore's Trenton Democratic Club," *American Quarterly*, Winter 1955, 332–344.

113 Obstruction of justice: *Washington Post*, May 16, 1954. Another son, Thomas J. D'Alesandro III, served as Baltimore mayor from 1967 to 1971; a daughter, Nancy Pelosi, became the first woman speaker of the House of Representatives.

113 Schmo: *The Sun*, Feb. 26, 1959.

113 Wonderful nicknames: Interview with Milton Bates, Jan. 7, 2003. Bates, a prolific writer, also recalled his growing-up years in articles for *The Evening Sun* and the *Jewish Times*.

113 His pride: Interview with Billy Lewis, Jan. 23, 2004.

113 Rap Wheatley: Interviews with Milton Bates and Billy Lewis. The *Afro-American* reported on June 23, 1951, that police broke up a softball game in Easterwood Park between the Mohawks and a U.S. Navy team because the latter had a black player. By that time a fair number of blacks had moved to the neighborhood.

115 Daniel W. Spaulding: *The Sun*, June 25, 1995; July 22, 1999. In 1958, Spaulding ran as a Republican for the Maryland House of Delegates.

115 Cracks: Interview with Bernadine Johnson, who lived on McCulloh Street in Sugar Hill, Oct. 8, 2004.

115 One-way thoroughfares: *The Sun*, Feb. 18, 1948.

116 Jewish friend: Interview with Erla McKinnon, Feb. 8, 2008. Deed MLP 7825/594. Maurice "Mo" Lipman, who ran Adams's real estate firm, most likely facilitated the purchase.

116 Not happy: Interview with Gilbert Sandler, July 11, 2003. He dated a girl from around the corner.

116 He was born: Much useful material is contained in the *Afro-American*, June 5, 1954, and July 18, 1959. See also Antero Pietila, "Willie Adams Built on Risks, Strategy," and, "An Old Adams Secret—Keeping a Low Profile," *The Sun*, Mar. 19, 1979.

117 Notorious Negro: Frank R. Kent, *The Story of Maryland Politics: An Outline of Big Political Battles of the State from 1864 to 1910* (Baltimore: Thomas and Evans Printing, 1911), 308.

117 Black King: Mentioned in *New York Times*, Oct. 14, 1923.

117 Smith's patrons: A photo of the shrine is in the *Afro-American*, Sept. 10, 1938.

117 Smith Realty: *Afro-American*, Aug. 5, 1921.

117 Squeezing: *Washington Post*, Mar. 30, 1938. *Afro-American*, Aug. 20, 1938, *The Sun*, Aug. 13, 1938; interviews with Crockett between Dec. 13, 2002, and 2009. Mark Bowden, "Bossin' Around: A History of How Things got Done in Baltimore," *City Paper*, Aug. 1, 2007.

118 51 percent stake: The only exception was Parks Sausage Company, in which Adams and Henry G. Parks had an equal ownership interest. Adams, however, owned the company's fleet of delivery trucks, thus assuring that he would be in control.

120 Paid the price: Adams was not on the premises but was arrested when he rang the doorbell of the numbers headquarters during the raid. Officers said that keys to two strongboxes containing the number slips were found in his pocket, according to the *Afro-American*, Nov. 26, 1949. He was acquitted. A well-known nightclub owner and Adams operative, Walter Rouse, took the fall. He received a fine and a suspended 60-day jail term. Fifteen others also were fined. *Afro-American*, Apr. 1, 1950. The *Afro-American*, May 29, 1954, pointed out that the numbers headquarters of Austin Scarlett was raided after the Adams associate bought a 123-acre farm in Westminster, the white county seat of Carroll County, turning it into a country club for blacks. The Kefauver Committee asked repeated questions about Adams's connections with Scarlett and whether he in fact owned the country club in Westminster. Adams denied any ownership. See transcript of his testimony: http://www.archive .org/stream/investigationofo17unit/investigationofo17unit_djvu.txt.

120 Overturned: *The Sun*, Mar. 19, 1979.

120 Back taxes: *Afro-American*, June 5 and 12, and Dec. 18, 1954. See also July 18, 1959.

121 Local yokels: *Afro-American*, July 9, 1949.

122 Citywide basis: *New York Times*, Oct. 8, 1955.

122 Stampede: *The Sun*, Sept. 17, 1954. Harry Bard, "Observations on Desegregation in Baltimore: Three Years Later," *Teachers College Record*, vol. 59, no. 5 (February 1958), 1–14. Table 1, "School B." The school was located on the grounds of Western High School (now Frederick Douglass) at Gwynns Falls Parkway and Pulaski Street.

122 Terminated their leases: Interview with Sidney Hollander, Jr., Apr. 5, 2003.

122 Political aftershock: James Fleming, *An All-Negro Ticket in Baltimore* (New York: Holt, Rinehart and Winston, 1960), 1–28.

123 Buying houses: Interviews with Morton Pollack, Nov. 7, 2005, and A. Robert Kaufman, who was among subsidized renters, Sept. 10, 2003.

123 Shaarei Tfiloh, Interview with Rabbi David E. Herman, June 5, 2008. At that time Shaarei Tfiloh was coming back. Its membership was growing again thanks to whites moving into gentrifying areas.

124 Irvin Kovens: See several entries in C. Fraser Smith: *William Donald Schaefer: A Political Biography* (Baltimore: Johns Hopkins University Press, 1999). Kovens was later convicted of racketeering and served time in a federal prison before being exonerated. Also convicted was Mandel, who had his conviction overturned after serving time. He spend his remaining years in private law practice in Annapolis.

124 Parks Sausage: The company was named after Henry G. Parks, who rose to become a City Council member. In the waning days of Jim Crow, when he began his business career, someone gave the fair-complexioned Parks a tip: Say that you are from Brazil and you will have fewer problems. Parks did not take the advice. Reflecting on his career, he said that his biggest mistake was

to seek public office because that called attention to him. He said that a black had an easier time in business if he kept a low profile.

124 Adams's empire: *The Sun*, Mar. 19, 1979.

125 Adams avoided: Ibid.

125 Adams's other: Interviews with John Luetkemeyer, Jr., Apr. 13, 2004. The Kefauver Committee repeatedly asked Adams about safe deposit boxes he might have. He replied that he had only one, at Union Trust. Downey Rice, associate counsel, kept on pressing:

Mr. Rice. What do you have in the safe-deposit box?

Mr. Adams. I really wouldn't know offhand.

Mr. Rice. You are the man who has a key.

Mr. Adams. It has been quite sometime since I have been in there. I use it for keeping more important papers. I have had it for a long time. Before I had my office set up, I more or less used to keep deeds to property in there.

Mr. Rice. Do you keep any cash in there?

Mr. Adams. Very little.

Mr. Rice. Very little?

Mr. Adams. Yes, sir.

125 Luetkemeyer: Profile, *Washington Post*, Feb. 11, 1973. Frank DeFilippo, "Who Runs Baltimore?" *News American*, Dec. 17 and 18, 1967, identified Luetkemeyer as the head of an informal network of 133 businessmen and lawyers who called the shots in Baltimore. They were mostly Anglo-Saxons, members of Protestant and Catholic churches, alumni of Ivy League schools, and mainstays of exclusive private clubs. They controlled the local financial and civic institutions through interlocking board directorships, DeFilippo wrote; they were connected to City Hall, state decision-makers in Annapolis, and the Catholic archdiocese, and some had influence in Washington. DeFilippo identified fewer than ten Jews among the group, and no blacks.

127 State contracts: *Washington Post*, May 18, 1991.

127 Adams's membership: Interview with James Crockett, who was present at the meeting, Oct. 1, 2008.

127 Pallbearers: Interview with John Luetkemeyer, Jr.

Chapter 9. Fighting Anti-Semitism

128 Having grown: Richard N. Goodwin, *Remembering America: A Voice from the Sixties* (Boston: Little, Brown, 1988), 15.

129 Art of magic: A. D. Glushakow, *A Pictorial History of Maryland Jewry* (Baltimore: Jewish Voice Publishing, 1955), 18–19.

129 Solomon Etting: "Maryland in Liberia; A History of the Colony Planted by the Maryland State Colonization Society Under the Auspices of the State of Maryland, U.S., at Cape Palmas on the Southwest Coast of Africa, 1833–1853." A paper read before the Maryland Historical Society, Mar. 9, 1885. http://www.archive.org/stream/marylandinliberioolatr/marylandinliberioolatr_djvu.txt (1885).

129 Political milestone: *New York Times*, Oct. 28, 1907.
129 Isaac Lobe Straus: Calcott, *Negro in Maryland*, 126–130.
129 Schaefer's Gentile: BJC 132, JMM.
130 Employment ads: "Discriminatory ads in Sunpapers, December 19, 1941–July 1942," BJC 197, JMM. A collection of such ads is in BJC 201, JMM.
130 Barred Jews: Kalb to Anti-Defamation League, Apr. 30, 1940, BJC 323, JMM.
130 Dividing issues: Deborah R. Weiner, "A Club of Their Own: Suburban and Woodholme Through the Years," *Generations*, 2004, 5–21.
130 Caste system: Fein, *Making of an American Jewish Community*, 233–237.
131 Very strange: Anita Kassof, et al., "Lives Lost," 21.
131 Adopted quotas: *PM*, Jan. 25, 1946, and May 19, 1946; *Dartmouth Review*, July 22, 1999, and *Yale Daily News*, Apr. 4, 2001.
131 Doggerel: Cited in Thomas F. Gossett, *Race: The History of an Idea in America* (Dallas: Southern Methodist University Press, 1963), 372.
131 Wilson Shaffer: "Memorandum from Leon Sachs Concerning the Johns Hopkins University" (undated), Civil Rights Folio II, BJC, JMM. "Regardless of the merits or demerits of the University's position, it is noteworthy that this is the only instance of which I am aware in which a university discussed its problem with the Jewish community before imposing a quota. This much must be said for the integrity of the College," Sachs wrote.
131 Leon Sachs: Biographical information from an August 1976 interview, OH 8136, MHS.
133 Kelly Miller: *Johns Hopkins Gazette*, Jan. 16, 2001. Miller became a respected mathematician and sociologist.
133 Sachs was told: Sachs to Alex Weinstein, Dec. 13, 1949, BJC 932, JMM.
133 Pre-med applications: Sachs, Sept. 27, 1951, BJC 932, JMM.
133 Formal and deliberate: Walter R. Heart, "Anti-Semitism in N.Y. Medical Schools," *American Mercury*, July 1947, and "The 'Distinctive Name' Method of Determining Jewish Enrollment in Medical Schools," *CLA Reports*, both BJC 883. See also "The Quota System in Medical Schools," *CLA Reports*, BJC 694, JMM.
133 The quota initially: Memorandum from Sachs; letter from Dr. Kenneth Zierler, *Hopkins Medical News*, Spring 1995, 3.
133 Hopkins maintained: Bowman to Louis Singer, May 12, 1948, BJC 932, JMM. There is less evidence that Johns Hopkins discriminated against Jews in faculty positions, though that too did happen.
133 Not true: In an e-mail to the author, Hopkins archivist James Stimpert wrote, "However, oral tradition both here at Hopkins and from contacts in the local Jewish community, agree that Hopkins did indeed admit prescribed numbers of Jewish students per year. I have never been sure what that number—or percentage—was but I'm confident it did exist."
133 Drop a question: Sachs, Sept. 27, 1951, BJC 932, JMM.
133 Still worried: Ibid.
133 Student newspaper: *News-Letter*, Nov. 16, 1951.

133 Jewish ceiling: "University of Maryland Medical School, number of Jewish students in graduating classes," BJC file 932, JMM.
133 Dean said: *The Sun*, Oct. 9, 1949.
134 Segregationist president: Byrd to Sachs, Apr. 22, 1950, BJC file 932, JMM.
134 Practice of anti-Semitism: *The Sun*, May 13, 1949.
134 Byrd pledged: Byrd to Sachs, Apr. 22, 1950, BJC file 932, JMM.
134 Meadowbrook: *Jewish Times*, Jan. 19, 1953. In 2008, Michael Phelps, the Olympic gold medalist, acquired what by then had become the Meadowbrook Aquatic and Fitness Center, his longtime practice facility.
134 City Council meeting: *Jewish Times*.
134 Denied admission: *The Sun*, June 16, 1953.
135 Business reasons: *Jewish Social Directory*, 4, JMM.
135 Offered his services: *Jewish Times*, June 19, 1953.
135 Telephone interview with Stephen Sachs, Nov. 11, 2005.
135 Urinal: Telephone interview.
135 Dirty little secret: "Chronology of BJC negotiations with Marylander Apartments," undated, BCJ 344, JMM.
135 April 29: Report marked Apr. 29/48, BJC 349, JMM.
136 Should exclude: Undated draft, BJC 349, JMM.
136 Joseph Meyerhoff: John F. Kelly, "You Can't Take It with You," *The Sun Magazine*, Sept. 12, 1982.
137 Teetered: Hirsh M. Goldberg, *Joseph Meyerhoff: A Portrait* (Baltimore: privately printed, 1987), 34.
137 Pivotal moral position: *The Sun*, Feb. 4, 1985.
137 Council refused: Sachs to Harry Greenstein, report marked Dec. 12, 1949, BJC 349, JMM.
137 Meyerhoff's business: Report marked Dec. 30, 1949, BJC 349, JMM.
137 Meyerhoff once told: Report marked Dec. 23, 1949, BJC 349, JMM.
138 Any weakening: *Baltimore Real Estate News*, August 1936.
138 Deal was struck: Waesche, *Crowning the Gravelly Hill*, 114–151.
138 He was broke: Ibid.
139 Blackmail: "Meeting on restricted housing, Madison Avenue Temple Center," July 7, 1948, BJC file 349, JMM.
139 Not once offering: "Steering Committee Meeting—June 29 (1949), Lord Baltimore Hotel," BJC 249, JMM.
140 Misunderstood: "Conversation with Jos. Meyerhoff in his office, July 19, 1949," BJC 349, JMM.
140 Squirmed and recanted: Sept. 21, 1949, BJC 349, JMM.
140 Dinner meeting: "Memorandum of meeting on restricted covenants" (Jan. 5, 1949), BJC 349, JMM.
140 His impressions: Ibid.
140 Nothing more: Letter dated Feb. 6, 1950, BJC 349, JMM.
141 Quota for Jews: Draft "Statement of the Baltimore Jewish Council Concerning the Restrictive Rental Policy at the Marylander Apartments" (undated); report marked May 2, 1951; Steering Committee Meeting, June 29, 1951.

141 Moss told Sachs: "Conversation with Mr. Hunter Moss concerning the Marylander," Mar. 6, 1951, BJC 344, JMM.

141 Feelings were hurt: Interview with Walter Sondheim, Dec. 1, 2007.

141 Rouse protested: Rouse to Sachs, Aug. 22, 1951, BJC 344, JMM.

142 Vice presidents: Dun & Bradstreet report, Mar. 29, 1950, BJC 348, JMM.

142 The young man: Irving Sarnoff to Sachs, July 6 and July 25, 1951, BJC 344, JMM.

142 Father complained: Sachs to Frenkil, July 10, 1951, BJC 344, JMM.

142 Controversy persisted: Joe Katz in "Marylander Apartment Statement," Aug. 21, 1951.

142 Broadview too: "Chronology of BJC negotiations with Marylander Apartments," undated, BJC 344, JMM.

142 Similar flexibility: See "Steering Committee Meeting—June 29, Lord Baltimore Hotel," BJC 349, JMM.

143 Until years after: It is not known who that first Jewish buyer was. The first black resident arrived in 1974, when Kenneth L. Johnson, a lawyer who later became a judge, bought a huge Victorian house in an unlisted sale from a Johns Hopkins professor. The Johnsons moved in at 206 Woodlawn Road over the Fourth of July weekend that year.

143 In general: Sachs to Sidney D. Cohen, Sept. 29, 1953, BJC 345A, JMM.

143 Answer was negative: Wootton to Sachs, Dec. 7, 1953, BJC 345A, JMM.

143 Separate multiple listings: Interview with Herbert A. Davis, May 28, 2008. A dispute over commissions contributed to the formation of the separate service; e-mail from Len Bernhardt, July 26, 2009.

Chapter 10. A Brotherhood of Profit

144 Building permits: "Topic: Neighborhood Stabilization," BJC file 1585A, JMM.

144 Until 1960: Malcolm Sherman, who was the Real Estate Board's treasurer at the time, said that integration came about because membership applications had been inadvertently sent to some African Americans. He persuaded the board to use that as an opportunity to desegregate the organization. Interview Aug. 21, 2003.

144 Wrote in 1957: Louis V. Blum, M.D., to Leon Sachs, Jan. 29, 1957, BJC 1585A, JMM.

144 Referral fee: Interview with Mal Sherman, Aug. 21, 2003.

145 Reminded me a little: Interview with Sidney Hollander, Jr., Apr. 5, 2003.

145 Straw buyers: Report dated June 12, 1952, BJC file 1604, JMM.

145 Quite accidentally: Interview with Richard Swirnow, Dec. 4, 2003. Swirnow became a major developer of waterfront condominiums.

146 James Crockett: Interview with Crockett, Dec. 13, 2002.

146 Stanley Sugarman: Interview with Sugarman, Dec. 28, 2002.

147 First black family: Interview with Homer Favor, June 17, 2003.

148 Dance lessons: *The Sun*, Oct. 15, 1948.

148 Federal penitentiary: *The Sun*, Mar. 26, 1959.

148 Wasting your time: Interview with Manuel Bernstein, May 14, 2004. Much of the subsequent description of Manning-Shaw is based on that interview and on documents belonging to Melvin J. Sykes.

149 Misrepresenting: *James R. McDonough Jr. and Wife v. Manning-Shaw Realty Company*, Real Estate Commission of Maryland complaint, September 1958 (Sykes's private collection). Also, interview with Sykes, Jan. 20, 2003.

149 Already been broken: Ibid.

150 His father: Monroe N. Work, *The Negro Year Book* (Tuskegee, Ala.: Tuskegee Institute, 1913), 242; *The Sun*, Jan. 17, 1924.

150 Sympathetic social activist: Mae Gellman's report, Dec. 1 and 3, 1954, BJC 1584, JMM.

150 Abortionists: *Afro-American*, Sept. 10, 1955. Interview with James Crockett, Apr. 9, 2004.

150 Responsible citizens: Leon Sachs to Robert L. Mainen, Dec. 13, 1954, BJC 1584, JMM.

150 Sale fell through: The Ashburton activists mobilized pressure on lending institutions. "Never in the history of our organization has so much pressure been applied to us," a representative of one building and loan association told the *Afro-American*, Dec. 11, 1954.

151 Pilot project: Michael L. Mark, *But Not Next Door—Baltimore Neighborhoods Inc.: The First Forty Years* (Baltimore: Baltimore Neighborhoods, Inc., 2002), viii.

151 Dysfunctional: The information and quotations in this section are from the Feb. 5, 1959, transcript of *Ex Parte in the Matter of Joseph Jerome Carter*, Circuit Court of Baltimore City (Sykes collection).

151 Seventeen head: *The Sun*, Feb. 25, 1959.

152 Suspended the licenses: Manning-Shaw's business went on under another broker's license, according to Crockett.

152 Judge said: *Manning-Shaw Realty Co. v. Real Estate Commission of Maryland*, Baltimore City Court, June 4, 1959 (Sykes).

153 They appealed: June 13, 1960.

153 Rejected that too: Oct. 10, 1960.

153 Bernstein maintained: Interview with Manuel Bernstein, May 14, 2004.

153 Big spread: *Saturday Evening Post*, Apr. 4, 1959.

154 Gamely bragged: Judith Sykes, in an interview Jan. 20, 2003, said she was told that by a neighbor who either did not remember she was Jewish or did not care.

154 Sykeses were black: *The Sun*, June 18, 1973. Ultimately only one white remained. She was Miriam Konigsberg, who had lived in Ashburton since 1941 and had experienced the various transformations. "When we moved in, Ashburton was all Christian, and it didn't take long for them to run away from 'the Jews.' When African Americans came to the neighborhood, I again witnessed a flight. I stayed and couldn't imagine living anywhere else," she said. She died at ninety-six, in 2005, having left Ashburton only after Alzheimer's disease struck her. *The Sun*, Apr. 1, 2005.

154 Repeatedly arrested: William L. Adams participated quietly and behind the scenes, making available $100,000 in bail money.

154 Radical public profile: *The Sun*, Nov. 12, 14, and 23, 1961; Jan. 3, 1962; *Washington Post*, Dec. 24, 1961.

155 Chauffeur-driven: Interview with George Collins, June 11, 2003. See also *The Sun*, May 20, 1964, and Aug. 1 and 5, 1966.

155 Transparently slick: Interview with Walter Dean, Jr., June 18, 2003.

155 Dabbling in politics: *Afro-American*, May 25, 1964. The paper did not endorse Shaw—perhaps there was nothing to endorse. His proposals and positions, as reported in news stories, were unfocused and shallow. He did not even offer fire and brimstone about civil rights. "We are not yet convinced that we ought to or are able to elect a congressman," the *Afro-American* editorialized, saying that increasing African-American representation in the City Council was more important.

155 Bernstein didn't think: Interview with Manuel Bernstein, May 14, 2004.

155 Shaw himself: *The Sun*, Mar. 26, 1966.

155 Constant attacks: *The Sun*, Feb. 1, 1969.

156 Born in Oberlin: This section relies heavily on four pages of answers Laura J. Smith prepared to my questions. "Neither my brother [Master Sergeant Allen E. Shaw, U.S.A., Ret.] nor I . . . have substantial information on the activities of my brother . . . from the time he left Oberlin past his high school, during his army career nor during specified other periods of his life," she wrote. Also interview with Smith, Oct. 12, 2003.

156 Moved to California: Interview with Laura J. Smith.

156 The ancestor: William H. Rogers, *Senator John P. Green, and Sketches of Prominent Men in Ohio* (Washington D.C.: Arena Publishing, 1893), 61.

156 Everybody knew: Interview with Theodosia Stokes, Aug. 2, 2004.

157 Childhood chum: Telephone interview with Howard Jones, June 20, 2003.

158 Shared the glory: *Afro-American*, Oct. 21, 1961.

158 Happiness: *Afro-American*, Dec. 14, 1957.

158 His wife: Also a real estate agent, Cecelia Shaw was corresponding secretary of Victorine Adams's Woman Power organization.

158 Larceny: *The Evening Sun*, Mar. 25, 1970.

158 His health: By then, Shaw's former lover was dead. Virginia Groff Gerhold, forty, had been found slain in her car in 1968. She had been strangled and shot twice at close range with a small-caliber pistol. The case seemed unsolvable. Years later her husband was convicted of having arranged a contract on her. He wanted to cash in her life insurance policy and, for $1,500, found a minor hood to get rid of her. The husband was caught only because he tried to hire someone to kill his subsequent wife as well. *Washington Post*, Feb. 10, 1968, and July 12, 1989.

158 Funeral: The book of condolences, in the possession of Laura J. Smith.

158 Enlisted: According to army enlistment records (ancestry.com), Shaw enlisted Oct. 18, 1945.

Chapter 11. Ordinary Lives

160 Impossible to predict: Interview with James Crockett, Jan. 13, 2003.

160 Recalled Morris Goldseker: Deposition, Jan. 5, 1972, in *Montebello Community Association vs. Morris Goldseker*, U.S. District Court for the District of Maryland. National Archives, Philadelphia.

161 In his prime: Thomas W. Spalding, *The Premier See: A History of the Archdiocese of Baltimore, 1789–1989* (Baltimore: Johns Hopkins University Press, 1989), 337.

161 Superior recruiter: *The Evening Sun*, Nov. 20, 1969.

161 Streetcar: E-mail from Jerry D. Kelly, who grew up in Edmondson Village. I also benefited from the recollections of Joe Lamp, who grew up on a white Edmondson Village block that was among the first to change racially.

161 No third owners: W. Edward Orser, *Blockbusting in Baltimore: The Edmondson Village Story* (Lexington: University Press of Kentucky, 1994), 31, 72.

161 Baseball: Interview with Thomas Cripps, a Lutheran from Goose Hill, who was recruited for the team, Apr. 2, 2006.

162 Volume of homebuilding: *Residential Development in Baltimore City and Baltimore County* (Baltimore: Maryland State Planning Commission, 1953), 26.

162 Tommy Tucker: *Afro-American*, Apr. 30, 1960.

162 Smelled of death: Undated note from Reutter.

163 Never cross the bridge: Telephone interview with Albert Rechelt, Mar. 15, 2003, a parishioner at St. Bernardine's; interview with Monsignor James J. Cronin, July 23, 2003.

163 Telegram: Interview with Father Richard Lawrence, who was assigned to St. Martin's, Jan. 29, 2004.

163 Discomfort: Spalding, *Premier See*, 379.

164 Cowards: Interviews with Reichelt and Monsignor Cronin.

164 Dear uncle: Orser, *Blockbusting*, 108.

164 Tumultuous period: Spalding, *Premier See*, 403.

164 Unhappy place: Interview with Father Witthauer, Aug. 8, 2003.

164 Size of black families: Ira De A. Reid, "The Negro Community of Baltimore: A Social Survey," Baltimore Urban League, Oct. 2, 1934, 27. Ruth Blumenfeld McKay, a George Washington University anthropologist, noted one significant exception to larger black family sizes in the 1960s and 1970s. According to a study reported in *The Sun*, Feb. 11, 1975, professionally trained "elite" blacks, whose children belonged to the Jack and Jill chapter, typically had 1.54 children. Because those families delayed childbearing into later years, they tended to have daughters. The shortage of mates often caused these light-skinned offspring to marry below their peer group in terms of social and economic status and skin hue.

165 Slow to desegregate: Interview with Monsignor Cronin.

166 Economic fears: Interview with Father Witthauer.

166 Largest advertiser: Interview with George Collins, who was the newspaper's city editor, June 11, 2003.

166 Introduced himself: Interview with Stanley Sugarman, Dec. 28, 2002.

166 No English: The Goldseker deposition, Jan. 5, 1972, suggests he may not have fully understood the question about his education:

Q: Could you briefly describe for me your educational background, grammar school, high school . . .

A: No school.

Q: The school of hard knocks.

A: Briefly.

Q: How briefly.

A: As I said briefly.

Sheldon Goldseker, in *Morris Goldseker, 1898–1973* (Baltimore: privately printed, no date), 4, contends that his uncle "attended elementary and parochial school, since his parents hoped that he would become an important and successful man."

166 Collateral: Sheldon Goldseker, *Goldseker*, 4.

167 Forced to forfeit: Sheldon Goldseker's version is different. In *Goldseker*, the nephew says, "Morris was able to save the few pieces of property that were in his own name," page 4.

167 Made sure: Goldseker deposition, Jan. 5, 1972.

167 Big break: Sheldon Goldseker, *Goldseker*, 9.

168 Sweeping language: Exhibit 6, Standard Lease and Option Contract between the Kenneth Company, a Goldseker subsidiary, and Lawrence and Louise Getling, Sept. 5, 1963, *Goldseker & Company Case No. 21552*, U.S. District Court of the District of Maryland.

168 Among methods: The various Goldseker mechanisms are described in Exhibit C, *Goldseker & Company Case No. 21552*.

168 Options: Exhibit Six, Standard Lease and Option Contract between Lee Realty Inc., a Goldseker subsidiary, and Isaac C. and Marie Smith, Nov. 4, 1966, *Goldseker & Company Case No. 21552*.

169 Two mortgages: See James D. Dilts, "Inflating Home Costs with the 'Black Tax,'" *The Sun*, Sept. 20, 1971.

169 No building: Interview with Stanley Sugarman.

170 Ground rents: Ground rents were widely used throughout the city to reduce the initial acquisition price for homeowners. Investors linked its predictable yield. After a probe by *The Sun* in 2006, the legislature tightened ground rent rules but abuses persisted. See *The Sun*, June 17, 2009.

170 Put out: See complaints about Goldseker in BJC 306, JMM.

170 Did not show: Interviews with James Crockett and Stanley Sugarman.

170 Paid more: *The Sun*, July 27, 1924, included the quotation.

171 Later studies: "Confidential Report of a Survey in Baltimore, Maryland" (Home Owners' Loan Corporation, 1936), 10 (HOLC City Survey File, Record Group 195, NA). Seven years later a governor's advisory panel came to the same conclusion. "Report of the Governor's Commission on Problems Affecting the Negro Population," March 1943. VF Housing–Baltimore, EPFL. See also "Rent and Housing Conditions by Race, Baltimore, Md. 1960," Baltimore Urban Renewal and Housing Agency, September 1963. VF Housing–Baltimore, EPFL.

171 Other cities: Arnold R. Hirsch, *Making the Second Ghetto: Race & Housing in Chicago, 1940–1960* (Cambridge, England: Cambridge University Press, 1983), 29.

171 Black tax: The process is described in *The Sun*, Sept. 20, 1971. See also Leonard Downie, Jr., *Mortgage on America: The Real Cost of Real Estate Speculation* (New York: Praeger, 1974), 12–41. The "black tax" later came to denote price gouging in insurance and other services as well.

Chapter 12. Uneasy Allies

172 About the same: Henry B. Suter, "Howard Park," a mimeographed chronicle published by the Howard Park Civic Association, 1971, 23. Also, interview with David Yaffe, whose family stayed in Howard Park for more than fifty years and still lived there in 2009, Jan. 4, 2009.

173 Prevent overcrowding: *The Evening Sun*, Apr. 12, 1956.

173 Firm position: "Baltimore Jewish Council position on problem of changing neighborhoods," undated 1957, BJC 1585A, JMM.

174 Dire economic consequences: Cited in Mark, *But Not Next Door*, 3.

174 Also voted: *The Sun*, Jan. 18, 1966.

174 Majority defeated: *The Sun*, Apr. 4, 1960; *The Evening Sun*, June 29, 1960.

175 The truth: Allen and another African-American real estate broker involved in racial change, Linwood Koger, were vice presidents of the Citizens Planning and Housing Association. *Housing*, January and February, 1944.

175 Center Club: Interview with Walter Sondheim, Oct. 28, 2004.

175 Young architect: Interview with M. J. Brodie, Aug. 5, 2003. BJC 1585A, JMM, describes how David Janofsky and Alvin Snyder did this in Windsor Hills around 1955. They evicted fifteen non-Jewish and three Jewish families from an apartment building they owned, and "caused violent anti-Semitic reaction from tenants."

176 Director pleaded: Edward L. Holmgren to Edward J. Myerberg & Co. (Apr. 5, 1962), BJC 1557, JMM.

176 Stakes were high: Sachs to Judge Joseph Sherbow; Eugene M. Feinblatt's telegram to three apartment complex owners, all dated May 28, 1962, BJC 1557, JMM. The owners were Samuel Kalis (Virginian Apartments), Edward Myerberg (Greenwood), and Dr. John Rosin, a colon and rectal surgeon (Woodland). Charles Siegfarth (Greenlyn) did not receive a telegram because "[we] do not believe he is Jewish."

177 Another force: *Newsletter* of Baltimore Neighborhoods, Inc., June 1962.

177 Offensive: Walter C. Schmidt to Sachs (Jan. 17, 1955), BJC 197, JMM.

177 Newspaper's duty: Baltimore Neighborhoods, Inc., minutes, Feb. 5, 1962. When discriminatory real estate ads finally withered away around 1970, it

was because the Real Estate Board asked its members to drop racial classifications from ads.

178 Sent a letter: Hollander to White, Sept. 18, 1947, BJC 1675, JMM. The Mitchells quickly learned about the letter, according to Clarence M. Mitchell, Jr., OH 8209, MHS, and saw it as an attempt to muzzle her.

179 Issue was control: Gunnar Myrdal, *An American Dilemma: The Negro Problem and Modern Democracy* (New York: Harper & Row, 1960), 819, 1406.

179 Verbal violence: James Rouse, OH 8175, MHS.

180 Famously said: Cited in *City Paper*, May 17, 2000.

180 She graduated: A predecessor of Baltimore's Frederick Douglass High School.

180 Crisscrossing: Langston Hughes, *Fight for Freedom: The Story of the* NAACP (New York: W. W. Norton, 1962), 176–177.

180 First time: Andor Skotnes, "The Black Freedom Movement and the Workers' Movement in Baltimore, 1930–1939," unpublished Ph.D. dissertation, Rutgers University, 1991, 181–193. According to the University of Maryland law professor Larry S. Gibson, Thurgood Marshall, just out of law school in 1933, represented Costonie, who had sued a Pennsylvania Avenue storekeeper for libel. The suit went nowhere.

180 De facto leader: Bruce A. Thompson, "The Civil Rights Vanguard: The NAACP and the Black Community in Baltimore, 1931–1942," unpublished Ph.D. dissertation, University of Maryland, 1996, 149.

182 Headline read: *Afro-American*, Jan. 12, 1934.

182 Aghast: *The Crisis*, February 1936.

182 Department stores: *The Crisis*, April 1936.

183 Better treatment: Ibid.

183 Leon Sachs: OH 8136, MHS.

183 Bordering on dishonesty: Leon Sachs, OH 8136, MHS. Such was the white fear of buying "tainted" clothes that might have been tried on by blacks that in 1943, when the NAACP made an attempt to outlaw Jim Crow practices in stores, the legislature's bill was not sent to the judiciary committee but to the "hygiene committee," where it was promptly killed. See Paul A. Kramer, "White Sales: The Racial Politics of Baltimore's Jewish-Owned Department Stores, 1935–1965," in *Enterprising Emporiums* (Baltimore: Jewish Museum of Maryland, 2001).

183 German-language scholar: Pietila, "Baltimore Afro-American," *Buncombe*. The *Afro-American* reprinted the article on Sept. 23, 1972, under the headline: "WHITE SUN REPORTER WRITES ABOUT THE AFRO."

183 Nazi Germany: Ibid.

184 Full-time job: Interview with Clarence M. Mitchell III, Feb. 25, 2003. Bernstein confirmed this.

184 Apartment buildings: After Jackson's death in 1975, the Mitchells inherited the properties. They became notorious slumlords who did not pay their property taxes and were repeatedly sued by their tenants.

184 Clash erupted: *Afro-American*, Jan. 31, 1961.

184 Took exception: Ibid.

185 Separate socials: Interview with Sidney Hollander, Jr., Dec. 1, 2003.
185 Cycle repeated: *Windsor Hills: A Century of History, 1895–1995* (Baltimore: Windsor Hills Neighbors, 1995), 15–18.
186 Four years later: Interview with John Pumphrey, Aug. 26, 2005.
186 No Welcome Wagon: Ibid.
186 Racial diversity: Mark, *Not Next Door*, 12, 13. Also, interview with Martin Dyer, a longtime Windsor Hill resident and activist in Baltimore Neighborhoods, Inc., Apr. 18, 2003.
186 Loan pool: Minutes of the BNI executive committee, June 15, 1961, BNI file, UB/Langsdale. Interview with John Michener, May 20, 2009.
187 No limit: *The Evening Sun*, Mar. 12, 1956.
187 Matter of time: Interview with Thomas Ward, a longtime Bolton Hill resident, former City Council member, and a judge, June 23, 2003.
187 Supreme Court: "Motion of the Mount Royal Protective Association, Inc. for leave to file brief as amicus curiae" (October term, 1947).
188 Direction changed: Martin Millspaugh and Gurney Breckenfeld, *The Human Side of Urban Renewal* (New York: Ives Washburn, 1960), 82–83.
188 Democratic goal: Ibid.
188 Stock corporation: Ibid. *The Evening Sun*, Mar. 5, 1957.
188 Overwhelmingly white: In the late 1970s the area west of Linden remained "about 99 and 44 one-hundredths percent white," reported *The Sun*'s Carleton Jones on Jan. 28, 1979. Along Eutaw Place, several rows of mansion-size nineteenth-century houses were demolished in the 1960s and 1970s and replaced with subsidized housing complexes catering to blacks. In the early 2000s, one of them, in turn, was razed and replaced with a modern rowhouse community for homeowners, Spicer's Run. Bolton Hill eventually became Baltimore's best-known historic revival neighborhood.

Chapter 13. From Dream to Nightmare

189 Flickering images: http://teachingamericanhistorymd.net/000001/000000/000033/html/t33.html; *New York Times,* July 13, 1963.
189 Struck a waitress: *Washington Post*, Feb. 12, Mar. 20, June 21, 1963; Aug. 4, 1991. *Time*, Feb. 22, 1963.
190 First white man: *Washington Post*, Sept. 15 and 17, 1963.
190 Pastoral letter: *Catholic Review*, Mar. 1, 1963.
191 Four months later: Also arrested at Gwynn Oak Park was Michael Schwerner, a young New Yorker. He would become a martyr a year later, when he and two other civil rights workers, James Chaney and Andrew Goodman, were murdered in Mississippi.
191 Overflow crowd: *The Sun, The Evening Sun*, Jan. 14, 1966.
192 Catholic majority: Ibid.
192 Rebellion grew: Cited in Barbara Mills, *"Got My Mind Set on Freedom": Maryland's Story of Black and White Activism, 1663–2000* (Bowie, Md.: Heritage Books, 2002), 564.

192 Another reason: Interview with the Reverend Marion C. Bascom, an important civil rights activist, Sept. 20, 2004. Dr. King's main liaison in Baltimore was the Reverend Logan Kearse, a controversial figure who was not trusted by Morgan student activists in particular.

193 Needed him: Activists for Fair Housing to Dr. King, May 9, 1967, Southern Christian Leadership Conference file, Reel 5, Box 38, frame 0521. The letter was signed by William L. Hankins, chairman of the Federation of Civil Rights Organizations; Cleveland A. Chandler, chairman of Activists for Fair Housing and a Morgan professor; the Revered Vernon Dobson, chairman of the Activists advisory board and pastor of the Union Baptist Church; Eugene L. King, of the Baltimore County League for Human Rights; the Reverend Frank L. Williams, of the Metropolitan Methodist Church; and the Reverend Chester L. Wickwire, a white cleric and the Johns Hopkins chaplain.

193 Planning commission: He served in those positions from 1957 to 1963.

193 See Joe: *New York Times*, Feb. 6, 1961.

194 Proven fact: Undated "Statement by Joseph Meyerhoff on Pending Open Housing Legislation," BJC 124, JMM.

194 Abruptly canceled: *The Evening Sun*, Nov. 30, 1966.

195 Their appeal: An intriguing first-person account of those times is contained in Mills, *Freedom*.

195 Windy City: See Beryl Satter, *Family Properties* (New York: Metropolitan Books, 2009), 169–214.

195 His telephone rang: Interview with William L. Hankins, Aug. 11, 2005.

196 Israeli immigrant: He was Jack Goldensohn, a friend of the author's.

196 Radio station owner: He was Robert C. "Jake" Embry, Sr. Interview with his son, Robert C. Embry, Jr., May 7, 2005.

196 Petrified wife: The lawyer was William L. Marbury, Jr., who had risen to become a Harvard overseer. A celebrated liberal, he was the son of William L. Marbury, the segregationist lawyer.

196 Mayhem: "A Report of the Baltimore Civil Disturbance of April 6 to April 11, 1968," Maryland Crime Investigating Commission, June 10, 1968, 1, EPFL.

196 Indiscriminate pillaging: "Statistical Analysis of the Baltimore Riots," April 1968, Baltimore Jewish Council, JMM.

196 Anguish gripped: *Washington Post, New York Times*, Apr. 12, 1968.

197 All races: Mills, *Freedom*, 576.

197 Alinsky began: See Sanford D. Horwitt: *Let Them Call Me a Rebel: Saul Alinsky, His Life and Legacy* (New York: Alfred A. Knopf, 1989).

197 Thorny problem: John Foot, "Mapping Diversity in Milan: Historical Approaches to Urban Immigration," Fondazione Eni Enrico Mattei Working Papers, www.bepress,com/feem/paper11.

198 A trusted friend: He was the important French Catholic philosopher Jacques Maritain, who had befriended Montini while serving as the French ambassador to the Vatican from 1945 to 1948. Alinsky and Maritain, for their part, had become fast friends in Chicago, where the Frenchman spent the war years in exile. See Lawrence J. Engel, "The Influence of Saul Alinsky on the

Campaign for Human Development," *Theological Studies*, vol. 59 (1998), 636–661.

199 Dr. King lacked: Horwitt, *Alinsky*, 468–470.

199 Senior thesis: http://www.gopublius.com/HCT/HillaryClintonThesis.pdf

200 Barack Obama: Interview with Arnold Graf, May 18, 2009. In running for president, Obama took advantage of his training. In Iowa, his breakthrough state, he turned long-ignored caucuses into a feat of organizing. As he raced toward the White House, he received important help from the Association of Community Organizations for Reform Now (ACORN), which had changed its original name, Arkansas Community Organizations for Reform, and spread outside the South after merging with the National Welfare Rights Organization. Another Alinsky-inspired organization, Andy Stern's Service Employees International Union (SEIU), was Obama's strongest labor supporter. After the election Obama continued mobilizing. His campaign machine, Organizing for America, was given a new mission: build coalitions of mutual self-interest around health care and other initiatives.

200 Alinsky's tactics: Sampson Green, "Purpose and History of Activists Incorporated," undated, unsourced (private collection of Kenneth L. Johnson).

200 Data-gathering hunt: "Baltimore Under Siege: The Impact of Financing on the Baltimore Home Buyer (1960–1970)," a mimeographed thirty-five-page report issued by Activists, Inc., in 1971. Various public library copies have been pilfered; I relied on a copy provided by Johnson.

200 Stay of exploitation: *The Evening Sun*, May 4, 1969.

201 Green told: Ten-page transcript of an interview with Sampson Green by W. Edward Orser, June 13, 1983 (Johnson collection).

201 Splendid scapegoat: Interview with Walter Dean, Jr., June 18, 2003.

201 Evil system: *The Sun*, Mar. 10, 1972.

201 Mandel resigned: *The Sun*, Sept. 24, 1971.

202 Goldseker qualified: Interview with John Luetkemeyer, Jr., June 11, 2005.

202 Luetkemeyer marveled: *The Sun*, Feb. 5, 1978.

202 Activists, Inc., study: "Baltimore Under Siege," iii.

202 Mother of six: *The Evening Sun*, Jan. 26, 1972.

204 Withdrew its suit: Orser's interview with Green, June 13, 1983 (Johnson collection).

204 Celebrated by buying: *Afro-American*, Mar. 21, 1972.

204 Public bludgeoning: Over a sixteen-month period, WJZ-TV reporter Christopher Gaul did a series of hard-hitting exposés on Goldseker, who sued the station and the reporter but failed to stop the reports.

205 Edwin J. Wolf: http://www.msba.org/departments/commpubl/publications/bar_bult/2007/jul/nowitsend.asp.

205 Jewish lawyers: Interviews with Mark Sissman and Samuel I. "Sandy" Rosenberg, Jan. 1, 2004.

206 Categorically denied: Interview with Mandel, June 25, 2003.

206 First black: *New York Times*, Nov. 5. 1970.

206 After a tough campaign: See Smith, *Schaefer*.

207 One detail: Orser's 1983 interview with Green.

Chapter 14. Exiting the City

211 Whites fled: U.S. Censuses, 1950 and 1970.

211 Marginalize: W. Edward Orser, "Neither Separate Nor Equal: Foreshadowing *Brown* in Baltimore County, 1935-1937," *Maryland Historical Magazine*, Spring 1997, 4–35.

212 Petty corruption: In the summer of 1976 I benefited from several long conversations about the Democratic machine with P. David Hutchinson, a son of the east side political warhorse, Delegate Preston A. Hutchinson.

212 Flood plains: Neal A. Brooks and Eric G. Rockel, *A History of Baltimore County* (Towson: Friends of the Towson Library, 1979), 371.

212 Even in Washington: Richard M. Cohen and Jules Witcover, *A Heartbeat Away: The Investigation and Resignation of Vice President Spiro T. Agnew* (New York: Viking Press, 1974), 4.

214 Carnal bribe: *The Sun, The Evening Sun,* Feb. 2, 1974.

214 Sexual needs: According to testimony at the trial, Green told the women in job interviews: "If you don't fuck, you got to suck. If you don't blow, out you go."

214 Antique etching: *Washington Post,* Feb. 26, 1974.

215 Meyerhoff regained: *The Evening Sun,* Feb. 6, 1954.

215 Agnew: Theo Lippman, *Spiro Agnew's America* (New York: W. W. Norton, 1972), 33.

216 Little known: Joseph Albright, *What Makes Spiro Run* (New York: Dodd, Mead, 1972), 65.

216 Metropolis: A seven-foot fiberglass statue of Superman was erected on the town square after the town claimed to be the hometown of the fictional comic book hero.

217 The city grew: Ralph S. Weese, "Report on the Housing Market, Baltimore, Maryland, Standard Metropolitan Area, as of September 1, 1953" (Washington, D.C.: Federal Housing Administration), 8, EPFL.

217 Bowling alley: *The Evening Sun,* Feb. 16, 1960.

218 Gloom: Interview with Walter Sondheim, Apr. 10, 2003.

219 Headquarters campus: E-mail from Larry DeWitt, the Social Security Administration's historian, Apr. 7, 2003.

219 Transportation nightmares: *Report of the Urban Planning Conferences Under the Auspices of The Johns Hopkins University* (Baltimore: Johns Hopkins University Press, 1944), 51.

219 He proposed: Robert Moses, *Baltimore Arterial Report,* Oct. 9, 1944, EPFL.

219 The first major: *1962—Year of Dynamic Accomplishments in Downtown Baltimore* (Baltimore: Committee for Downtown, 1962), 7. The business community combated the malaise by launching a downtown revitalization project, Charles Center.

219 Acquired and demolished: "Housing Needs and Resources for Displaced Families," Monograph V, Baltimore Urban Renewal and Housing Agency, 1965, 4.

220 National City Lines: The NCL story spawned many conspiracy theories. A summary may be found in Stephen B. Goddard's *Getting There: The Epic Struggle Between Road and Rail in the American Century* (New York: Basic Books, 1994), 120–137.

220 Mysteriously: "Preliminary Report: Investigation of the Service and Facilities of the Baltimore Transit Company and the Baltimore Coach Company, Jan. 10, 1953" (VF in the Baltimore *Sun* library), 1–27.

220 Two-minute intervals: E-mails from Martin Van Horn, a streetcar enthusiast and scholar, June 25, 26, 28, 2008.

220 Ridership declined: "Preliminary Report," 1–27.

221 Cutting routes: E-mails from Van Horn, June, 26, 2008.

221 New supermarkets: Taped recollections of Ed Kane, a perceptive observer who lived in Arbutus and Govans before moving to Fells Point where he operated a water taxi company, April 2003.

Chapter 15. Metropolis

222 White noose: *The Sun*, Aug. 13, 1974.

223 Anderson's outlook: Paul M. Angle, *Bloody Williamson: A Chapter in American Lawlessness* (Urbana: University of Illinois Press, 1992), 142. I also relied on my personal observations of the area, having gone to graduate school at Southern Illinois University, Carbondale.

224 Hangman's offer: *Washington Post*, July 8, 1928; *Chicago Tribune*, Oct. 7, 2001.

224 Good family: E-mail from Don Anderson. Dale's brother was still living in Metropolis as a Baptist preacher, Apr. 29, 2008.

224 Sundown towns: Many such towns remained all white until the 1980s. See Loewen, *Sundown Towns*; also, Jaspin, *Buried in the Bitter Waters*.

225 Terrible temper: Interview with Thomas Toporovich, an insider as the County Council's executive secretary, Feb. 20, 2008.

225 Rezoning was done: Gilbert Sandler, "Not much happened at the Penn. Honest!" *The Evening Sun*, Aug. 29, 1995.

226 Made an error: *The Sun*, Aug. 29, 1995.

226 In a single month: Lippman, *Agnew's America*, 68–69.

226 Disappeared: Ibid., 44.

227 Practically no rowhouses: The legislation called rowhouses "group housing" and limited each row to a maximum of seven homes. See *The Evening Sun*, Aug. 29, 1952; *The Sun*, Sept. 30, 1952.

227 Confined rowhouses: High-density zoning was also practiced in the Arbutus-Catonsville area, which had a substantial concentration of blacks.

227 Anderson believed: See *The Sun*'s editorial, Sept. 30 and Nov. 19, 1952.

227 He agreed: Oliver Herman Laine, "Towson: A Geographic Survey of an Urban Community," unpublished Ph.D. dissertation, Clark University, 1953, 222–223.

227 Fratricide: *Union News*, Apr. 18 and 25, 1958.

228 Attractive alternative: Lippman, *Agnew's America*, 40.

228 Agnew pledged: "Statement of Spiro Agnew," November 1963, Agnew–Civil rights, folder 1166, UMCP.

228 Agnew ousted: "Statement of Spiro Agnew," Dec. 18, 1965, Agnew–Civil rights, folder 1166, UMCP.

228 Open occupancy: Ibid.

229 The idea: Laine, "Towson," 222–223.

229 Communist conspiracy: *New York Times*, Apr. 25, 1965.

229 Cockey operated: Interview with Joshua Cockey, Mar. 18, 2009. See also a profile in the *Daily Record*, Sept. 5, 2005.

230 No subsequent: *The Sun*, Dec. 23, 1971; *The Evening Sun*, May 31, 1982.

230 Political repercussions: *New York Times*, Apr. 25, 1965. Wahbe ultimately served as the state's planning secretary under governors Agnew and Mandel.

230 Segregationist vote: Albright, *Spiro*, 120; *The Sun*, Sept. 2, 1966.

231 No middle ground: *New York Times*, Oct. 20, 1966.

231 A foundation: *Toward Equality: Baltimore's Progress Report* (Baltimore: Sidney Hollander Foundation, 1960), 11–12.

231 Without access: *The Sun*, June 2, 1968.

231 Zoning: Yale Rabin, "Expulsive Zoning: The Inequitable Legacy of Euclid," in *Zoning and the American Dream: Promises Still to Keep* (Chicago: Planners Press, 1989), 101–121.

231 Removals of blacks: Yale Rabin, "The Roots of Segregation in the Eighties: The Role of Local Government," in Gary A. Tobin, ed., *Divided Neighborhoods: Changing Patterns of Racial Segregation* (Newbury Park, Calif.: Sage, 1987).

232 Textbook example: Louis S. Diggs, *From the Meadows to the Point* (Baltimore: Louis S. Diggs, 2003), 17.

232 Detected patterns: *The Sun*, Aug. 19, 1970.

232 In 1970: *Hearing Before the United States Commission on Civil Rights*, Baltimore Aug. 17–19, 1970 (Washington, D.C.: U.S. Government Printing Office), 700–729.

232 Segregated pockets: *Hearing*, 393, 399, 402.

233 Anderson rebuffed: *The Evening Sun*, Apr. 9, 1969.

233 He rejected: *Hearing*, 72–93.

234 No entity: John Michener's recollections in a memo to Malcolm Sherman, Mar. 6, 2007. Michener's private collection contains original correspondence between SSA and various officials, copies of SSA's housing policies, and bulletins.

234 In 1972: *The Sun,* Sept. 6, 1972. The Social Security Administration built a new auxiliary complex in the city.

234 Accused them: Interview with George Gavrelis, Mar. 22, 2004, and Les Graef, Sept. 13, 2007.

235 Did not buy: *The Sun*, Aug. 27, 1972.

235 Anderson ordered: He canceled the order a month a half later. *The Evening Sun, News American*, Sept. 19, 1972.

235 Unspoken pact: *The Sun*, Feb. 15, 1992.

Chapter 16. Persistent Patterns

236 Tug-of-war: Interview with Theodore G. Venetoulis, Apr. 9, 2008.

237 Cycle began: Rowe to Carl Gray, Administrator of Veterans Affairs, Aug. 17, 1950, BJC 933A, JMM.

237 Friction: See Sachs to Benjamin Jacobs, Feb. 4, 1959, and Sachs to Rabbi Jacob A. Max, May 10, 1960, BJC 933A, JMM.

237 Steered elsewhere: Interview with Malcolm Sherman, Aug. 21, 2003. See also a series by Mark Reutter, Antero Pietila, and Gene Oishi, "Corridor in Transition," *The Sun*, Feb. 5–9, 1978.

238 Semi-rural: This historical information comes from the Baltimore County Public Library's website, http://www.bcpl.info/info/history/hist_ra_history .html.http://www.bcpl.info/info/history/hist_ra_history.html.

238 Fear and trepidation: Minutes, Mar. 5, 1968, "Lochearn Troubled Area," Baltimore Neighborhoods, Inc., Box 1, UB-Langsdale.

239 Leading the harassment: Minutes, Mar. 5, 1968, "Kimberly Area," Baltimore Neighborhoods, Inc., Box 1, UB-Langsdale.

240 Resegregation today: Unpublished 2008 article, Gregory Smithsimon, "The Benefits of Blockbusting: A Reconsideration of Racial Transition in the Suburbs," 38. Demographic data from Baltimore Metropolitan Council community profiles, http://www.baltometro.org/CP/RPD312CP.pdf.

240 Backlash developed: Jewish Community Relations Council of Greater Philadelphia, "Report on Conditions in Pikesville, Maryland," Oct. 15, 1964, unnumbered BJC file; "Civil Rights Bill; National States Rights Party, Pikesville, Md.," Box 34, JMM.

242 Contiguous zip codes: 1999 Jewish Population Survey. http://baltimore .ujcfedweb.org/local_includes/downloads/10221.pdf.

242 Turnover rate: Lata Chatterjee, David Harvey, Lawrence Klugman, *F.H.A. Policies and the Baltimore City Housing Market* (Baltimore: Urban Observatory, 1974), 1.1-2-7.

242 St. Ambrose: The Reverend Paul Zaboroski's 2008 video history of the parish, http://www.stambrose.org. He said inclusion of blacks in parish activities began after the 1968 riots.

243 Racial changeover: Chattarjee, Harvey, Klugman, *F.H.A. Policies*, 1.1.–4.4.

243 Epicenter: Ibid., 3.3.

243 Six months later: Interview with Gunther Wertheimer, one of the developers of the project, Jan. 7, 2009.

244 Decline accelerated: Documented evidence of this emerged during a long trial against HUD that ended in 2005. In his decision, federal judge Marvin Garbis determined that HUD had systematically consigned black public housing to segregated neighborhoods in Baltimore. But he also recognized that the situation could not be remedied unless public housing was spread more equitably. "Baltimore City should not be viewed as an island reservation for use as a container for all of the poor of a contiguous region, including Anne Arundel, Baltimore, Carroll, Harford and Howard Counties," Garvis wrote. "It is high time that HUD live up to its statutory mandate to consider the effect of its

policies on the racial and socio-economic composition of the surrounding area and thus consider regional approaches to promoting fair housing opportunities for African-American public housing residents in the Baltimore Region." "Memorandum of decision, *Thompson v. HUD*, Civil Action no. MJG-95-309," U.S. District Court for Maryland, 11–15.

245 Area consisted: This section relies on the organizational records of NECO in the special collections of the University of Baltimore Langsdale Library.

246 Big ad: *Catholic Review,* Nov. 19, 1971.

246 Alinsky's teachings: *The Evening Sun,* Nov. 4, 1970; *The Sun,* Dec. 6, 1970; Jan. 31, Feb. 4, and Sept. 20, 1971.

247 Economic demands: Interview with Arnold Graf, May 25, 2009.

248 Catholic church created: Monsignor Geno Baroni had a key role in SECO's creation. He founded the National Center for Urban Ethnic Affairs. He later served as an assistant secretary of the U.S. Department of Housing and Urban Development in the Carter administration, the highest rank achieved by a Catholic priest in the federal government at the time. See Lawrence M. O'Rourke, *Geno: The Life and Mission of Geno Baroni* (New York: Paulist Press, 1981).

248 Organization's godmother: In 1976, Stockholm's *Dagens Nyheter* sent a reporter and a photographer to document white working-class alienation and Mikulski's political ambitions in the heart of the SECO target area. The resulting newspaper series was reprinted in a book, *Highlandtown: Gilla oss eller stick* (Stockholm: Bo Cavefors, 1976). That Swedish title is a literal translation of a bumper sticker that the journalists found: "Highlandtown, Love It or Leave It."

248 Low turnover: Interview with Adolph Simmons, Apr. 5, 2004.

249 Mass transit: Governor Schaefer was a big booster of light rail, which he saw as key to the success of the taxpayer-financed stadiums that the city built for the Orioles baseball team and the football Ravens; Josef Nathanson, interview, June 18, 2009.

249 To placate: Interview with Ronald Hartman, who ran the Transit Administration at the time, Apr. 18, 2008.

250 Frustrated judge: *The Sun,* Nov. 4, 2003. In 2009 legal wrangling still continued.

253 One day: Interview with Crockett, Aug. 9, 2008.

Epilogue: An American Dilemma

255 A new day: Gunnar Myrdal, *An American Dilemma: The Negro Problem and Modern Democracy* (New York: Harper & Row, 1960), xxvi, 1021.

255 A survey: The survey was commissioned by Baltimoreans United in Leadership Development (BUILD). Interview with Arnold Graf, May 18, 2009.

256 Worst economic mess: *Dr. King's Dream Denied: Forty Years of Failed Federal Enforcement.* 2008 Fair Housing Trends Report, National Fair Housing Alliance, www.nationalfairhousing.

256 Two-tier system: See Gregory D. Squires, "Do Subprime Loans Create Subprime Cities? Surging Inequality and the Rise in Predatory Lending," *Economic Policy Institute Briefing Paper*, February 2008, 2.

257 Race was: Ibid., 4. According to the Massachusetts Affordable Housing Alliance, 55 percent of black and Latino borrowers in metropolitan Boston who obtained loans for single-family homes from seven lending institutions had subprime loans. Only 13 percent of white borrowers did. In many cases the purchase prices and mortgages far exceeded the value of the underlying real estate. *Boston Globe*, Mar. 16, 2007.

257 Baltimore became: John B. O'Donnell, "House Prices Soar, Sometimes in a Day: Quick-buck Artists Selling Crumbling Baltimore Homes at Inflated Prices Create the Illusion of a Robust Real Estate Market," *The Sun*, Aug. 1, 1999.

258 In both scenarios: E-mail from Ken Strong, July 26, 2009; *New York Times*, Jan. 8, 2008.

258 First city to sue: *The Sun*, Jan. 9, 2008.

259 Some blacks: *New Amsterdam News*, Nov. 15, 2007.

259 Laboratory for integration: *New York Times*, Sept. 7, 2008.

259 Blacks moved: *Sun Reporter*, May 24, 2007.

259 Highest in California: *New York Times*, Aug. 9, 2008.

260 Voluntary withdrawal: Myrdal, *American Dilemma*, 631.

261 Millennial Generation: Morley Winograd and Michael D. Hais, *Millennial Makeover: MySpace, YouTube and the Future of American Politics* (New Brunswick: Rutgers University Press, 2008), especially 66–67.

Index

Hillbillies, 78, 81–82, 187
Hiss, Alger, 106
HOLC (Home Owner's Loan
    Corporation), 61–68, 68, 70–73,
    280–281, 281
Holder, Eric, 256
Hollander, Sidney, Jr., 145, 184
Hollander, Sidney, Sr., 178, 179
Home auctions, 95, 100
Homeland community, 36, 67, 138–139
Homeowner covenants. *See* Covenants
Homeownership, 34, 66, 109–110. *See
    also* Lending practices
Home Owners' Loan Corporation. *See*
    HOLC
Home Owners' Refinancing Act of
    1933, 62
Hopkins, Charles, 206–207
Hopkins, Johns, 132
Housing projects, 83–86, 144, 233, 299,
    305
Housing shortages, 66–67, 79–80,
    83–86, 91–92, 97–98
Housing speculators. *See* Blockbusters
Housing surpluses, 260
Howard, Joseph C., 204–205
Howard Park, 172
Howell, William, 44
Hoyt, Homer, 62–64, 280
HUD (Department of Housing and
    Urban Development), 244, 305
Hunting Ridge, 73–74, 134
Hutzler, Albert, 184
Hypothecation, 169

Immigration, 42–46
Industrialization, 33
Integrated neighborhoods, 188
Israel, Edward L., 182
Israeli Prime Minister's Medal, 194

Jackson, Howard W., 53–54, 55, 79–80,
    118
Jackson, Juanita. *See* Mitchell, Juanita
    (nee Jackson)
Jackson, Kenneth T., 71
Jackson, Lillie May Carroll, 178–183,
    181

Jackson, Robert H., 105
James Keelty Company, 160–162
Jeffries, James J., 6
"Jew Hatred among Negroes" (Israel),
    182
Jewish Social Directory, 15
Jewish Times (newspaper), 108
Jews: barred by covenants, 47; barring
    of African Americans by, 47; caste
    system among, 130–131; Davenport
    on, 43–44; and Democratic Party
    machine, 112, 117–118, 122–124;
    discrimination by fellow Jews,
    135–143; discrimination of by FHA,
    73–74; discrimination of by *The
    Sun*, 38; and Eutaw Place, 10–11;
    and Fulton Avenue home sale, 90;
    HOLC rankings of neighborhoods,
    71–72; and the Ku Klux Klan, 224;
    in Maryland, 128–129, 129; and
    McCulloh Street, 15; and proximity
    to synagogues, 244; and quotas at
    universities, 131–133, 290; relations
    with African Americans, xii, 47,
    129–130, 178, 182–183; and Roland
    Park, 36; in the suburbs, 109,
    240–242; and succession patterns of
    neighborhoods, 15, 18, 56–57; and
    three tier real estate system, xi. *See
    also* Anti-Semitism; Baltimore Jewish
    Council
Jim Crow laws, 156–157, 255, 298
Jobs lost to county, 221
John Birch Society, 230
Johns Hopkins University, 10, 12,
    131–133, 290
Johnson, Jack, 6
Joseph Meyerhoff Corporation, 194. *See
    also* Meyerhoff, Joseph

Kahl, Christian H., 227
Kansas City, Missouri, 33–35
Kaufman, Herbert, 97, 100
Kearse, Logan, 155, 299
Keelty, James, 160
Kefauver committee, 120, 288, 289
King, Martin Luther, Jr., 192–193, 195,
    199

A NOTE ON THE AUTHOR

Antero Pietila was born in Helsinki, Finland, and studied at the School of Social Sciences in Tampere. After visiting New York City in 1964, he returned to the United States in 1967 to attend graduate school at Southern Illinois University. In 1969 he joined the *Baltimore Sun*, where he worked for thirty-five years as a reporter, a foreign correspondent in South Africa and the Soviet Union, and a member of the editorial board. He and his wife live in Baltimore.